D0745906

The Economy
of Kuwait

The Economy of Kuwait

Development and Role in International Finance

M. W. Khouja and P. G. Sadler

HC
497
K8
K48

© M. W. Khouja and P. G. Sadler 1979

All rights reserved. No part of this publication may be
reproduced or transmitted, in any form or by any means,
without permission

First published 1979 by
THE MACMILLAN PRESS LTD
London and Basingstoke
Associated companies in Delhi
Dublin Hong Kong Johannesburg Lagos
Melbourne New York Singapore Tokyo

Typeset in Great Britain by
PREFACE LTD
Salisbury, Wilts
and printed by
BILLING & SONS LTD
Guildford, London and Worcester

British Library Cataloguing in Publication Data

Khouja, M W
The economy of Kuwait
1. Kuwait — Economic conditions
I. Title   II. Sadler, P G
330.9′53′6705   HC497.K8

ISBN 0-333-22561-9

This book is sold subject
to the standard conditions
of the Net Book Agreement

To our families

Contents

List of Tables

Preface

The opportunity to write this book presented us with an exciting challenge, the true nature of which only unfolded as our work progressed. We were to write about an economy under development. Yet the tremendous body of theoretical and general literature on development economics at present available is devoted to circumstances which are almost totally inapplicable to Kuwait. In particular, most works on the subject presume a shortage of capital relative to the ability to save. However, Kuwait, and many of its fellow oil exporting states, are not faced with this problem. Instead, they need to find ways whereby the capital made available to them may be deployed to provide the maximum benefits for their countries, both now and in the future. We found it necessary, therefore, to develop a conceptual model which would reflect the aspirations of such countries, and to use it as a framework to guide our investigations.

The statistical information available to us was quite extensive and was much more than experience elsewhere might have suggested we would find. In order to put the facts available into an ordered perspective, we needed to undertake much fieldwork and many interviews to understand the motivation and objectives of those in different sections of the economy whose advice and decisions were crucial to its operation or affected its relationships with the rest of the world. This was probably the most interesting part of our work and we hope that, through our interpretation of the facts of Kuwait's development, readers will gain a greater insight into the country's activities as expressed in its policies on conservation, internal development and foreign investment. We do not pretend that there is an overall guiding policy which dictates the activities of the various sectors and institutions which comprise the economy, but our interviews indicated the development of a general philosophy from which such a policy will undoubtedly arise. We detected elements of this development among officials at all levels and in all branches of governmental activity, as well as in the private and the joint sectors. Often the evidence was confined to the expression of an opinion on present policy or doubts about the future, but in most cases there appeared to emerge a general consensus on the need to integrate resource exploitation, internal development and foreign investment so as to secure the country's future well-being and its rate of growth in the long term. It is from this consensus that we have evolved our approach to the investigations which provided the basis of this book, and which also instigated the construction of the more formalised behavioural model which we feel is capable of more general application than to Kuwait alone.

We illustrate elsewhere in our acknowledgments the debt we owe to so many people and institutions in Kuwait for their advice, helpful discussion and willingness to make so much of their time available to us. From these discussions, we quickly realised that a whole new approach to economic development was unfolding while our investigations were proceeding and that it was the relationship between events that we were recording which were much more important than the events themselves. It is the pursuit of these relationships which have provided us with the greatest stimulus and satisfaction and we hope that the results of this pursuit are adequately recorded in what follows.

Thus we hope that those who wish to learn more about contemporary Kuwait, for political or commercial reasons, or for purely personal interest, will find the information they need adequately presented within the framework we have chosen and that our interpretation of data, contemporary events, and policies will contribute to greater understanding of Kuwait by those who read our work.

Kuwait, June 1978   M. W. Khouja
                                                       P. G. Sadler

Acknowledgments

Contributions to the development of this book have been so varied that it would be impossible to do justice in an acknowledgment page such as this to all who have helped us. The interest shown by our colleagues at the Kuwait Fund and at the University of Aberdeen, their constant encouragement, suggestions and frequent discussion of ideas single them out as two groups for special mention. But, above all, we must thank Mr Abdlatif Al-Hamad, Director General of the Fund, who conceived the idea of joint authorship of this work by a western academic and a practising economist in Kuwait. His constant personal interest in our work and his willingness to discuss and comment on it as it progressed have been invaluable. He provided much help in suggesting sources of information and arranging introductions and made many comments on our final manuscripts. We must also thank the Kuwait Fund and the University of Aberdeen for the accommodation and hospitality they afforded whenever each of us visited the other's institution and for the lenient view they both took of the time we devoted to the book's completion.

Dr Zacharia Nasr, Director of Research at the Fund, gave us much advice and assistance too, and also read and made invaluable comments on our final drafts as did Professor David Pearce of the University of Aberdeen, Mr Maurice Scott of Nuffield College, Oxford, and Professor H. A. Kheir-el-Din of Kuwait University. Mr Saad Andary, both while a Research Officer at the Fund and now while researching at the University of Aberdeen, has made a unique contribution and we owe much of our data to his research efforts and constant assistance over the whole period of the book's compilation. Mr Ron Edwards of the Department of Political Economy at Aberdeen rendered invaluable support in the computation and continual refinement of the mathematical model appearing in Chapter 7 and also made many helpful contributions generally.

The many interviews which we were granted in institutions in Kuwait make it impossible to thank all our respondents by name, but mention must be made of OAPEC, the Central Bank of Kuwait, the Ministry of Planning, the Kuwait Oil Company and the Kuwait Chamber of

Commerce and Industry as well as many of the commercial banks, ministries and national and semi-national institutions who provided us with data. We must thank too the many friends in so many institutions with whom discussions were held on a social or an informal basis. We hope neither group would be offended if we were to acknowledge the special contributions made by Mr Nasser Al-Sayer, Deputy Director-General of the Kuwait Fund, Mr Khalid Abu Saud, Financial Advisor to the Prime Minister, Dr. Bourhan Chatti formerly of the Planning Ministry and now Director of the AFESD/UNDP programme at the Arab Fund, Dr Hassan Al Ebraheem, Director of Kuwait University and Mr Majed Jamal el-Din, advisor to the Chamber of Commerce, all of whose advice and assistance was such that we feel we must record them separately. We owe a special debt of gratitude too to the Kuwait Ministry of Information with whom the concept of this work was originally formulated and would pay personal tribute to Mr Hatim Abdul Ghani for the great and varied help which he afforded us. We thank the staff of the library at the Kuwait Fund for their willing assistance and also Mrs Sameeha Al-Humaidhi and Mr Naseer Geilani for help in research.

We acknowledge with gratitude the painstaking and patient efforts of Mr K. X. Joseph and his colleagues at the Fund for their prodigious efforts in typing and re-typing drafts and final manuscripts and also Mrs Helen Perren at the University of Aberdeen for her efforts in this regard, and Mrs Shirley Tucker for her construction of the explanatory diagrams. Lastly, to our wives we owe a special debt for their patience, tolerance and constant support since our joint effort commenced.

In spite of the copious assistance and encouragement we received, however, we must stress that the final responsibility for the interpretation of the data at our disposal and for the opinions expressed lies exclusively with us and the latter in no way represent the views of the Kuwait Fund or any other institution in Kuwait or elsewhere. We accept entire responsibility for what has finally been written, as we do equally for all errors and omissions.

Note on the Kuwaiti Dinar

Until 1970 the Kuwaiti dinar was equivalent to $2·8. It increased to $3 in 1971 and 1972, reaching $3·37 in 1973. During the last four years it rose gradually to more than $3·5 in 1977. In converting some values to dollars an average for each relevant period was often used.

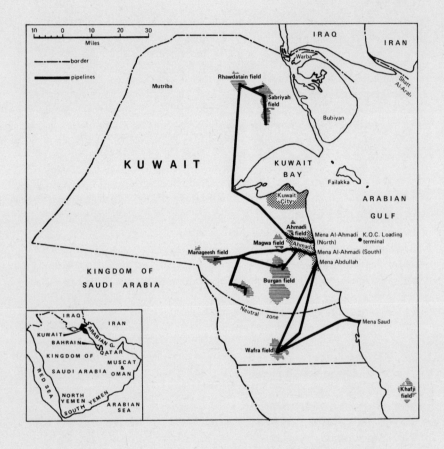

1 Introduction

Since 1973 the oil-producing countries of the Arab world seem constantly to have reached the headlines in the world's press for reasons varying from oil price rises and conservation measures to large-scale operations in financial or real estate markets. Much of this publicity has been achieved against these countries' will, and the reactions which were generated would have been far more rational had more attention been paid previously to the changes in the world order which had helped to bring them about: changes of which the events commencing in 1973 were but a consequence. The changes to which we refer were not isolated and unrelated, but were a part of the whole process of transformation of the relationships, both political and economic, which previously existed between the oil-producing countries and those companies and countries which controlled the extraction and marketing of their oil resources. This process had commenced a decade or more before 1973, yet much of it seems to have passed unnoticed by the world at large and little, if any, recognition was accorded it as the vehicle of more profound changes in the world economic order such as those of 1973 onward, many of which we must now admit should have been obvious.

It is to this process of change we would address ourselves rather than to the changes themselves, and contend that, had greater attention been paid to the historical evolution of the process, many of the events in the recent history of oil which appeared to have been isolated responses to changes in world affairs would have been better understood and would have provoked a different response. Thus, Kuwait's involvement in the recent apparently turbulent events of the world's oil politics and their market ramifications must be set against the changes in its political and economic relationships both with the former concessionaires who extracted and marketed its oil and their home countries, and also the growth of new relationships with partner states who, like Kuwait, had achieved greater control of their own resources. For this reason, we have dwelt upon the formation of OPEC as an integral part of this change. The oil boycott which accompanied the Arab/Israeli war of 1973 was in fact a part of the changes which were taking place and certainly indictated to the oil producers the power which they held to raise

1

prices and to control production. OPEC had been formed in 1960. Price changes had already been taking place since the late sixties, and the Tehran Agreement of 1971 had already given prices an upward jerk. The rapid increases in prices in 1973 in the face of reduced supply were in fact an acceleration of an inevitable process as the evidence of increased prices in the face of shortages at the consumption end of the market convinced producers that conservation was possible without a decline in income.

We intend, therefore, to trace the evolution of the Kuwait economy through the period when the country passed from one dependent upon royalties paid by oil concessionaires who developed and extracted its natural resource, via transitional stages when it gained first the control of those resources then their complete ownership, to the present day when it is able to formulate and execute policies for the integrated deployment of its wealth in order to secure the future well-being of its people and its place in world affairs. Each of the changes which have come about have presented Kuwait with a wider set of opportunities to shape its own destiny. From the political changes which commenced with the termination of the Protectorate in 1961 to the conservation measures applied to oil output in the second half of the seventies, all have stimulated further elucidation of Kuwait's aspirations, the realisation of which became successively more possible as these changes took place.

Even though for analytical purposes it may be convenient to treat social, political and economic affairs separately, the overall aspirations of Kuwait cannot be divided into compartments labelled economic, political, and social, nor can the Kuwait economy be examined without reference both to the social and political forces which give it life and the social and political environment in which it operates. The transformation of mineral wealth into disposable funds is in effect substituting a negotiable asset for a physical one and this can be deployed by economic means to achieve social and political ends both at home and abroad. Disbursement of aid to the developing world is an acceptance of its responsibility as a member of the world's family of nations, but the respect which this has earned throughout the world is also a contribution to the protection of its sovereignty. The allocation of resources at home is dictated by economic needs, yet at the same time may have social and political consequences, in that economic development may require a further large influx of population which will vitally affect the social structure and political fabric of the state, while the allocations of funds abroad may affect interest rates and equity markets in such a way that broader consequences might ensue. The development of the Kuwait economy, therefore, is an inseparable part of the overall development of the country and this overall development may be seen as the evolution of the state's aspirations for the future; we would thus prefer to view economic development in the light of that evolution rather than as a series of events which can be chronologically catalogued.

This is not an easy task, for so often aspirations are not made explicit but have to be deduced from contemporary events. However, early in our work and especially in discussions with many responsible for formulating policy, we felt we were recording an unfolding pattern consistent with the type of evolution we have postulated. In the early chapters, therefore, a tentative model of an economy in a stage of rapid development unconstrained by capital shortage is described. This is used as the basis for many of the events which are described in later chapters, but it remains always the basis of our investigation only, rather than a hypothesis which we test against data. It is essentially behavioural, with objectives which are not easy to define and which take account of such factors as world responsibility and national well-being, as well as more usual economic matters. The model may be said to evolve as the work proceeds rather than being derived *a priori* from a body of abstract theory. However if, as we believe, the model is capable of explaining the behaviour of a resource-rich developing economy, then it may well evolve further into a normative tool for the guidance of national policy-makers in Kuwait and elsewhere.

In particular, we sought an explanation of the deployment of oil resources, internal investment and investment overseas which would accord with a rational allocation to attain a preconceived set of objectives. Such aims were obviously present in the minds of those responsible for this deployment and their actions, as evidenced from available data, are in accord with this view. This alone has important consequences in that, apart from a period during 1974 and possibly a little of 1975, investments abroad were based upon a consistent set of preconceived policies, and even those funds temporarily lodged in 1974/5 were later redeployed into other means of holding wealth, so that the concept of 'surplus funds' of the oil-exporting countries, often called the 'oil surpluses', as funds looking for a home because they are 'surplus to requirements' is completely erroneous, as in reality they represent the transfer of one form of wealth, oil, into another, financial assets. Thus, for the financial markets to seek to handle these surpluses by the conventional methods as if they were merely balance of payments surpluses is to tackle a problem which does not exist. Instead, what is needed is an acceptance of radical changes in order to accommodate a new phenomenon of long term flows on to the capital markets from oil producers which are not temporary symptoms of balance of payments surpluses to be corrected by the usual methods, but are flows of claims requiring the eventual transfer of ownership of part of the world's resources permanently to new owners.

The chapter layout of the book follows a pattern which accords with the approach we have adopted, rather than a chronological one, and we have described various sectors and divisions of economic activity rather than specific periods of time. Chapter 2, therefore, is not merely a historical description of Kuwait pre-oil, but also an attempt to describe the moulding of the Kuwaiti character and its social and political institutions upon which the forces of change impinged and which decisively influenced the direction which change and development followed after 1946, when the first oil began to flow. Chapter 3 commences our analysis and description proper, and, together with Chapters 4 and 5, describes the development of the institutions, the infrastructure and other aspects of the national scene. But, although these developments are entirely dependent upon oil, stress is laid upon the developments which began before the latest price increases, and which undoubtedly formed the basis which made recent rapid strides possible. The oil developments themselves are only touched upon here to illustrate their relationship, via national income, with the other developments which have taken place, notably the expansion of the Welfare State, the emphasis placed upon diversification, the influx of labour due to construction, the distribution of wealth and Kuwait's changing regional and international relationships. Some consequences for the future in the light of the problems raised are also touched upon. While developments in these chapters are closely related, and generally occurred concurrently, especially in the early phases of the economy's evolution, it was deemed appropriate to present them in three separate chapters to highlight the major features of each.

Chapter 6 deals specifically with the development of oil, but very much in its world context, relating it as much to the change in the world order and the rise of OPEC as to the actual effect upon Kuwait's monetary income. It is obvious, of course, that the oil revenues are fundamental to the changes which have taken place, yet this chapter is merely designed to illustrate their growth and the consequences of other changes, some of which made the price rises and overall ownership of its resources by Kuwait possible, and some which were themselves made possible by the increases in revenue. It is to the former to which this chapter is mainly addressed, however, as the latter occupies a substantial part of the remainder of the book.

Chapter 7 contains an aggregative econometric model for the investigation of the Kuwait economy and its salient features. It illustrates vividly the imbalance in the Kuwait economy and not only the dependence upon oil, which is obvious, but the essential cleavage which exists between the oil and non oil sectors. Many of the parameters generated are of interest and of importance to planning, but it is stressed that the model is an investigatory rather than a forecasting instrument. Chapter 8 analyses the structural growth of the economy and the economic institutions, while Chapter 9 deals with the specific economic sectors and the economy's absorptive capacity. The rationale of development, and its relationship with other aspects of national changes including those of a political and social nature, are developed in the former while the latter provides a description of the existing economy and some of the problems it faces.

The local financial sector is given a chapter of its own, Chapter 10, due to its obvious importance both in the internal economy and its relationships with the outside world. It is essentially a review of the background to the current organisation and an analysis of its structure and operations. It also dwells on recent developments in the monetary institutional framework, and sets the current structure in the overall context of Kuwait's economic development. In view of the vast proportion of Kuwait's financial resources which are being channelled abroad, three separate chapters have been devoted entirely to various aspects of international finance and cooperation in which Kuwait is actively engaged. In Chapter 11 we review Kuwait's role in international finance and illustrate the growth of her power together with that of other oil-exporting countries. Here more than anywhere else, however, we try to emphasise the fact that her foreign investments form part of her overall strategy for the future and that her activities abroad form an integral part of her overall developmental activity.

Chapters 12 and 13 cover the role of Kuwait in foreign assistance to the LDCs, in both the Arab and the non-Arab worlds. The first deals with the development and organisation of aid in Kuwait, its pattern and objectives, while the second is devoted entirely to the organisation and activities of the Kuwait Fund for Arab Economic Development, one of the world's major aid-giving agencies, and whose remit extends beyond the Arab nations to include LDCs generally. 'The Fund', of course, is the main source through which much of Kuwait's concessionary flows to the developing world are channelled.

Chapter 14 is in the nature of an overview of the problems that seem to us to have been made apparent from Kuwait's point of view as our work proceeded. We can only point to these problems and perhaps eluci- date some of their causes and consequences. It is not our wish to prescribe policy, although we may occasionally have transgressed in this in our discussion of 'future prospects' which forms the second half of this, the final chapter.

Our hope is that readers will read this volume in a 'developmental frame of mind', and we hope that the descriptive model of explanation of Kuwait's behaviour that we have offered, and which has guided our investigations, will in turn serve readers as a frame of reference for the interpretation of much that follows.

2 A Background to Development

The origins of Kuwait as a state are not comparable with most of those of the great majority of other states which have achieved international recognition of their sovereignty in the years since World War II. The boundaries of so many of the emergent nations of the former colonial territories were fixed during the colonial period by conquest or agreement between the colonial powers and these boundaries usually bore no relevance to ethnic or social divisions of the peoples which lived within them, indeed the reverse was often the case. Tribes and even whole peoples with no linguistic or cultural affinity one for another might find themselves in a grouping of convenience made solely on the basis of a useful colonial administration and that grouping might well now form the basis of an emergent 'nation' which in fact might have no historical foundation at all. Many of the emergent states therefore had few of the elements of cohesion so necessary for political stability and ordered progress. Even where an efficient civil service had been built up during the colonial period, this was usually structured to facilitate the maintenance of a *status quo* rather than to provide an executive arm for an independent government of a sovereign state primarily concerned with indigenous development. This, however, was not so in Kuwait. Even though the indigenous population came from similar Arab tribes to those of its neighbours, their history provided them with those elements of cohesion that have maintained the social and political unity of Kuwaiti society for more than two centuries.

To appreciate Kuwait's current attitude to its neighbours and to the rest of the world it is necessary to understand the social and political genesis of the Kuwaiti people. Kuwait was never a colony, but for around sixty years was a British Protectorate. However, even under the protectorate, the British presence was minimal and at no time were there any British troops or other forms of imperial presence in the country. Thus, while its development has been coloured by its relationships with the western industrial powers, those relationships were of a rather special kind which we shall examine later in this chapter.

Very little is known of Kuwait in early history. Archaeological findings on the Isle of Failaka indicate a Greek presence some time during 400 to 100 B.C. While the nature of this presence has not been determined with exactitude, it is believed that the island was reached by the fleet of Niarchus during the time of Alexander the Great. Whether it was a fortress or merely a stopping place is not known, but it is probable that during this and other periods Failaka may have been a staging post on the trade routes which existed between the West and the East. To use an island for such a purpose rather than a coastal site would only make sense if there was need of a natural defence system, and this the sea would provide. This fact in itself might tell us something of the nature and character of the area during those early times. If the mainland areas were inhabited by warring tribes to whom fixed settlements might even be regarded as offensive intrusions, especially if they controlled watering places, then an organised defence of any such site would obviously be necessary. It is known that the Portuguese built a fort at Kuwait in the sixteenth century, but no trace of this exists now, and whether it was a staging post or an outpost to protect trade routes is not known. But no matter how limited historical evidence on Kuwait's early history is, it all points to Kuwait being an important junction on the trade routes no matter to which period the evidence available relates. It is, of course, only through painstaking historical investigation that more will be learned of Kuwait's early history, and speculation will serve no useful purpose. But suffice to say that Kuwait, placed at the head of the Arabian Gulf close to the Shatt El Arab, not only occupied an important place in the development of trade between West and East, but also held a strategic position in the Arab world itself. This second point must be noted, for even during the days when the Suez Canal supplanted the overland routes as the vital link between the Mediterranean and the East, the interest in the Gulf of the powers depending upon East–West trade was in no way diminished as it was realised that they depended upon the Middle East as a whole for the furtherance of their overall strategies. Kuwait, therefore, in spite of its diminutive size, always had a special position in the world political scene during the nineteenth and early twentieth centuries before the advent of oil, and the way in which it used that position to maintain its separate existence has played an important part in forming its attitude and outlook to the present day.

The origins of modern Kuwait can be traced back to the settlement of the area by a clan of the Anaizz tribe from the northern part of central Arabia.[1] When this settlement took place is not precisely known, but it is held to have been some time just before or at the beginning of the eighteenth century. At that time the area of modern Kuwait was part of the province of Al Hasa and under the dominance of the Bani Khalid tribe. The authority of the Sheikh of Kuwait gradually emerged during the eighteenth century and appears to have been absolute not long after 1750. The Sheikh was appointed by tribal election and the first was chosen from the Sabah family. Ever since, this family has provided the ruling Dynasty. A number of factors facilitated the establishment of independence for Kuwait and its Sheikh from the influence of the Bani Khalid. First the rise of the Wahabis. These were a religious sect dedicated to basic purity of the Islamic faith and advocating a return to religious fundamentalism. At the time of Kuwait's emergence they were locked in struggle with the Bani Khalid, thus keeping the latter preoccupied on a wider scale so that the development of a separate authority on such a small scale as Kuwait posed a relatively minor threat. Secondly the antagonism between rulers in the southern part of the Gulf and their almost perennial conflicts kept them preoccupied also; and lastly Kuwait's physical smallness which belied its true importance.[2] Soon Kuwait was to develop into an important port for the northern Gulf with better natural facilities than Basra or Bushire from whom it initially drew trade; also it was the only feasible port for Jabal Shammer (the northern area of Arabia). Thus it became a centre for the desert caravans crossing the area.[3] This strategic position was particularly important after the events of the 1770s. Firstly Basra was hit by the plague and then in 1776 was occupied by the Persians. These twin events with the scattering of the population from Basra and the anxiety of foreign commercial interests over the city's trustworthiness as a local centre for their activities gave an important impetus to the development of Kuwait where sovereign rule had but recently been established by the Sabah. Local autonomy in such a small, closely-knit state with the possibility of quick adjustment and response to opportunities enabled Kuwait to take immediate advantage of any possibilities offered by the changing fortunes of other states in the area. Only a state as small as Kuwait can exercise the necessary flexibility with sufficient speed in this way.

POLITICAL EMERGENCE

However, the factors contributing to the political emergence of modern Kuwait took root in the latter part of the nineteenth century. Indeed the

end of this period, which was marked by intense imperialist interest in
the Gulf by the major European countries, saw the rise of a remarkable
ruler who is held by most historians to be the father of modern Kuwait.
True, he was in full conformity with the Kuwaiti tradition of exploitation of opportunities which presented themselves, but the world order
was changing in such a way that these opportunities arose in a world
dimension and for the first time, but certainly not the last, a Kuwaiti
ruler began to play for stakes on the world stage, skilfully exploiting the
rivalry of the great powers who sought his favours and turning that
rivalry to his country's advantage. That ruler was Mubarak.

Mubarak was one of eight sons of Sabah II who was the fourth ruler
of Kuwait. On the death of Sabah II in 1886 his son Abdullah
succeeded him but died in 1892 to be succeeded in turn by Muhammad
who ruled with the assistance of his full brother Jarrah. These were
essentially pro-Turk, Muhammad even accepting the title of
Quaimaqam (Deputy Governor), a title which had previously been
given to Abdullah by the Turks. He devoted little time to government
and effectively handed over the administration of the Sheikhdom to an
expatriate from Iraq. In May 1896 Mubarak murdered his half brothers
Muhammad and Jarrah and seized the throne. Whether this was
through his own ambition or his half brothers' weaknesses is not really
clear and historians are divided on this issue, but Kuwait found a leader
who could withstand both the pressures of the Turks and those of the
rivalry of the Saudi and Al Rashid families in Arabia. In fact the
succour which he gave to Wahabi exiles fleeing the persecution of the Al
Rashid changed the course of the peninsula's history, for these exiles
included many of the foremost members of the House of Saud including at one time Abdulaziz Ibn Saud, who was later to establish the
Saudi Dynasty, and whom he helped to re-establish the Saudi family's
position in the Najd. Later, he became less interested in his role in inter-
Arab conflicts and became a champion of the Arab cause against the
Turks, thus incurring the enmity of Ibn Saud, who saw himself in that
position.

At the same time as he was establishing himself in the Arab world
Mubarak also realised that his country's fortunes lay with the British,
the growing power in the Gulf at that time. However, by skilful states-
manship, he made his friendship as necessary to the British as theirs was
to him and was able to ensure that the British were never able to exercise
direct interference in the internal affairs of Kuwait. As quoted by Al
Ebraheem,[4]

Thanks to the exceptional ability of Sheikh Mubarak and to but little less extent of his successors, the political agent at Kuwait has never been called upon to make representation to the ruler of Kuwait affecting the internal administration of the principality. Gun-boats and aeroplanes have protected the town against Wahabi incursions, but no troops have ever been landed. ... In no part of the Persian Gulf have the relations alike of the Sheikh and his people with British government, its representative and with British merchants been more uniformly pleasant and cordial.[5]

A crucial element in world power politics at this time was the German aim to establish a railway linking Germany and the central European system with the Gulf in order to counter Britain's control of sea routes to the east via the Mediterranean and the Suez Canal and to further her own commercial interests. This proposal relied crucially on the support of the Turks, as the new railway would of course cross the Ottoman Empire. The history of these proposals and the inter-power rivalry which they created is a classic example of how world power politics were conducted at that time.[6] With Central European powers and the Ottomans denied access to the non-industrial areas of the world either as sources of raw materials or markets for finished products many of the alliances forged during that period were concerned not so much with mutual protection as with the furtherance of common commercial aims. The alliance of Germany with the Turks grew from their common interest, Germany's increasing commitment to the area through railway building in Anatolia.

To complete the outlet from central Europe to the East required a suitable terminal port in the Gulf, and Kuwait was the first and major choice. Far from being a pawn in the game, however, Mubarak used his position to further his country's interests. Having destroyed his pro-Turkish predecessors he was in no way endeared to the Turks and sought some guarantee of his own position. The British, anxious lest their interests be endangered by the access of the railway to the Gulf, sought actively to thwart the German plans. Russia, meanwhile, viewed with disfavour the prospect of Turkey, her southern enemy, having rapid rail access to Russia's southern frontier in the Middle East, especially when that access was provided by international capital that would have a vital interest in its protection. Mubarak therefore attempted to use the British antagonism towards the German plans as a weapon against the Turks, and sought British protection. In 1899, after pressure on the home government from Curzon, the Viceroy of India, an agreement was signed by which Kuwait became a British Protectorate in all but name. As part of the agreement Kuwait 'agreed not to lease, dispose of, or give concessions to any individual power of, land in the Sheikhdom for any purpose without British permission, nor to receive agents or representatives of foreign governments without British agreement'. This effectively gave Britain the right to control the development of both Kuwait and its foreign policy.

By 1913, however, the British had cooled in their attitude towards the railway somewhat and a draft agreement with Turkey was prepared which actually recognised Turkey's suzerainty over Kuwait, but which also included the recognition by the Turks of British interests in the Gulf and guaranteed Mubarak's existing agreements with Britain. This agreement remained unratified when the war broke out in 1914, however, and Mubarak sided with the British in their attack on the Turks in the Mesopotamian campaign. As a result, Kuwait was recognised by the British as an independent state under British protection. Meanwhile, in October 1913 Britain had received an extra strengthening of its power regarding oil in a letter from the Sheikh agreeing not to cede any power over oil except to an appointee of the British government. This letter was to be of vital importance in future oil negotiations, as is explained later.

In 1915 Mubarak died, but the relationships forged with the British remained substantially intact until the cessation of the Protectorate agreement in 1961 and it was on the agreements which he made that the British interests in Kuwait were based.

COMMERCIAL DEVELOPMENT

During the nineteenth century Kuwait's economic activities were centred entirely on trade and the sea. By 1800 the Kuwaiti sailors were very prominent on the sea routes to India and East Africa, handling a goodly proportion of the Gulf trade, which in that year was estimated at sixteen million Bombay rupees per year. By no means all the trade carried was via Kuwait, however, and Kuwait's ships handled much of the imports and exports of the other Gulf states. The trade between India, East Africa and the Gulf varied in its fortunes, but was vital to the last mentioned area, where for the most part the possibilities of indigenous development were extremely limited and the majority of necessities were imported.

Throughout the nineteenth century the trade routes from the Gulf itself and the journeys of the Kuwait mariners followed definite patterns. The trading season started around September and continued for about ten months. The usual trading cargo commenced with dates bought at Basra and traded down the Gulf coast either for money or other trade goods and the trade continued across the Indian Ocean to India or down the east coast of Africa as far as Zanzibar and Dar-es-Salaam. The return journey was then usually direct, carrying for the most part timber and this usually mangrove poles for building.[7] However it would be a grave error to assume that the whole of Kuwait's trading activities were confined to this type of 'journey out—journey home' pattern. The whole of the Indian Ocean was a vast trading area, with sailing routes linking the countries which surrounded it. Kuwait's dhows plied these routes constantly, and there grew up a most intricate trading system in which Kuwait took a substantial part. Also, the general relationships between mariner, shipowner and merchant were important. Often, but not always, the last two would be the same person, but in any event there was a vital basis of mutual trust between the captain and his shipowner, as with the absence of rapid communication he was his owner's agent and traded on his behalf, often accepting or selling trade goods when prices made either expedient, and accepting cargoes on his own initiative in foreign ports. At the same time the rights of each, and of the crew, were rigidly defined, and certain forms of trading would be part of the crew's 'perks'. At the end of a voyage, the final share of the profit was a most intricate operation. It was the merchant-shipowner, however, who was the financier of a voyage. He advanced the money for the purchase of trade goods, provided for the victualling of the ship and also for the funds required on voyage.

Given the form and pattern of trade, it was natural too that merchants would establish links in the market areas in which they operated. Thus, many of them established agencies in the main ports around the Indian Ocean, often headed by family members, and these agencies became centres for wholesaling activities. Not only would value added be increased, but cargoes could be received and stored rather than sold straight from the dhow at what might be a much lower price if the market was unfavourable. Similarly, purchases could be made if advantageous and stored to await shipment.

Kuwaiti merchants also reached back toward the sources of trade goods for investment opportunities, with some purchasing date plantations, others financing crops by providing growers with working capital and similar financial ventures. For example, many Kuwaiti merchants took an important part in the development of trade in Basra, when that port was prominent in the trade of the Gulf.

Thus, the Kuwaiti merchant families grew up as trading dynasties, centred on Kuwait, but with an intricate network of relationships, often based on kinship, which spanned the Middle East and a greater part of the Indian Ocean, and it was these merchant families which provided that echelon of social and political leadership to the country and gave it that special brand of mental adroitness and financial astuteness which characterises it today.

Added to this, the mariner–owner relationship touched upon earlier added its own contribution to the working of the social structure. Based as it was upon 'interdependent trust', it combined a peculiar blend of independence and individuality with a loyalty that was almost absolute.

The only other major activities in pre-oil Kuwait were pearling and fishing. Pearling provided Kuwait's sailors with an important supplement to their incomes. Even after the Second World War a sailor might only get fifty US dollars for a nine months voyage, so an additional income, no matter how meagre, was welcome. In three months, a pearling fisherman could earn a further thirty-five dollars. This was important, as the total income took the Kuwaiti sailor out of the class of the peasant in the developing countries, whose equivalent income at that time was much lower. Also, it was a monetary income and he enjoyed a far greater independence than a peasant tied to his land and receiving income in kind only. The industry had flourished for centuries in the Gulf area and, while little is known of its early history, it is recorded that in the 1940s Kuwait still sent about a hundred boats to the pearling grounds in spite of the set-backs of the great depression, development of the Japanese cultured pearl industry, and of course the outbreak of the Second World War.

In discussing the economic problems of the inter-war period, most emphasis is usually placed upon the Depression. However, the First World War saw the end of a social system in which the aristocracies and the great families of Europe were the natural leaders of society. The distribution of wealth was altered drastically by the war and by the social upheaval which it created. With the introduction of mass production, so many branches of industry produced at a lower quality for the masses and competed with the high quality craftsmanship which had hitherto produced only for the wealthy few. Cultured pearls and mass produced automobiles were all part of the new syndrome and the wearing of pearls or the ownership of an automobile was no longer a mark of high social distinction. Fashions changed and pearls no longer enjoyed the same regard as in pre-war days. Thus, the pearl market would undoubtedly have suffered even if the great Depression had not happened. When incomes in the Western economies fell so dramatically this was an added blow and the war itself imposed further downward pressure on an already depressed industry. There is no doubt that in spite of the hundred boats visiting the pearling grounds during the 1940s the industry was doomed and only remained active because of the lack of alternative opportunities. Also, whereas a peasant in an agricultural but poor country may at least have had his land on which to produce something, the foodstuffs consumed by the sailor and his family would be essentially restricted due to the severe lack of natural endowments ashore. Thus, Kuwait was forced into further reliance on the sea. Fishing, then, was another major activity, but it cannot be described as an industry in the same way as pearling. Essentially fish was a part of the food supply of the local population, rather than a commodity of trade. Catches were sold at local markets or consumed by the fishermen themselves, and fish would form part of the essential protein supply of the people and be in the same category as the produce of the land consumed by peasants elsewhere who were engaged in subsistence agriculture. The only other sources of indigenous foodstuffs were milk and meat from the herds obtaining a meagre living from the desert. Consequently any supplementation of the local diet would need to be purchased and imported. With such a low monetary income, and limited opportunity for food production, the lot of the Kuwaiti fisherman and his fellows was very hard, although as mentioned above he was certainly not in the same category as a peasant in the underdeveloped world.

The other activity which some writers have surprisingly classed as an 'industry' was a form of smuggling. This was of course a sideline for the Kuwaitis, and undoubtedly was made necessary as an alternative source of income by the harsh conditions of the time. To a great extent it consisted of the importation of gold into India, especially up to 1947, and for some time thereafter. Import and export of gold was not illegal in Kuwait. Indeed, this would be inconsistent with any state having a large interest in maritime trading. In India, gold was both an adornment and a store of value as in other countries, but its use and veneration was woven into the social fabric in a way that made its position rather special. The Indian rupee was legal tender in the Gulf itself, and for long was the official currency. Consequently, payment for gold sold in India could be made in rupees, and all rupees surplus to requirements could be cashed quite legally through the Bank of India. Conversely gold could be purchased in India for rupees and sold on the world market by Kuwaitis in exactly the same way when gold prices made this expedient. Control by India, and later by India and Pakistan, was impossible. Kuwaiti traders were able to buy gold in Beirut and other markets of the Middle East and Europe. Kuwait itself acted as a trade centre for Arab goods, much of which might be traded in gold, and Kuwaiti dhows were trading down the coast of Africa where gold was a uniquely acceptable currency and marketable commodity. Any outlet for furthering profit on the results of trade would naturally be exploited to the full. The gold trade was so prevalent that in 1947 Pakistan and India both banned Kuwaitis, but this proved to be entirely ineffective and even when a distinctive rupee currency was introduced in the Gulf in 1959 the difficulties created were easily circumvented.

Wherever there is a demand for a commodity complete control can never be guaranteed, but one thing is certain, where any commodity is in demand control and restriction will drive up its price and make evasions more profitable. Thus it was with gold, and in the immediate years post-1945, gold traders could reckon to make profit even when losing one in four cargoes. In fact the odds and the profits were such that it was possible to insure consignments against confiscation.[8] Due to the prevalence of the gold trade and its relationship with other seafaring activities of the Kuwaiti fleet it may be classed as an industry in the sense that it contributed a large if unknown proportion of Kuwait's income.

All these activities were later to be overshadowed by developments in oil, the magnitude of which could never have been imagined in those harsh times. It is to the history of the oil developments, therefore, that we turn in the next section. However, the combination of Kuwait's political and commercial history is the main foundation of the Kuwaiti character, and should be remarked upon here. The constant need to tread a path between antagonists has given it a flavour of 'neutral independence' and an ability, born of necessity, to turn affairs quickly to its own advantage. At the same time, the harsh forces of nature, and the type of activities open to its people, bred a very rugged type of citizen able to withstand much adversity. Trade of the type we describe required a solid basis of mutual trust between owners, captains and merchants, while at the same time the merchant community depended upon the rulers of Kuwait to maintain favourable conditions for them to develop their activities. In return, they provided the rulers with their revenue.

The modern Kuwait reflects in great measure all these elements. The state welfare system is a reflection of that pattern of inter-related responsibilities without which the commercial enterprises of the pre-oil era could never have survived. At the same time it is a basis of support for a free enterprise system in which citizens are able to exploit opportunities as they arise and turn them to advantage, just as any merchant mariner would have done if faced with a good trading prospect, rather than a reflection of any socialist ideology. This intricate inter-relatedness, which pervades the commercial and political structure, does more to explain the modern attitudes and methods of approach to major economic and political problems than any other single factor.

OIL AND THE FIRST OIL AGREEMENT

To put an actual date on the discovery of oil in the Middle East would in many ways be misleading. The existence of bitumen in the desert was obviously well-known to Arab tribesmen at the earliest times and it is often speculated that the 'burning bush' of biblical times could easily be explained by a freak ignition of a seepage of natural gas. But the history of oil in Kuwait, or more correctly the entry of Kuwait oil into history, may really be dated from about 1911. Britain had committed itself to oil as a future fuel for the Royal Navy and the safeguarding of existing and future supplies of this fuel as an essential sinew of war was vital to British security. The Anglo-Persian Oil Company (APOC) represented British oil interests in the area of the Gulf and in November 1911 the British political resident in the Gulf was asked to inquire of the Sheikh of Kuwait (Sheikh Mubarak) if an oil concession was obtainable and if so to apply for a prospecting licence. Due to the political problems in the area at the time, the political representative advised against pursuing this matter immediately, but in March 1913 Mubarak permitted a group of Admiralty experts to carry out a geological survey. The survey was 'not unfavourable' according to Chisholm[9] and in November of that year a British Admiralty commission led by Admiral Slade visited Kuwait to discuss the state's oil possibilities with the Sheikh. Prior to the meeting with the mission the Sheikh had received, and replied to, a letter from the political representative and this exchange was of vital significance to the future history of oil in Kuwait.

The letter from the political representative (Lt. Col. Sir Percy Cox) was in fact a confirmation of a discussion of the previous day (26 October, 1913). In it he confirmed his request that a delegation be permitted to view the places of seepage of bitumen in the Burgan and elsewhere in Kuwait and '... if there seemed in his view a hope of

obtaining oil therefrom Your Excellency agrees not to give a concession
in this regard to anyone other than a person nominated and
recommended by His Majesty's Government.' Replying the same day,
the Sheikh agreed to accept the mission and '. . . if in their view there
seems hope of obtaining oil therefrom we shall never give a concession
in this matter to anyone except the person nominated by the British
Government'. It was these two letters, together with the 1899
Agreement as strengthened with the 'Declaration of Protection' of 1914
which was the basis of Britain's special claims on Kuwait.

However, the outbreak of war in 1914 and the protracted
negotiations after 1918 of the peace settlements in the Middle East
consequent upon the break-up of the Ottoman Empire meant that little
was pursued in the matter of Kuwait oil until 1920–1. Meantime, Sheikh
Mubarak had died in 1915, but before his death he had established the
system which exists today whereby the country's leadership was to be
drawn from his descendants. He was thus succeeded by his son Sheikh
Jabir who died in 1917 and was succeeded by his brother Sheikh Salim
who in turn died early in 1921. Sheikh Salim's successor, however,
Sheikh Ahmad Al-Jabir, ruled not only throughout the period of the
subsequent oil negotiations but right up to 1950 which saw the start of
the influx of his country's great wealth from oil exports.

In early 1922, terms and proposals for suitable concessions were the
subject of discussion both between APOC, the British government and
the political representative in the Gulf, as well as between the political
representative and Sheikh Ahmad. In March APOC provided the
former with a draft agreement for presentation to the Sheikh which
incorporated almost all the modifications he had requested to previous
proposals. However, while the political representative was still
considering these proposals before submission to the Sheikh the latter
was approached by Major Frank Holmes representing a small
company, Eastern and General Syndicate Ltd (EGS), a London
prospecting company which had just obtained concessions in Saudi
Arabia from Ibn Saud. Holmes was not an experienced oil man; he had
little knowledge of the Middle East and did not speak Arabic. However,
he was to become one of the most persistent and important figures in
Middle East oil for the following decade. His approach to the Sheikh
was via a telegram simply asking him to grant no concessions until he
had considered proposals from EGS. These followed immediately by
letter and were considerably more favourable than those offered by
APOC.[10] There were other factors besides monetary ones which
persuaded the Sheikh to lean towards Holmes rather than APOC. The

former had good relations with Ibn Saud who had recently proposed to the Sheikh joint exploration of the Neutral Zone[11] for oil purposes. Also, with APOC's involvement with the British government the Sheikh did not wish his own state's development to depend upon the interests of those of Persia which were bound to be paramount in the eyes of APOC as it was there their major operations were centred. With the approval of his Council the Sheikh decided not to accept the British offer, but of course he was aware of his obligation not to accept other offers unless they were received from nominees of the British government. Holmes meanwhile assured the Sheikh that he would be able to obtain the necessary approval, as indeed he had done previously in his negotiations with Ibn Saud on the EGS Arabian concession. In a series of letters between the British government and the Sheikh it was agreed by Britain that the Sheikh might, if he chose, accept terms from Holmes provided that they were better than those offered by APOC. This made the way clear for the Sheikh to enter into competitive negotiations with both APOC and Holmes, a situation which he viewed with much pleasure. He was obviously in no mood to hurry his agreement with any successful bidder, and he was also in separate negotiations with Holmes and Ibn Saud over the development of the Neutral Zone. Consequently negotiations, if indeed they even amounted to such, continued haphazardly until 1926. Holmes and EGS by this time seemed to have been overstretched with interests in Bahrain, Hassa and the Neutral Zone and in February 1926 they offered the whole of their interests in the area to APOC for £50,000. These terms were not acceptable to APOC and after unfavourable reports by their geologists on the possibilities of oil developments in the area they broke off negotiations with EGS. EGS then sought American backing. However, this was not forthcoming either but Holmes succeeded in persuading Gulf Oil (Pennsylvania) to maintain an interest which eventually came to life when Holmes under the guise of a 'public-spirited act' of drilling for water found traces of oil in the drillings. In November 1927 Gulf Oil bought an option on all EGS interests in the Gulf. Sheikh Ahmad was immediately confronted with a totally different situation. Previously he was faced with a choice between, on the one hand, a powerful company backed by the government to which he was politically committed and of which his country was a Protectorate, and on the other, a doubtful organisation which, while offering him better terms, had no financial backing with which to exploit the concessions he might give, and therefore might well prove unable to fulfil their obligations to him. Now, however, he had two large companies vying for his favour, both backed by their respective powerful governments and both with sufficient finance for any operations that they might wish to undertake. Also, not only did it mean that he had the economic stakes for which to play and to balance these against the political consequences, but he could now play for political stakes at the same time, as no matter which of the two companies he chose this would imply some form of political commitment to his state in view of the size and importance of the companies' activities in general. He therefore leaned towards Gulf as a means of exploiting the new situation in order to reduce Kuwait's dependence on the British. Holmes continued negotiations on behalf of EGS but in view of the Gulf Oil option the situation was entirely transformed as far as Britain was concerned.

The astuteness of the Sheikh should be noted here, as this policy of maintaining the interests of two parties at the same time was to pay handsome rewards. Nowhere else in the Gulf did this occur and yet of course it meant that not only did they compete for his favour, but also that the one would provide protection against pressure from the other.

In November 1928 the political agent in Kuwait informed Holmes that the British government would require a 'British nationality clause' in any agreement he made. This would in fact preclude any American participation in such an agreement and of course would debar a transfer to an American company of any concessions obtained. (Simultaneously EGS were informed in London that this would also be required in their Bahrain concession in which they were being backed by Standard Oil of California.)

While this set-back was anticipated somewhat by the Sheikh it was to impede his efforts to increase his country's income by competitively bidding up the terms of the rivals' offers at a time when the pearling industry was hit by a series of poor years and he was also being embarrassed by a blockade of trade with the interior by Ibn Saud. Meanwhile with the stock market crash of 1929 Gulf saw no reason to press ahead through political channels to break Britain's insistence on the nationality clause and APOC were quite willing to let matters drift as long as Gulf (through EGS) remained inactive. Relationships between all parties seemed to remain intensely cordial, but cordiality was not sufficient to assist the Sheikh in his efforts.

In 1929 the British government removed their insistence on the nationality clause in the case of Bahrain and Holmes confidently expected similar treatment in respect of the moribund Kuwait negotiations to follow quickly. This however was not the case. It must be remembered that oil did not occupy the paramount position in world affairs that it does today. It is very possible that the British attitude to a Kuwait concession passing into the hands of a non-British company might be to regard this as the introduction of non-British interests into an area which might militate against the interests of Britain. It might not have had the same attitude towards Bahrain. It must be remembered too that no oil had been discovered on the Arabian side of the Gulf apart from the traces noted by Holmes so that the actual oil interests would possibly have figured quite low in the British government's calculations and assessment of its policy.

It was not until April 1932 that the British finally removed their insistence and this only after heated and repeated representation by the American government that was being pressured by the strong oil lobby. America regarded the British attitude as another facet of the unjust treatment it had received in the Middle East at the hands of both Britain and France after the cessation of hostilities in 1918 when she was effectively kept out of the division of the Ottoman spheres of interest, even though she had been a member of the victorious allies during the First World War. The persistence of the Sheikh in constantly negotiating for improved offers was justified when oil was struck in Bahrain on 31 May 1932 in commercial quantities. This fact transformed the situation in the Gulf and vitally affected the situation of Kuwait. Oil was now known to exist on the south side of the Gulf and Holmes' eternal optimism was vindicated while the pessimism of so many better qualified 'experts' was proved to be unfounded. Still however APOC were reticent, preferring to offer the Sheikh a sum for prospecting rights only. In view of his internal problems (the continued slump in the pearl industry and the blockade to landward) the Sheikh insisted that only proposals for a long-term concession of around seventy years would be acceptable. Proposals were then made to him by both APOC and EGS and these, together with his comments, were in the hands of the British government for five months until January 1933 when British permission was given to APOC and EGS to resume their negotiations. By this time, however, overtures had been made between Gulf and APOC for a possible combined effort in Kuwait, but both continued to strive for the concession for themselves, at least up to the time when a joint effort could actually be agreed upon and mounted.

In May 1933 after an inexplicable suspension of negotiations by the Sheikh there was agreement between Gulf and APOC on a standstill in their competitive negotiations. This standstill was to last until December when their jointly-owned Kuwait Oil Company (KOC) was founded, and in February 1934 Holmes and Chisholm (who formerly represented APOC) arrived in Kuwait as joint representatives of the new company.

The company had an initial capital of £50,000 and was to have three directors from each side and an annually appointed chairman chosen from each alternately. The company was to remain a British company and the concession was not to be transferred without British approval. Unfortunately the new company instructed these negotiators to commence negotiations with monetary offers at levels lower than either of the offers made in the final submissions of the two parent companies before the standstill commenced. Naturally the Sheikh took exception to this obvious collusion and after negotiations the offers were quickly improved. This collusion also prompted the Sheikh to make a number of new demands, one concerning a directorship on the board of the new company for a nominee to be decided by him. He also demanded a much higher royalty payment than the one being offered. But while these plans were being considered a new company was found to be negotiating with the Sheikh. It was called Traders Ltd, and was an entirely British-registered company. This was said to be offering much better terms than KOC. The entrance of this company on the scene was regarded by Holmes as an APOC 'plot' to maintain a completely British interest[12] and by others as a ruse by which the Sheikh sought to force the hand of KOC. It was in fact neither, but was a genuine company offering to enter the market for the concession. It had the effect of crystallising KOC into action, however, and by December, once it had been confirmed that the new company had actually applied to the British government for permission to negotiate, their representatives in Kuwait were instructed to accept unaltered the Sheikh's complete proposals, which by now no longer contained an insistence on a directorship. The final agreement was signed on 23 December 1934. Holmes was quickly appointed the Sheikh's representative in London, a post he occupied until his death in 1947.

This agreement granted the Sheikh 475,000 rupees (i.e. around $178,000) on signature, 3 rupees (around $1·13) per ton 'won and saved' or 95,000 rupees (about $35,000) per annum whichever be the larger until oil be declared obtainable in commercial quantities and after that date 250,000 rupees (about $94,000) per annum or the 3 rupees per ton royalty whichever be the greater plus, in lieu of all taxes and dues, 4 annas (9c) per ton of oil on which royalties were payable. This agreement was written for a period of seventy-five years.

The history of these negotiations, much of which has been disclosed for the first time by Chisholm, shows Sheikh Ahmad as the prime architect of the 1934 agreement and the vast benefits it has brought to Kuwait. The achievement of his objectives, despite the existence of a definite division in Kuwait public opinion, which was so obviously very active during the whole of the period, is evidence of his adroit handling of both the political and commercial aspects of his state. As in the case of Sheikh Mubarak, Ahmad followed in the traditional Kuwaiti mould of the astute ruler of a small state using the strategic position granted it by contemporary conditions, be they in international politics, trade or oil, and turning these to the state's advantage. Chisholm's record, as he himself states,[12,13] shows Sheikh Ahmad in a new light as the driving force of the long and protracted negotiations and the role of Holmes, and consequently his position in history, is correspondingly lessened. His subsequent appointment as the Sheikh's representative in London is seen to have been a genuine reward for years of friendship and counsel instead of what euphemistically were hitherto called 'services rendered'.

We have dealt at length with the negotiations leading to the first oil agreement as they are not only a fascinating portrayal of contemporary relationships between states and international business interests, but more importantly they highlight the manner in which the Sheikh of Kuwait played the role of statesman so adroitly on behalf of the country when faced with such superior power. This effective neutralising of the power of his adversaries seems a skill inherent in the Kuwait character and the whole of this historical review portrays occasions when this skill has been skilfully exercised. However it must be emphasised that at the time of the signing of the agreement oil had still not been discovered in Kuwait!

The quest for oil commenced in the following year and the first well was drilled at Bahrah in May 1936. This proved dry, but oil was discovered in February 1938 in the Burgan, later to be recognised as the world's largest single field. Eight more wells were drilled on the same field and one on what was to become the Magwa field, but in 1942, because of the critical situation reached by the war in the Middle East, the wells were plugged and work was not commenced again until the war was reaching its close in 1945. From that point on, however, activity was feverish and the rapid developments which resulted will be described in following chapters.

Up to the Second World War, of course, the KOC were the sole concessionaires in Kuwait oil. However the Kuwait government also had a half interest in the Neutral Zone between Kuwait and Saudi

Arabia and a concession for exploiting this was granted to the American Independent Oil Company (Aminoil) in 1948. This was quite different from the KOC agreement, with a minimum of $625,000 per annum, $7.25 million on signature, $2.50 per long ton plus other miscellaneous payments. Further concessions were granted later, e.g. to the Arab Oil Company in 1958, a Japanese owned company, to exploit offshore oil in the territorial waters of the Neutral Zone and in 1961 to Royal Dutch Shell to exploit the coastal waters off Kuwait's coast itself. Each agreement was a substantial improvement on its predecessor and marks both the process of change in the balance of power in the oil world and also the great increase in the importance of oil to the industrial countries since those early days when APOC first began its negotiations. It is to the next stage of development in Kuwait, from 1946 onward, which evolved while many of these changes took place, that we turn in the next chapter.

3 The Emergence of Modern Kuwait

The emergence of Kuwait's modern economy goes back to 1946 when the first oil shipment was exported. The country's growth since then has largely mirrored the smooth and swift exploitation of its vast oil reserves. Within a span of no more than fifteen years its population came to enjoy living standards normally considered the prerogative of the most developed among the industrialised countries. The pattern of growth that Kuwait has experienced since 1946, the development of its infrastructure, institutions and the welfare system that has evolved are unparalleled in modern history. This chapter is thus devoted to analysing the main features of the country's economic growth and development as the commercial production of oil commenced and the modern economy of Kuwait began to evolve.

Oil was not only the leading sector after 1946 but it also quickly substituted for many of the country's traditional activities, particularly pearling, seafaring and fishing. The swiftness with which oil exports acquired a predominant role was essentially due to the small size of the economy (estimated GNP in 1945 was less than $5 million) and the rapid increase in the oil revenues.[1] This development was enhanced by the limited scope for expanding the country's traditional activities; because of technological progress elsewhere and other factors mentioned earlier in the case of pearling, or inferior remuneration and working conditions as is the case of seafaring and fishing. In view of these considerations the economy had no inherent resistance to the transformation process that was about to take place. On the contrary, the outward-looking attitude of the people and the absence of major reluctance or scepticism towards foreign investment by the rulers and the business community paved the way for a fruitful cooperation with the oil companies and a rapid development of oil resources as well as the required build-up of the country's infrastructure. Table 3.1 illustrates the growth of oil production and government oil revenues during the years 1946–77.

As the table shows, oil production was increasing steadily until 1973

TABLE 3.1   Growth of oil production and revenues, 1946—77

Year	*Crude Oil Production*		*Government Oil Revenues*	
	(Million US Barrels)	*(Annual Increase %)*	*(Million $US)*	*(Annual Increase %)*
1946	5·9	—	0·76	—
1947	16·2	174·0	2·07	172·3
1948	46·5	187·0	5·95	187·4
1949	89·9	98·0	11·52	93·6
1950	125·7	39·0	16·09	39·6
1951	204·9	63·0	18·00	11·8
1952	273·4	33·0	57·00	216·6
1953	314·6	15·0	169·00	195·6
1954	349·7	11·0	194·20	14·9
1955	402·7	15·0	281·70	45·0
1956	405·5	0·6	293·70	4·2
1957	424·8	4·7	308·00	4·8
1958	522·4	23·0	356·00	15·5
1959	525·9	0·6	419·40	17·8
1960	619·1	17·7	445·80	6·3
1961	633·3	2·2	467·40	4·8
1962	714·6	12·8	484·40	3·6
1963	765·2	7·0	513·80	5·7
1964	842·2	10·0	554·40	7·9
1965	861·5	2·3	567·50	2·4
1966	907·2	5·3	598·30	5·4
1967	912·4	0·6	648·80	8·4
1968	956·6	4·8	736·70	13·6
1969	1011·7	5·8	690·20	−6·3
1970	1090·6	7·8	784·00	13·6
1971	1116·4	2·4	963·00	22·8
1972	1201·6	7·6	1650·00	71·3
1973	1102·5	−0·8	1795·20	8·8
1974	929·3	−15·7	7094·90	295·2
1975	760·7	−18·2	8641·20	21·8
1976	785·2	3·2	9802·80	13·4
1977	718·0	−8.5	8963·10	−8·0

SOURCES: 1 I. Najjar, *The Development of a One Resource Economy: A Case Study of Kuwait*, 1969. An unpublished dissertation, Indiana University.
2 *Kuwait Annual Statistical Abstract*
3 Central Bank of Kuwait, *Quarterly Statistical Bulletin.*

but its rate of growth was subject to noticeable fluctuations. Apart from factors relating to new discoveries by the first concessionaire (KOC) and subsequently by new concessionaires (Aminoil and the Arabian Oil Company), the main causes underlying these fluctuations were external. Hence the economy was exceedingly vulnerable to factors beyond its control, associated with the international oil market and the policies of the major oil companies that exerted a substantial degree of influence. In more recent years, however, a decline in production has developed because of the adoption of a conservation policy which the country could well afford after the rise in oil prices and the nationalisation of the oil companies.

Evidently, the steady increase in Government oil revenues in the 1950s set the stage for the expansion of the economy. Although there are no reliable estimates of GDP before 1961/2, the growth of the economy was clearly manifested in the rapid increase of imports, population and government expenditure. Imports expanded quickly to reach by 1952 a per capita level of over $280; a high rate for many present-day developing countries and a clear indication of the country's potential dependence on foreign-produced goods. The value of total imports more than quadrupled during the 1950s reaching a per capita level of over $780 by 1960. The growth of imports was sustained during the 1960s despite some fluctuations in their rate of increase. The country's import requirements represented in 1970 almost 50 per cent of its exports and over 25 per cent of GDP with per capita imports exceeding $1000 annually. The pattern of imports conformed closely to the process of development that was taking place. Hence, goods and construction materials became increasingly more prominent among imports during the build-up of the country's infrastructure.

The 1961/2 estimate of GDP was KD610 million (approximately $1·708 billion). Based on a population size of approximately 330,000, per capita GDP at KD1848 ($5174) was already one of the highest in the world. This is a clear indication of the phenomenal growth that the country experienced during the period from 1946 to 1961. However growth in the following eight years came down to more normal levels averaging an annual rate of 5 per cent. With the massive influx of labour, population increased by more than 20 per cent during this period and per capita GDP could not be sustained, falling to KD1300 ($3640) by 1970/1. Apart from the fact that the growth of Government oil revenues was considerably lower than that which the country experienced in the 1950s, there were also clear indications that the oil sector was becoming less effective as an engine of growth.[2] Oil revenues continued to provide the bulk of the country's foreign requirements. However its role as an income-generating force was being rapidly eroded. This development was perhaps due to the process of saturation that was taking place in such sectors as construction, services and public administration and the lack of an effective diversification programme to supplement oil receipts with income from other sources.

The evolution of the modern state of Kuwait can best be explained in terms of major developments that have taken place since 1946 which portray a host of social and economic indicators. Many of the changes which these indicators represent were inter-related and occurred concurrently. However, the rapidity with which this evolution took place was made possible by the presence of one common factor — the gradual relaxation of the constraint on the availability of capital. This was an important consideration in the allocation of resources for infrastructure, diversification and welfare development. There are significant implications for population growth and labour force composition as well as the balance of payments and regional economic relations which will all be discussed in the following two chapters. Emphasis is placed in this chapter on the general developments in the earlier years of the emergence of the modern economy. Other features relating to the structure of the economy, its organisation and sectors of production, and Kuwait's role in international finance, as well as its provision of foreign assistance in more recent years, are covered at greater length in appropriate chapters which occur later.

Moreover, even though the rate of growth of oil revenues and pace of development have fluctuated over the last thirty years, the ways in which changes in the other spheres of economic and social activity occurred were such that the whole of the period represented in large measure a single continuous process. It is therefore misleading to divide it into separate phases marked by large changes in oil revenues, as these essentially represented successive relaxations of a combination of constraints on this process rather than being the instigators of it. Further, the process is still developing as contemporary activities in the fields of infrastructure and diversification testify.

Finally, it should be noted that, during the period of the developments which we will describe, there have been two changes, and very recently a third, in the leadership of the country. Sheikh Abdullah Al-Salim succeeded Sheikh Ahmad Al-Jabir on his death in 1950 who in turn died in 1965 to be succeeded by Sheikh Sabah Al-Salim. Sabah Al-Salim ruled Kuwait from 1965 until his death in 1977. On 31 December 1977, Sheikh Jaber Al-Ahmad became Emir of Kuwait. The country's development continued unhindered by such important political changes. On the contrary, the smooth transition and continuity inherent in the system provided greater confidence and an added impetus to the growth of the economy, particularly as in each instance the new ruler had been active in the country's economic affairs prior to his assuming office.

DEVELOPMENT OF INFRASTRUCTURE

For a desert country where there had been an ever-present need for water, it was only natural to give top priority to solving this acute problem. Kuwaitis had depended for centuries on the salt brackish water of the desert wells, collected rain water and irregular supplies from Shatt-Al-Arab by boat. However as soon as the Government had the necessary means sweet water was brought on a more regular basis from Shatt-Al-Arab in traditional boats. The supplied water was very dear and often contaminated. Hence, the Government immediately started to look for alternative sources of supply. In 1953 the Government commissioned the first desalination plant with a designed capacity of almost a million gallons per day of potable water from the sea. Supply of water has continued to enjoy the highest priority in all government plans. The growth of this activity is truly phenomenal; production increased from about 250 million gallons in 1957 to 2·2 billion in 1964 and 6·6 billion by 1970. Kuwait's production of desalinated water is the highest in the world reaching in 1978 a capacity of 102 million gallons per day. This supply is supplemented by underground sweet water at Raudhatain in the north and Shagaiya in the west at a combined daily rate of 8. million gallons.[3]

Due to technical reasons the introduction of desalination plants also paved the way for the development of the country's power sector.[4] The growth of the power generating capacity is also phenomenal. From 2·5 mW in the early 1950s, Kuwait's generating capacity rapidly increased to 160 mW in 1962, to over 500 mW in 1967 and a staggering installed capacity of 2618 mW is scheduled for the end of 1978. The rise in people's income coupled with the climatic conditions of the country resulted in an ever-increasing demand for electricity and produced one of the most tangible indicators of affluence.

In 1954, a town plan was formulated and began to be implemented almost immediately. It envisaged the transformation of the city of Kuwait from a town of 200,000 people to a modern city bursting with activity stretching over 20 km along the Gulf and the demolition of the old town to make way for the building of a new business centre. In spite of some modifications recent developments clearly demonstrated the foresight displayed by the government and its advisors in formulating the plan. The government was not only willing to conceive and adopt such a plan but it was prepared to allocate the necessary funds to implement it. High priority was given to building a modern road network, schools, dispensaries, hospitals and an up-to-date system of communications. In addition, three new oil terminals were constructed and the Kuwait harbour expanded on more than one occasion to cope with the rapidly increasing imports. The land acquisition programme, which will be discussed later, was also partly designed to expedite the development of modern Kuwait by making funds available to the private sector for the construction of houses and commercial buildings. It should be emphasised that even though the town plan mentioned was of such a fundamental and far-reaching nature, many of these developments were accomplished within about fifteen years of its formulation, and revisions as well as supplementary developments were already becoming necessary in fields not covered by the plan. In the last few years, many of these too have been implemented.

INSTITUTIONAL DEVELOPMENTS

Within a period of ten years from 1946, Kuwait had been able to accomplish sufficient progress in the field of infrastucture for the economy to enter a new phase of development.[5] By the late 1950s the country was already preoccupied with such long-term problems as sustaining economic growth and diversification. Hence, the government decided in 1961 to set-up the Shuaiba Industrial Zone to help promote industrialisation. Moreover, the title of the Development Board established in 1952 to plan and coordinate construction activities, especially with respect to public utilities, was changed to the Planning Board and became responsible for such functions as planning, advising the government on economic policy and the identification of new development projects. Both the Planning Board and its predecessor contained representatives from the private sector of the economy as well as representatives of government bodies.

With the achievement of full independence in 1961, the country was also becoming more concerned with other matters of national interest.

These included safeguarding its oil-export earnings, creating an independent monetary system and strengthening economic relations with other Arab countries. As well as developing its role in OPEC which it had joined, prior to independence, in 1960, the government took immediate steps to substitute a national currency for the Indian rupee and to establish its aid organisation — the Kuwait Fund for Arab Economic Development.

Obviously, this rapid pace of progress could not have covered such a broad spectrum of activities without creating and developing a new government machinery. This was also one of the country's highest priorities and most remarkable achievements. Measures were soon introduced to expand and modernise the civil service to perform new functions and shoulder greater responsibilities called for by the growth of the economy. In addition to the need to staff the numerous infrastructure projects that were being implemented and the public service ministries and departments that were rapidly expanding, the government was also expected to provide all the requisites of a state, including ports and telecommications, public works and townships, a judicial system and a security force. Added to these, a foreign service and a military force were required from 1961 onwards.

The task was staggering and would not have been possible to accomplish without the influx into the country of Palestinians, Egyptians, Indians and Iranians and others. The formal collaboration of some other Arab countries was also required. This, however, had some major consequences for later years, often unnecessarily superimposing on Kuwait the slow and bureaucratic systems of countries with obviously different conditions and backgrounds. Although the country was able, because of its social fabric, to overcome many of these drawbacks, there is fear that the inherited problems are increasingly constituting an impediment to the growth and development of the country. Hence, there has been public demand for major administrative reforms in recent years.

THE EVOLUTION OF THE WELFARE STATE

The tribal customs and traditions which have long prevailed in this desert country largely explain the paternal attitude that the government has assumed since 1946.[6] This attitude more than any other factor has been responsible for the country's commitment to the creation of a state welfare system. The outline of this system in its present form had been established by 1956 and has been developed and expanded ever since. A description of the main developments that have taken place in various social services is given below.

Health

Kuwait like many other developing countries in the region had suffered considerably from two of the most serious endemic diseases of the desert, namely smallpox and tuberculosis. Given the limited means available prior to 1946, particularly in respect of health services and hygienic care, the struggle against disease had been most difficult. Hence the government was determined to utilise oil revenues to do everything possible to improve health conditions in the country. The Emiri hospital, completed in 1949, was the first step in the country's concerted effort in this field. This was soon followed by the construction of sanatoria, mental hospitals, maternity units and a new general hospital (Al-Sabah) that were supplied with the most advanced diagnostic and therapeutic equipment available.

In less than a decade after the first export of oil, the people of Kuwait were enjoying, free of cost, health services which few other countries in the region were able to provide.[7] Further, in spite of increasing costs, the community was determined to maintain free medical care and to continue improving the standard of the service. As was proven in more recent years, this has not been an easy task. In fact, there are indications that with the increased influx of people, not only has the quality of the services declined but also the infrastructure and facilities have not kept pace with the country's requirements.[8] Although efforts have very recently been made to rectify this by constructing a new major hospital and expanding some existing ones, more fundamental changes are needed, especially to improve the quality.[9]

Education

Efforts in the field of education constitute a major component of the welfare system. However the main objective underlying these efforts has been the development of the country's human capital which is regarded as the main requisite for its social and economic progress. Government's preparedness to bear its responsibilities in this field by providing free education at all levels to Kuwaiti nationals has made it possible not only to realise this objective, but has also enabled lower income groups to aspire to better economic opportunities.

Soon after oil revenues began to flow a massive school construction plan was implemented. With forty-one schools completed by 1954, a comprehensive educational programme covering all levels from primary to university was formulated. The results became quickly apparent; the student population increased from about 3600 in 1945 to 45,000 in 1960, 78,000 in 1965 and about 250,000 by 1975.[10]. The story of female education is even more spectacular, their percentage of the student population increased from an estimated 5 per cent in 1945 to about 30 per cent by 1965 and to more than 45 per cent by 1975. However, in spite of these remarkable achievements, the number of illiterate Kuwaitis over ten years of age increased considerably with the influx of large numbers of illiterate tribesmen into the country. This prompted the government to institute in the 1960s a major adult education programme aimed at eradicating illiteracy, which is now regarded as one of the most advanced programmes in the world.[11]

The University of Kuwait, established in 1966, was an ambitious step to raise the level of education in the country and to help improve the cultural standard of the community. It has expanded into new fields of study including engineering and medicine and the student body has increased from about 400 in 1965/6 to over 6000 by 1976/7. In addition, a large number of Kuwaitis have been studying abroad, either with the financial support of the government or their families, since the 1940s, and the number reached its peak prior to the opening of the University.

Housing

The Government has since 1953 been active in implementing programmes designed to provide housing to low-income Kuwaiti families. The programme consists of constructing model-type housing which are allocated to low-income applicants at highly subsidised prices on very easy credit terms. A total of about 4662 of such dwellings were allocated over the period from 1953 to 1964. By 1975, the number had increased to approximately 15,000 dwellings. On the basis of an average family size of five, the total number of Kuwaitis benefiting from this scheme up to 1975 was estimated at 75,000 people, representing about 15 per cent of the Kuwaiti population. There are still, however, more than 20,000 families waiting to benefit from the government-supported housing programmes, with a rate of increase in the order of 1800 annually. Hence, the government has recently announced plans to intensify its efforts aiming to provide housing to all qualified applicants by the early 1980s.

In addition, the government-owned Credit and Saving Bank extends soft loans to eligible Kuwaitis to enable them to purchase land at highly subsidised prices and to construct their houses. During the years from

1961 to 1975 it provided several thousand loans for housing construction totalling KD48·6 million. The capital of the bank was doubled to KD300 million in 1976 in order to expand its activities in the real estate field and improve the housing situation in the country.

Financial Support to Needy Families

Government financial assistance to needy Kuwaiti families started as early as the mid-1950s. The programme has expanded in recent years to provide aid to about 9600 families.[12] The amount of assistance increased from a total of KD2 million in 1967 to approximately KD6·7 million in 1976, i.e. an average of about KD700 (equivalent to $2500) per family anually. The cost of this programme which is administered by the Ministry of Social Affairs and Labour totalled about KD51 million during the years 1965 to 1976.

Subsidies

The consuming public in Kuwait have long enjoyed many government subsidies irrespective of their incomes. These subsidies cover such basic services as water, electricity and gasoline. In the case of water the subsidy amounts to about KD0·4 ($1·4) per 1000 gallons sold to the public whereas electricity is subsidised to the extent of about 5 fils ($0·018) per kWh.[13] In addition, the price of gasoline which has remained almost constant for over a decade obviously includes a substantial element of subsidy. Due to inflation, the subsidy system has been extended in recent years to cover many of the essential food products (rice, sugar, milk, meat, vegetable oil, etc.). The cost of the food subsidy programme has varied but it is estimated to be in the order of KD20 million per year.

Employment

Securing employment for all Kuwaiti citizens in the labour force has long been regarded by the government as a national commitment. In spite of its social merits, this policy has had many drawbacks. Overstaffing of government departments is common and labour redundancy is now a major problem for most government establishments. In addition, a feeling of indifference, apathy and the lack of sufficient incentives have afflicted a significant part of the civil service to which reference will later be made.

Social Security

A social security programme has recently been introduced covering Kuwaitis in the private and government sectors. So far, benefits proposed include generous retirement pensions which may be obtained at a comparatively early age. Other social security measures are expected to be adopted as the programme develops. The Social Security Authority was created in late 1976 to administer the funds contributed to this programme. No attempt has been made to quantify the benefits accruing from these measures, but they are expected to be substantial, especially in view of the fact that the government and other employers provide the major part of the contributions.

It should be noted at this juncture that the welfare system Kuwait evolved during the last thirty years has been far-reaching, costing by 1975 an estimated KD130 million which represents about 20 per cent of total government expenditure.[14] The average cost per Kuwaiti citizen is approximately KD275 (over \$960) per year, financed almost exclusively from government oil revenues rather than from the usual sources of taxation.

DIVERSIFICATION

The need to diversify sources of income and develop new productive activities is self-evident for a country as dependent on a single exhaustible resource as Kuwait. With oil accounting for over 95 per

TABLE 3.2   Indicators of the economy's dependence on oil
1961/2–1976/7

	Oil Exports/ Total Exports (%)	Oil Revenues/ Govt Revenues (%)	Share of Oil in GDP (%)
1961/2	97·8	92·3	NA
1962/3	97·3	91·2	NA
1963/4	97·3	91·9	NA
1964/5	96·8	92·8	NA
1965/6	97·2	92·0	63·1
1966/7	96·8	92·2	59·9
1967/8	91·5	84·1	54·4
1968/9	95·8	90·6	55·7
1969/70	95·5	91·5	56·3
1970/1	96·2	86·6	67·9
1971/2	95·0	92·4	67·1
1972/3	93·8	92·2	59·9
1973/4	96·4	92·5	68·6
1974/5	93·6	96·9	77·2
1975/6	93·0	98·1	70·0
1976/7	92·3	85·7	NA

cent of its foreign exchange earnings, 90 per cent of government revenues and about 60 per cent of GDP during most of the years shown in Table 3.2, it was essential to make every effort to broaden the economic base. Although the picture is complicated by changes in the price of oil, Table 3.2 gives an indication of the degree of progress that had taken place prior to the major increases in the oil prices in 1973/4 and the gradual government take-over of the oil industry as of 1974/5.

Progress towards diversification began in the early 1950s with the setting-up of the water desalination plant at Shuwaikh. This provided an impetus for the development of small scale industrial operations, e.g. aluminium casting, bottling of oxygen, manufacturing of building materials, etc., many of which actually started in small workshops. However major efforts to promote industrialisation started in 1961 when the government decided to set-up the Shuaiba Industrial Zone. A site for the Zone covering an area of 8·4 sq. kms was selected in 1962 and soon afterwards work started on such supporting services as communications, water, electricity and port facilities. In the meantime it was also decided to establish a petrochemical industry to become a nucleus for a variety of related industrial activities. In spite of all government efforts in this direction, the pace of industrialisation was slow for reasons that will be discussed later.

Industrialisation, however, has not been the only means of diversifying the country's sources of income. Such services as trade, banking, finance, insurance and shipping were rapidly developed over the last three decades. Finance and real estate have had particularly impressive growth records in recent years. The growth of services was to a large extent enhanced by the inherited venturesome, outward-looking and merchant-minded attributes of the Kuwaitis. As already indicated, the extreme niggardliness of nature and their country's strategic location between India and the Eastern Mediterranean countries compelled Kuwaitis to engage in such service activities as trade and shipping which enabled them to acquire the necessary skills for promoting a service-oriented economy.

4 Socio-Economic Development

The origins of the Kuwaiti people and the development of their social structure and attitudes have already been described in Chapter 2. However, the recent marked economic changes have brought about equally rapid changes in the social conditions in Kuwait, including changes in the size and composition of the population, the composition of the labour force, employment levels and the distribution of wealth and income. It is to these topics we turn in this chapter.

POPULATION GROWTH

Few social and economic indicators mirror the growth of the economy as accurately as population growth. The size of the population increased almost eight-fold over a period of about twenty-five years, from an estimated 90,000 people in 1946 to approximately 740,000 people by 1971 and over one million by 1975. The growth of the population is best illustrated by reference to Table 4.1.

Kuwait's population has been increasing at a compounded annual rate of more than 8 per cent for the last thirty years. The growth rate was below this average in the early years of the period but started to increase rapidly with the expansion of the economy and reached a peak of 16 per cent per annum in the late fifties. From 1961 onwards that rate was more uniform ranging between 8 per cent and 10 per cent per year. This phenomenal growth is due to two main developments: (1) The influx of workers from other countries in the region to help in the construction of new infrastructure projects and staff jobs created by the expansion of public services. (2) The increase in the number of Kuwaitis through a concerted effort to naturalise tribesmen scattered on the fringes of the country along with a limited number of qualified people who had resided in the country for an extended time (normally twenty years or more). This development is illustrated by the fact that the compounded growth rate of the Kuwaiti population (more than 6·5 per cent) is almost double the natural growth rate of other countries in the region.

TABLE 4.1 Kuwait's population

Census Year	KUWAITIS				NON-KUWAITIS				TOTAL		
	Males	Females	Total	% Kuwaitis	Males	Females	Total	% Non-Kuwaitis	Males	Females	Total
1957	59,154	54,468	113,622	55	72,904	19,947	92,851	45	132,058	74,415	206,473
	(52)	(48)	(100)		(79)	(21)	(100)		(64)	(36)	(100)
1960	84,461	77,448	161,909	50	116,246	43,466	159,712	50	200,707	120,941	321,621
	(52)	(48)	(100)		(73)	(27)	(100)		(67)	(33)	(100)
1965	112,569	107,490	220,059	47	173,743	73,537	247,280	53	286,312	181,027	467,399
	(51)	(49)	(100)		(70)	(30)	(100)		(61)	(39)	(100)
1970	175,513	171,883	347,396	47	244,368	146,898	391,266	53	419,881	318,781	738,662
	(51)	(49)	(100)		(62)	(38)	(100)		(57)	(43)	(100)
1975	251,700	250,600	502,300	47	323,400	239,600	563,000	53	575,100	491,300	1,066,400
	(50)	(50)	(100)		(57)	(43)	(100)		(54)	(46)	(100)

( ) Figures in parentheses are percentages of males and females of total population in each category.

As regards the structure of the population, the following observations may be made on Table 4.1:

1. the rise in the proportion of non-Kuwaitis to about 45 per cent in 1957, 50 per cent in 1960 and a constant 53 per cent thereafter;

2. the high percentage of males among non-Kuwaitis is due to the preponderance of workers in this category;

3. the relative increase in the proportion of females among the non-Kuwaiti population is an indication that the latter has become less transitory;[1]

4. the last observation is also borne out by the significant change in the age structure of the population, where the percentage of the non-working age group increased from less than 30 per cent in the fifties to about 38 per cent in the mid-sixties and over 43 per cent in the seventies.

The implications of these observations on the properties of the labour force are discussed in the next section.

LABOUR FORCE STRUCTURE

The growth of Kuwait's labour force during the fifties and early sixties was most remarkable, averaging about 9 per cent per annum during the years 1946–57 and over 16 per cent annually in the following eight years, reaching by 1965 a total of 184,297. This was to a very large extent due to the rapid growth in construction and infrastructure development rather than the growth of the oil industry. Also, the development phase of the oil industry ended during this period so that the requirement of a large labour force for oil-related construction gave way to the much lower requirements for the more capital intensive production phase. Thus, although in comparison to other countries the labour force continued to increase rapidly during the second half of the sixties and early seventies, the growth rate came down to rather lower levels averaging since the mid-sixties about 6·5 per cent annually. Further reasons for this slow-down were the slower growth of the economy and the increased restrictions on entry into the country.

According to the 1975 census, Kuwait's labour force numbered 304,582 of which Kuwaitis represented about 30 per cent and non-Kuwaitis 70 per cent. The corresponding figures for 1970 are 27 per cent and 73 per cent, and for 1965 23 per cent and 7 per cent. Apart from the inordinately high percentage of non-Kuwaitis, there are a number of significant points concerning the size and structure of the labour force evident from Table 4.2.

TABLE 4.2 Changes in labour structure

	Kuwaitis			Non-Kuwaitis			Total		
	M	F	T	M	F	T	M	F	T
1957 Census									
Population	55,111	52,135	107,246	66,680	16,868	83,548	121,791	69,003	190,794
Population 15–60	29,563	27,014	56,577	58,968	10,570	69,538	88,531	37,584	126,115
Labour force	24,218	384	24,602	53,993	1,693	55,686	78,211	2,077	80,288
Inactives	5,345	26,630	31,975	4,975	8,877	13,852	10,320	35,507	45,827
Labour participation rate	43·9%	0·7%	22·9%	81·0%	1·0%	66·7%	64·2%	3·0%	42·1%
Proportion of inactives	18·1%	98·6%	56·5%	8·4%	84·0%	19·9%	11·7%	94·5%	36·3%
1965 Census									
Population	112,569	107,490	220,059	173,743	75,537	247,280	286,312	181,027	467,339
Population 15–60	52,254	49,352	101,606	135,854	38,823	174,677	188,108	88,175	276,283
Labour force	41,926	1,092	43,018	133,603	7,676	141,279	175,529	8,768	184,297
Inactives	10,328	48,260	58,588	2,251	31,147	33,398	12,579	79,407	91,986
Labour participation rate	37·2%	1·0%	19·5%	76·9%	10·4%	57·1%	61·3%	4·8%	39·4%
Proportion of inactives	19·8%	97·8%	57·7%	1·7%	80·2%	19·1%	6·7%	90·1%	33·3%
1970 Census									
Population	175,513	171,883	349,396	244,368	146,898	391,266	419,881	318,781	738,662
Population 15–60	79,688	78,472	158,160	166,792	73,754	240,546	246,480	152,226	398,706
Labour force	63,314	2,055	65,369	162,286	14,542	176,828	225,600	16,597	242,197
Inactives	16,374	76,417	92,791	4,506	59,212	63,718	20,880	135,629	156,509
Labour participation rate	36·1%	1·2%	18·8%	66·4%	9·9%	45·2%	53·7%	5·2%	32·8%
Proportion of inactives	20·6%	97·4%	58·7%	2·7%	80·3%	26·5%	8·5%	89·1%	39·3%
1975 Census									
Population	236,600	235,488	472,088	307,168	215,581	522,749	543,768	451,069	994,837
Population 15–60	109,497	111,271	220,768	196,990	110,188	307,178	306,487	328,956	527,946
Labour force	84,367	7,477	91,844	185,009	27,729	212,738	269,376	35,206	304,582
Inactives	25,130	103,794	128,924	11,981	82,459	94,440	37,111	293,750	223,364
Labour participation rate	35·7%	3·2%	19·5%	60·2%	12·9%	40·7%	49·5%	7·8%	30·6%
Proportion of inactives	22·9%	93·3%	58·4%	6·1%	74·8%	30·7%	12·1%	89·3%	42·3%

SOURCE: *The Kuwait Annual Statistical Abstract*, 1976. Tables 25 and 54.

1. The relatively small labour participation rate—about 40 per cent in the sixties and less than one-third in the seventies—is due to three principal reasons:

(a) Social and cultural factors that normally discourage women from seeking employment. Evidence of this is found in the very low percentage of women in the labour force amounting to about 2·5 per cent in 1957 and 11 per cent in 1975.

(b) The large proportion of people under the age of fifteen relative to the total population, particularly in recent years. This group constituted almost 46 per cent of the population in 1975 compared with 40 per cent in 1965.

(c) The relatively high percentage of economically inactive people, particularly among Kuwaitis. This percentage for the total population was estimated at 42 per cent in 1975 and more than 58 per cent for the Kuwaiti population alone. However, because of the limited role of women mentioned above, a calculation of the male inactive proportion only is more meaningful giving a percentage of 12·1. Also the definition of the working-age group in Kuwait includes people between the ages of fifteen and sixty whereas elsewhere the definition normally excludes people under seventeen. But in the case of an affluent society, where there is considerable emphasis on education, this should be further restricted to exclude all people under the age of twenty.[2] Therefore a large proportion of those classified as inactive are obviously students in secondary schools and universities and, while it is true that a large number of Kuwaitis receive unearned income in the form of rents, dividends and interest payments, there are clear indications that the overwhelming majority of them are also engaged in productive activities which are not caught within the definitions used in compiling the census. In the census questionnaire there is a category headed *muktafi* meaning a person of sufficient independent means. Many in this category derive their income solely from rents, dividends and profits. They are often, in fact, quite active elements in the economy of the country and are in reality a part of the labour force, often managing and overseeing real estate developments, identifying investment projects and engaging in general entrepreneurial activities.

2. The decline in the labour participation rate from about 40 per cent in the late sixties to just over 30 per cent in 1975 can be largely attributed

to the increasing tendency among non-Kuwaiti men to bring their wives and children to settle in Kuwait as mentioned earlier. This is evident from the rise in the percentage of people under the age of fifteen to the total non-Kuwaiti population as well as the increase in the percentage of females, about 40 per cent and 41 per cent respectively in 1975 compared with 17 per cent and 20 per cent in 1957.

3. Some positive developments with regard to the role of women in the economy can be inferred from Table 4.2. In percentage terms the active female population rose from 5·5 per cent in 1957 to almost 11 per cent in 1975 consisting of increases from 1·4 per cent to 6·7 per cent in the case of the Kuwaiti female population and from 16 per cent to over 25 per cent in the case of non-Kuwaitis. The overall situation concerning the male population has changed only slightly since 1957, but an upward trend in the percentage of inactive Kuwaiti males has developed in recent years. This has been due to such factors as increased interest in higher education, a substantial rise in rents and dividends and a growing feeling of security associated with the welfare state.

EMPLOYMENT

Unlike any other facets of the economy, the employment structure in no way reflects Kuwait's true dependence on the oil sector. Due to increasing capital intensity, employment in the mining and quarrying sector, which in effect is the oil sector, fell from 7200 in 1965 to 4800 in 1975, and its share of the labour force declined from 4 per cent to 1·6 per cent in the same period. In terms of employment, 'services' has consistently been the leading sector in the economy, with such activities as public administration, trade, transport, finance and communications accounting for the greater bulk of the labour force. The service orientation of the economy has become more pronounced in recent years as the percentage of the labour force employed in this sector rose from 60 per cent in 1965 to about 64 per cent in 1970 and almost 73 per cent in 1975. The second most important sector in terms of employment has been construction followed by manufacturing industries, with respectively 10·6 per cent and 8 per cent of the labour force.

The second observation regarding employment is concerned with the concentration of the work force in government service, i.e. public administration, defence and social services, which represents 52 per cent of the people employed in the 'services' sector and almost two-fifths of the total labour force. This is largely explained by the government policy of maximising employment among Kuwaitis which is

TABLE 4.3   Labour classification by economic activity (1975 census)

	Kuwaitis			Non-Kuwaitis			Total	%
	M	F	T	M	F	T		
Agriculture and fishing	3,970	13	3,983	3,522	9	3,531	7,514	2·5
Mining and quarrying	1,767	12	1,779	2,953	127	3,080	4,859	1·6
Manufacturing industries	2,237	21	2,258	21,889	320	22,209	24,467	8·0
Electricity, gas and water	2,029	5	2,034	5,230	7	5,237	7,271	2·4
Construction	1,755	1	1,756	30,357	143	30,500	32,256	10·6
Wholesale and retail trade	6,297	30	6,327	32,364	868	33,232	39,559	13·0
Transport, storage and communications	4,305	262	4,567	10,853	265	11,118	15,685	5·2
Finance and insurance	1,295	82	1,377	4,548	598	5,146	6,523	2·1
Government and other services	56,011	6,879	62,890	72,203	25,188	97,391	160,281	52·6
Total employment	79,666	7,305	86,971	183,919	27,525	211,444	298,415	98·0
Unemployment	4,701	172	4,873	1,090	204	1,294	6,167	2·0
Active labour force	84,367	7,477	91,844	185,009	27,729	212,738	304,582	100.0
Unemployment rate (%)	5·6	2·3	5·3	0·6	0·7	0·6	2·0	

SOURCE: *Kuwait Annual Statistical Abstract*, 1977.

evidenced by the high proportion (about 54 per cent) of employees in government service being of Kuwaiti nationality. In addition Kuwaitis had until recently generally favoured administrative jobs in government service to most other types of employment; hence over 52 per cent of the Kuwaiti labour force is employed by the government. However, with salaries and wages in the private sector rising more rapidly than in the public sector, an increasing number of Kuwaitis have been opting for more challenging and lucrative non-government jobs. Self-employment among Kuwaitis has also expanded in recent years, constituting in 1975 over 10 per cent of the Kuwaiti work force. On the other hand, non-Kuwaitis are more evenly distributed among such major activities as government service, trade, manufacturing, services and construction.

Finally, as shown in Table 4.3, the unemployment problem is of minor importance with the overall rate estimated in 1975 at 2 per cent. This is to be expected in view of the rapid development of the country and the labour shortages experienced in many economic sectors. In addition, as evidenced from the exceedingly low rate of unemployment (0·6 per cent) among non-Kuwaitis, this is due in large part to the restriction of entry of non-Kuwaitis to those who had been promised work before coming into the country. On the other hand, the relatively high rate of unemployment as conventionally measured among Kuwaitis (5·3 per cent) is considered to be mainly due to their reluctance to accept low paid or unattractive jobs because they can depend on other sources of income. Hence, the relatively high rate of unemployment reported among Kuwaitis is not necessarily an indication of involuntary unemployment in the Keynesian sense.

DISTRIBUTION OF WEALTH

The paternal attitude of the government was not only apparent in the establishment of the welfare system but also in the government's determination to distribute national wealth among the Kuwaiti population. Purchase of land was considered the simplest and quickest method for achieving this objective. Thus a total of more than KD1 billion (equivalent to $3·4 billion) has been disbursed through the land acquisition programme during the years 1952–75. The government in fact distributed by this means about one-quarter of its total oil revenues during the period from 1946 to 1971. The funds allocated to this programme in these years exceeded the country's investment in foreign assets and were almost equivalent to all government development expenditure during the same period. There is evidence, however, that in its eagerness to spread the oil revenues as quickly as possible, the government was paying for the purchased land far in excess of what it was worth. In the early sixties, land was also acquired at a greater rate than actually required for utilisation in the construction of such public projects as roads, schools, hospitals and government buildings. In addition, in order to induce the private sector to become active in the field of housing construction, the government would subsequently sell back to the public the surplus land and recover only a fraction of the cost of acquisition. Wealth was quickly spread among hundreds of Kuwaitis both by selling land to the state and by constructing residential and commercial buildings on cheap land bought from the government.

The programme implemented in the sixties has been sharply criticised for being an indiscriminate and an inequitable way of distributing oil revenues and for failing effectively to invigorate the Kuwait economy because the private sector invested abroad a large part of the funds received under the programme.[3] In this connection some also felt that the programme 'tended to weaken entrepreneurial ability because of the growth of dependence on the government as a source of income.[4] Nevertheless, there are strong indications that the land acquisition programme not only succeeded in spreading the new wealth, which was the main objective, but also helped in stimulating economic activity particularly in such sectors as housing, trade and small scale industry. Indeed, the slow down of the economy in the late sixties is partly attributed to the decline in budgetary outlays in 1966/7, 1968/9 and 1969/70. The programme, however, has been revived since 1974 on seemingly more rational and systematic bases with allocations representing about 10 per cent of total government expenditure.

INCOME DISTRIBUTION

In spite of the high per capita income level in Kuwait, its economy, as mentioned above, still displays many of the characteristics of a developing country. These include the high dependence on a single commodity as a source of income, the lack of adequate public institutions and the absence of direct taxation. In view of these circumstances, and the country's adherence to the principles of a free-enterprise system, the Kuwait economy has not yet achieved a pattern of income distribution commensurate with the high level of per capita income reached as far back as 1960. In fact, as has been demonstrated, the pattern of income distribution suffers from a significant degree of inequality, which widened over time, partly because of the increasing proportion of non-Kuwaitis in the population. This is evident from the 1972/3 structure of family income shown in Table 4.4. As shown in this table, the top 6·3 per cent of the households receive about 30 per cent of total income compared with only 25 per cent of income received by over 56 per cent of households whose monthly income is less than KD200. The degree of inequality is also greater among the Kuwaiti segment of the population than it is among non-Kuwaitis. It is estimated that the top 10 per cent of Kuwaiti households receive more than 40 per cent of total income received by this group of families compared with about 30 per cent in the case of non-Kuwaiti families.

Table 4.4 also indicates that the incomes of Kuwaiti families are generally higher than those of non-Kuwaiti families. Median family income for the first group is estimated at approximately KD225 per month compared with slightly more than KD150 for the second group. In addition, only 44·3 per cent of the Kuwaiti families receive a monthly income of less than KD200 whereas there are more than 65 per cent of the non-Kuwaiti families whose incomes fall below this level. These

TABLE 4.4   Structure of family income, 1972/3

Monthly family income (in KD)	Kuwaitis		Non-Kuwaitis		Total	
	House-holds (%)	Share of income (%)	House-holds (%)	Share of income (%)	House-holds (%)	Share of income (%)
Less than 50	5·4	0·5	5·5	1·1	5·4	0·8
50-69	3·0	0·5	7·5	2·2	5·7	1·3
70-99	4·0	1·0	14·6	6·0	10·3	3·2
100-149	13·6	4·9	20·9	12·6	17·9	8·4
150-199	18·7	9·2	16·1	13·8	17·2	11·3
200-249	12·8	7·9	10·3	11·2	11·3	9·4
250-299	9·4	7·2	7·6	10·2	8·4	8·5
300-399	10·3	10·0	8·1	13·8	9·0	11·7
400-599	11·5	15·4	6·5	15·1	8·5	15·2
600-999	5·8	11·8	2·2	7·8	3·6	10·0
1000 and more	5·5	31·6	0·7	6·2	2·7	20·2
Total	100·0	100·0	100·0	100·0	100·0	100·0

SOURCE: *The Kuwait Annual Statistical Abstract*, 1977, p. 224.

findings may be attributed to a number of factors including: (1) the high percentage of non-Kuwaitis employed as labourers, (2) the receipt of unearned income (rents and dividends) by Kuwaitis which does not accrue to non-Kuwaitis because of restrictions on ownership of property and company shares, (3) the preferential treatment given by the government to Kuwaitis in regard to employment and salaries as part of its policy to raise income levels of Kuwaiti nationals,[5] and (4) the imposition of regulations that restrict non-Kuwaitis from operating certain businesses unless they have a Kuwaiti partner with 51 per cent share of the capital or a Kuwaiti sponsor who receives a fixed fee or a share of net profit.[6]

It should also be noted that, while the 1972/3 structure of family income is the only one available, it is presumed that the pattern of income distribution has been aggravated by the recent rise in the cost of living, particularly in regard to rents and prices of consumer goods. In addition, even though the pattern of income distribution is expected to improve if family incomes were revised to incorporate the welfare benefits mentioned earlier, there seems to be clear evidence that a significant degree of inequality would remain. The main reasons for the development of this pattern of income distribution, particularly in the case of Kuwaitis since 1946, include: (1) differences in the level of education, (2) differences in social background, (3) the presence of market imperfections in the economy with major barriers to entry in many business activities, (4) lack of appropriate fiscal and public policies, and (5) the land purchase programme which, while succeeding in spreading the wealth, tended to accentuate the pre-oil disparity in income.[7] It appears, however, that the government has aimed, through its welfare system which includes free education, medical care, subsidies, and a housing programme as well as its employment policies, to help satisfy people's basic needs without resorting to direct taxation or attempting to change the free-enterprise orientation of the economy. Thus, as will be shown later, the welfare measures are all financed from oil revenues and the role of fiscal policy in regard to income distribution has been restricted to the expenditure side of the budget only.

SOCIAL DEVELOPMENT

A complex social structure has emerged with the oil boom and the influx of thousands of Arabs and non-Arabs into the country. Although the buoyant economic situation enabled the settlement of the mass immigration to take place fairly smoothly, the assimilation process proved far more difficult leaving the incomers largely estranged from the Kuwaiti society. Without going into great details of the cause, it is probably fair to say that the resistance among the Kuwaiti population to the new inhabitants was largely attributed to the enormous magnitude of the influx as well as the Kuwaitis' concern to protect their own identity.[8] Kuwaitis became quickly fearful of the tremendous human movements into their country which in certain periods reached several thousands per month. Hence the heterogeneous composition of the present Kuwaiti society clearly calls for separate analyses of the dichotomised Kuwaiti and non-Kuwaiti communities.

In spite of the rapid economic growth which led to the emergence of a modern state, Kuwaitis have generally retained most of their traditional values and customs and have remained largely conservative and clanish in nature. The strength of the family as a social and economic unit is still paramount. Nevertheless a measure of social change has occurred with social stratification becoming less determined by family origin and tribal affiliation and more by personal achievement and other tangible forms of success. But the rapid economic and social progress, especially the provision of welfare and the creation of a sense of economic security, has had some adverse effects on young Kuwaitis who often tend to regard life lightly. A good percentage of Kuwaitis have now come to expect a great deal from the state and yet the disbursement of the oil wealth via public channels implies that these expectations are not hampered by the necessity to contribute to state expenditure through taxation.

One of the most significant changes has been in the role of Kuwaiti women. Due to the maritime and trading activities of their menfolk during the pre-oil period, it was the women who provided a strong focus for family life in Kuwaiti society. While they have retained this important position, Kuwaiti women have become much more active in economic spheres in recent years and their influence is now no longer confined within the family. There is no doubt that their role will continue to grow over the coming years and the liberal attitude of Kuwait in this regard is most noteworthy.

The non-Kuwaiti community consists of many national groups with rather weak ties among them. The structure and composition of their community has been affected by economic and political events in neighbouring countries. Palestinians remain the predominant group representing about 40 per cent of the non-Kuwaiti population and almost 20 per cent of the overall total. Although non-Kuwaitis are less transitory than before, they still generally find themselves living 'on the sideline'. With government policies not allowing them to own real estate or company shares they have not been able to participate fully in the fruits of increased economic prosperity. Hence a growing feeling of frustration and lack of belonging to the country in which they work and live has developed among them. There is evidence, however, that the Kuwaiti authorities are becoming more aware of the negative aspects of present attitudes and proposals to rectify the situation have been considered by the Ministry of Planning. Such proposals, many of which have already been adopted, include granting Kuwaiti citizenship to people who have contributed to the progress of the country and the provision of a greater sense of security for other non-Kuwaitis by relaxing residency regulations.

5 External Economic Relations

Not only were the internal economic and social structures of Kuwait transformed by the development of its oil wealth, but its relationship with the rest of the region and the world at large was fundamentally altered. While Kuwait's external economic relations encompass a broad range of economic activities its role in international finance and foreign assistance will be dealt with in separate chapters in view of their differing nature and special importance. Emphasis in this chapter is on such aspects as foreign trade, the structure of the balance of payments and regional economic relations. Kuwait had always been a trading country, with a network of relationships abroad out of all proportion to its size. The development of trade in oil, with its ramifications in the balance of world trade, has now added a new dimension to the Kuwait economic scene.

FOREIGN TRADE

From the outset we have stressed the importance of oil as the basis of Kuwait's wealth and much of our work relies on an analysis of how the participation of Kuwait in the changing fortunes of oil in the world economy has affected its direction and rate of development. While, of course, the history of oil only occupies a small portion of the time spanning Kuwait's history, it is oil that has effected the dramatic changes of recent years, and it is Kuwait's actions based upon the future of its oil which will determine its future progress. Oil of course, has almost exclusively been a commodity of foreign trade in Kuwait, and with such a limited domestic capacity for alternative production, oil exports have been almost synonymous with Kuwait's total exports since production commenced in commercial quantities. Thus, an analysis of this sector will provide further insight not only into Kuwait's development in the recent past, but her capacity for future development also.

50

TABLE 5.1 Evolution of trade 1955–77 (Million KD)

Year	Oil exports	Other exports	Re-exports	Total exports	Imports	Trade balance
1955*	232·5	—		232·5	33·7	198·8
1960*	285·4	8·3		293·7	86·4	207·3
1965*	444·1	14·3		458·4	134·7	323·7
1966*	465·8	13·6		479·4	165·3	314·1
1967*	469·1	15·3		484·4	211·9	272·5
1968	496·8	16·7		513·5	218·3	295·2
1969	527·0	23·1		550·1	231·7	318·4
1970	564·5	26·4		590·9	223·3	367·6
1971	859·4	8·6	25·8	893·8	232·3	661·5
1972	931·7	16·4	33·2	981·3	262·2	719·1
1973	1059·9	27·3	42·5	1129·7	310·6	819·1
1974	3097·5	59·1	58·1	3214·7	455·1	2759·6
1975	2492·6	81·3	89·1	2663·0	693·2	1969·8
1976	2658·5	—	241·8	2873·3	970·3	1903·0
1977	2587·0		197·0	2784·0	1123·0	1661·0

*Fiscal years beginning 1st April.
SOURCES: 1. IMF, *International Financial Statistics*, 1977.
2. Central Bank of Kuwait, *Quarterly Statistical Bulletin*.

Table 5.1 shows the development of Kuwait's foreign trade. Up to 1960 adequate records of non-oil exports and re-exports are not available, but it is almost certain that they were not in excess of the KD8·3 million recorded in that year, when they were little under 3 per cent of total exports, and even in 1970 they were not much above 5 per cent. Even this comparatively small amount belies the true situation, however, as a significant portion of exports were, in fact, re-exports and formed part of the *entrepôt* services on which much of Kuwait's past was founded (see Chapter 2). The exports of indigenously produced finished goods was a small proportion of even this small amount and the figures for 1971, the first year for which we could obtain data, showed that these were 25 per cent of non-oil exports only, and therefore 1 per cent of total exports including oil. The figures for non-oil exports, of course, show an extremely rapid rise from the period when figures first became available and, when examination is confined to the period when separate data are available for re-exports, the increase in indigenously generated exports is even more striking. From 1971 to 1975 the value of oil exports trebled, with a slight downturn from the

TABLE 5.2   Crude oil exports by destination

| | Million Barrels | | | | | | | |
Country Group	1970	1971	1972	1973	1974	1975	1976	1977
North America	15·4	11·5	16·1	19·2	11·2	9·1	6·3	13·1
Latin America	20·2	26·6	22·1	27·2	22·3	43·6	44·9	48·5
Western Europe	582·2	605·8	610·2	538·2	390·3	248·0	265·3	214·6
Eastern Europe	–	–	–	–	–	11·8	11·5	9·5
Middle East	19·4	12·9	14·2	7·6	12·3	5·7	7·1	8·5
Africa	1·1	0·4	0·4	0·3	–	–	–	0·7
Asia and Far East	266·3	329·3	378·3	336·4	336·2	315·5	301·8	282·4
Oceania	37·1	26·5	29·3	37·1	32·5	19·0	18·4	11·1
Total	941·7	1013·0	1070·6	966·0	804·8	652·7	655·5	588·4

SOURCE: Central Bank of Kuwait, *Quarterly Statistical Bulletin*.

high of 1974. However, indigenously generated exports other than oil increased by more than nine times. Imports, of course, were increasing also and from 1955 to 1976 they increased by over twenty-nine times! Simple comparison, though, of such rates and proportions would be of doubtful use and prognostication from the trends they indicate would be of little value. Much more detailed analysis of the components of exports and imports is required, and this should be set against the background of other developments, both economic and non-economic, before any worthwhile contribution to a more general analysis can be made. However, an important statistic in Table 5.1 is the trade balance. This has been positive for the whole of the period of the table but reached a staggering peak of 2·76 billion KD in 1974 (equivalent to almost 10 billion dollars). However, the trend has been downward since then, reflecting the country's rise in imports and its conservation policy in regard to oil production as well as the deterioration in the terms of trade in 1976 and 1977.

While we shall analyse the significance of the trade surplus later in the chapter in a discussion on the balance of payments, its upward trend has been marked by a pattern of unevenness which should be noted. Firstly, the increase in value of oil exports is a result of two trends, one in output the other in prices. Neither output nor prices, however, have consistently risen. The 'official' price of Middle Eastern Crude Oil (Ras Tanura) fell from $2·08 per barrel in 1958 to $1·80 in 1961, where it remained until 1970, and prices paid often fluctuated below this. Also, and more importantly, the government take, initially in the form of

				Per cent of Total				
70	*1971*	*1972*	*1973*	*1974*	*1975*	*1976*	*1977*	*Country Group*
1·6	1·1	1·5	2·0	1·4	1·4	1·0	2·2	North America
2·2	2·6	2·2	2·8	2·8	6·7	6·9	8·2	Latin America
1·8	59·8	57·0	55·7	48·5	38·0	40·5	36·5	Western Europe
–	–	–	–	–	1·8	1·7	1·7	Eastern Europe
2·1	1·3	1·3	0·9	1·5	0·9	1·1	1·4	Middle East
0·1	–	–	–	–	–	–	0·1	Africa
8·3	32·6	35·3	34·8	41·8	48·3	46·0	48·0	Asia and Far East
3·9	2·6	2·7	3·8	4·0	2·9	2·8	1·9	Oceania
0·0	100·0	100·0	100·0	100·0	100·0	100·0	100·0	Total

royalties and taxes, has been increasing as well as the price (see Chapter 6) culminating in complete ownership and control in 1976 and making the take 100 per cent of the selling price. Further increases in the value of oil exports from Kuwait's point of view must therefore come via price or output increases only.

Over the period during which Kuwait has been gaining control over its oil resources, the market for Kuwaiti oil and oil products has undergone a marked change as is shown in Table 5.2.

From the table it can immediately be seen that, while total exports were increasing up to 1972, they declined from then onward in accordance with the government's conservation policies remarked upon earlier. The deployment of the annual totals between the markets is, however, interesting. In 1970, Western Europe was by far the biggest importing area, taking around 62 per cent of Kuwait's total exports with a further 28 per cent going to Asia and the Far East. By 1977, however, even though these two areas were still dominating Kuwait's market, the latter was absorbing some 48 per cent of the total while the former was in second place with about 36 per cent. Within these figures, the most significant factor is the Japanese imports which now account for about 23 per cent of Kuwait's total oil exports.

As well as the fluctuations caused by the changing fortunes of the oil exports, others in the trade balance are caused by imports; for not only has the trend in imports been ever upward, but the prices of imports have tended to be consistently upward also. Thus, with import prices rising even during the time of falling or static export prices (i.e. of oil),

TABLE 5.3 Indigenous exports and import retentions 1971–6 (Value in Thousand KD)

		1971		1972		1973		1974		1975		1976	
		Exports	Retentions	Exports	Retentions	Exports	Retentions	Exports	Retentions	Exports	Retentions	Exports	Retentions
Food and live animals	Value	1,002	35,365	898	40,129	3,107	47,181	2,377	64,551	2,110	100,636	1,640	109,800
	(%)	11·7	17·1	5·5	17·5	11·3	17·6	4·0	16·3	2·6	16·7	2·9	13·5
Beverages and tobacco	Value	2	5,183	3	5,091	–	5,292	11	5,801	10	7,139	–	11,750
	(%)	–	2·5	–	2·2	–	2·0	–	1·5	–	1·1	–	1·5
Raw materials	Value	376	3,643	480	3,522	1,230	4,774	2,657	8,166	1,938	6,576	2,100	13,030
	(%)	4·4	1·8	2·9	1·5	4·5	1·8	4·5	2·1	2·4	1·1	3·7	1·6
Minerals, fuels and lubricants	Value	50	1,865	40	2,405	21	2,779	16	5,088	13	3,521	–	7,250
	(%)	0·6	1·0	0·3	1·1	0·1	1·0	–	1·3	–	0·6	–	0·9
Animal and vegetable oil	Value	13	1,094	13	1,006	18	1,029	35	1,811	28	2,420	50	2,870
	(%)	0·1	0·5	0·1	0·4	0·1	0·4	0·1	0·5	–	0·4	–	0·4
Chemicals	Value	5,824	10,025	11,549	11,952	18,889	12,644	45,800	18,000	64,655	2,573	31,200	27,760
	(%)	67·9	4·9	70·4	5·2	69·0	4·7	77·5	4·5	79·3	0·4	55·2	3·4
Manufactured goods	Value	1,051	48,197	3,034	50,400	3,526	55,732	6,781	102,930	10,104	106,104	16,040	169,770
	(%)	12·3	23·3	18·5	22·0	12·9	20·8	11·5	25·9	12·4	17·6	28·4	20·9
Machinery and transport equipment	Value	33	64,996	21	71,285	127	89,945	459	125,156	1,521	264,209	3,390	331,500
	(%)	0·4	31·5	0·1	31·1	0·5	33·6	0·8	31·5	1·9	43·8	6·0	40·8
Unclassified commodities	Value	220	36,127	365	42,194	433	42,266	943	58,723	1,150	79,446	2,090	139,280
	(%)	2·6	17·5	2·2	18·4	1·6	15·8	1·6	14·8	1·4	13·3	3·7	17·1
Total	Value	8,571	206,495	16,403	228,984	27,351	268,040	59,079	396,990	81,529	603,856	56,510	813,010
	(%)	100·0	100·0	100·0	100·0	100·0	100·0	100·0	100·0	100·0	100·0	100·0	100·0

the terms of trade were moving against Kuwait for much of the period of the table. But, with ownership now complete, the continuous protection of the terms of trade via oil price hikes cannot always be guaranteed. Thus the protection of import potential must be accomplished via other means.

If we examine the pattern of trade, however, we gain further insight into the underlying influences on imports and exports which make up the broader aggregates of Table 5.1. However imports for re-exports are not really affected by the Kuwait economy. Table 5.3 has been compiled which compared exports (other than oil) with imports net of re-exports (i.e. import retentions). It is these two categories which are functionally related to general economic activity. On the exports' side, chemicals show an increasing proportion (from 67·9 per cent in 1971 to 79·3 per cent in 1975) of a rapidly increasing total, their monetary value being KD5·8 million and KD64·7 million for the two years respectively. However a substantial decrease occurred in the export of chemicals in 1976 due to the oil conservation policy and greater home use. The only other category to maintain a proportion of double figures over the period was 'manufactured goods' which was static at around 12 per cent until 1975, but which doubled in 1976. This may be a significant sign for the future.

This pattern of exports illustrates vividly the dependence of the non-oil productive activities on the oil sector. The whole of the chemical exports are petrochemicals and some of the manufactured goods use petrochemicals as inputs as well as relying on the oil sector for power.

As for retentions, 'manufactured goods' and 'machinery and transport equipment' make up the greater proportion, with 'food and live animals' being the next most significant. 'Machinery and transport equipment' has maintained its proportional importance, and this is indicative of the government's development and diversification programmes. The net import of food and beverages, and to a great extent manufactured goods, is related to both population and generally increased prosperity, showing an almost threefold increase over the period. 'Machinery and transport equipment' however show a fivefold increase, much of this occurring in the last three years of the period, when the oil price rises and increases in trade balances opened up a new vista for Kuwait, and plans for development became capable of implementation at a faster rate.

BALANCE OF PAYMENTS

In view of the consistent balance of trade surplus that Kuwait has
enjoyed throughout the oil period, it is obvious that a favourable
balance of payments position would result. This is significantly more
evident in the figures for the period 1973 onward. This section is
designed to analyse major developments pertaining to Kuwait's balance
of payments as they reflect its changing role in the areas of aid and
international finance as well as the build up of its foreign assets all of
which have occupied a central position in Kuwait development.

Table 5.4 shows the development of Kuwait's balance of payments
during the years 1966–77. The main observations that should be made
on this table are as follows:

1. The substantial rise in the current surplus in 1971 which are due to
the Teheran Agreement and again in 1974 due to the extraordinary rise
in the oil prices.

2. The consistent increase in income from foreign assets held by the
government and the financial institutions which almost doubled
between 1966 and 1973 and more than tripled between 1973 and 1977; it
is estimated at about 44 per cent of total imports in 1977 in spite of the
rapid rise in import levels. It should be noted that the increase in income
from this source has more than outweighed the fall in the trade balance
which occurred toward the end of the period.

3. Current private transfers, of which remittances constitute a major
component, have been estimated for the years 1975–7 at KD80,92 and
106 million respectively. In earlier years, however, these transfers were
substantially more modest because of generally lower earnings. Nevertheless, as will be mentioned elsewhere, these transfers were significant
to the balance of payments positions of other countries in the region.

4. These current surpluses have been partially offset by capital transfers
carried out by the government, the private sector and such institutions
as the Kuwait Fund for Arab Economic Development and joint sector
investment companies. Of these transfers, the private sector including
all financial institutions accounted for about 62 per cent over the period
from 1966 to 1977. Government transfers consisted mainly of concessional and non-concessional flows to Arab countries and other
developing countries, as well as investments elsewhere abroad.

5. The remainder of the surpluses constitutes an addition to the foreign
assets held by the monetary system and government, of which the latter
has become increasingly the more significant accounting by 1977 for
over 80 per cent of the country's foreign assets. There are indications,

TABLE 5.4   Balance of payments, 1966—77

(Million KD)

Transactions	1966	1967	1968	1969	1970	1971	1972	1973	1974	1975*	1976*	1977*
Balance of current transactions	184·1	112·9	138·4	147·5	178·0	339·7	431·0	342·5	1775·7	1939·0	2104·0	1794·0
Transactions of the oil sector	315·4	319·2	315·5	344·2	351·3	527·9	548·5	672·1	2369·3	2289·0	2615·0	2587·0
Government oil revenues	292·1	293·5	277·7	291·6	321·1	500·7	504·2	577·2	2203·5			
Expenditure of oil companies	23·3	25·7	33·0	41·5	27·8	19·8	26·1	23·0	140·8			
Transactions of KNPC	—	—	4·8	11·1	2·4	7·4	18·2	71·9	25·0			
Other current transactions	−131·3	−206·3	−177·1	−196·7	−173·3	−188·2	−117·5	−329·6	−593·6	−340·0	−511·0	−793·0
Exports, FOB	14·5	15·5	20·9	27·0	26·4	37·8	53·3	79·2	130·5	170·0	213·0	197·0
Imports, CIF	−176·1	−219·0	−213·1	−255·9	−240·6	−241·2	−266·6	−336·2	−552·6	−685·0	−963·0	−1123·0
Freight, Insurance, Travel, etc.	−26·8	−23·0	−27·1	−23·0	−21·0	−12·4	−11·9	4·8	−12·4	−53·0	−73·0	−185·0
Investment income	75·2	81·6	89·5	104·5	102·8	108·7	125·5	141·4	202·6	334·0	441·0	492·0
Current government transfers	−15·3	−65·9	−49·1	−50·1	−40·9	−37·6	−43·0	−152·8	−286·7	−36·0	−37·0	−68·0
Current private transfers	−2·8	4·5	1·8	0·8	—	−43·5	25·2	−66·0	−75·0	−80·0	−92·0	−106·0
Balance of capital transactions	−126·2	−94·1	−77·7	−81·3	−53·0	−87·8	−261·8	−125·4	−660·9	−792·0	−1268·0	−349·0
Private capital transfers[1]	−114·7	−93·0	−75·1	−79·9	−59·3	−87·9	−238·7	−110·3	−447·6	−318·0	−677·0	−33·0
Government capital transfers[2]	−5·5	4·1	3·1	3·3	4·5	7·4	−6·1	4·4	−68·3	−377·0	−520·0	−231·0
K.F.A.E.D. loans and investments	−6·0	−5·2	−5·7	−4·7	1·8	−7·3	−17·0	−19·6	−145·0	−97·0	−71·0	−85·0
Balance of financial sector	−57·9	−18·8	−60·7	−66·2	−125·0	−251·9	−169·2	−217·1	−1114·8	1147·0	−836·0	−1445·0
Net commercial banks assets	−62·0	−1·6	−54·0	13·0	−24·5	−34·7	19·0	22·9	23·3	−27·0	94·0	−52·0
Government assets[3]	4·1	−17·2	−6·7	−79·2	−100·5	−217·2	−188·2	−240·0	−1138·1	−1120·0	−930·0	−1394·0

SOURCE: *Kuwait Annual Statistical Abstract* and the Central Bank's *Quarterly Statistical Bulletin.*

*A different method of compiling Balance of Payments figures was adopted in these years.

[1] Including transactions by investment companies and specialised banks.

[2] Including government loans and capital transactions of the oil sector.

[3] Including the Central Bank.

NOTE: Occasional discrepancies may be observed between this table and Table 5.3 due to slightly differing methods of compilation.

TABLE 5.5   Summary of balance of payments 1950–77 (Billion KD)

		1950–65*	*1966–77*	*Total*
	Balance of trade surplus[1]	1·7	9·0	10·7
	Investment income	0·3	2·3	2·6
	Current private transfers	−0·2	−0·4	−0·6
	Current government transfers	−0·3	−0·9	−1·2
(1)	Net current account surplus	1·5	10·0	11·5
	Capital Transfers			
	Government[2]	−0·5	−1·6	−2·1
	Private[3]	−0·4	−2·3	−2·7
(2)	Sub-Total	−0·9	−3·9	−4·8
	Net financial assets			
	Commercial banks	−0·3	−0·1	−0·4
	Central Bank	−	−0·9	−0·9
	Government	−0·3	−5·1	−5·4
(3)	Sub-Total	−0·6	−6·1	−6·7
	Grand Total (2) + (3)	−1·5	−10·0	−11·5

*Estimate
[1] Including non-factor services.
[2] Including government loans and portfolio investments, Central Bank loans to the IMF, and other official transfers.
[3] Including investment companies and specialised banks.

however, that the increase in these assets peaked in 1977 and have since been declining due, in part, to the decline in the trade surplus.

For the purposes of summarising the utilisation of Kuwait's current account surpluses for the entire oil period, Table 5.5 has been prepared from the data in Table 5.4 and estimates for years prior to 1966. As shown, the total of current account surpluses for the years 1950–77 was in the order of KD11·5 billion including income from foreign investments and after deducting remittances, other current private transfers and current government transfers. This surplus has been utilised to the extent of KD4·8 billion in capital transfers, of which concessional and non-concessional flows to developing countries by government and the private sector constitute a sum in the order of KD2·0 billion. It is estimated that about KD1·7 billion of the concessional and non-concessional flows were made by the government and KD0·3 billion by the private sector primarily in bonds. In addition, the Kuwait Government provided an estimated amount of KD1·0 billion in current transfers to developing countries during the years 1950–77. The balance of the capital transfers, estimated at KD2·8 billion, has taken the form of private and government direct investments, respectively KD2·4 billion and KD0·4 billion, mainly in the industrial countries.

The remainder of the current account surpluses formed additions to the financial assets held abroad of approximately KD6.7 billion by the end of 1977. This sum consists of foreign financial assets held by the monetary system of KD1·3 billion and KD5·4 billion by the government. From this it can be deduced that investments and financial assets abroad held by the government total about KD5·8 billion, by the monetary system KD1·3 billion, and by the private sector KD2·4 billion, giving a total of external assets held by Kuwait in the order of KD9·5 billion, to which must be added concessional and non-concessional capital flows of KD2·0 billion. The underlying principles which have dictated this distribution have evolved over the years in response to changing circumstances. These principles together with the detailed components of these aggregates will be discussed in the appropriate chapters to follow and they will form part of a conceptual model designed to explain the behaviour of the Kuwaiti authorities regarding oil policy, internal developments and investment abroad, given domestic and international constraints.

REGIONAL ECONOMIC RELATIONS

Complementarity in factor endowments between Kuwait and many countries in the region has resulted in mutually beneficial economic relations. Kuwait's abundant capital supply and labour shortage compared to most other countries in the region have long opened the way for the exchange of resources. Kuwait, as mentioned earlier, has relied heavily on labour imports from various countries in the region and Kuwaiti capital has been made available in the form of concessional and non-concessional flows to many countries suffering from capital shortage. In addition, differences in the patterns of production have induced the development of trade between Kuwait and a number of other countries. Tourism was another area that grew rapidly as a result of the rise in the incomes of Kuwaitis and other people living in Kuwait.

Apart from the fact that Kuwait's growth was facilitated by the influx of professional, skilled and unskilled expatriates, together with the importation of a range of food products, these regional economic relations have provided an impetus to development in many countries in the region. However, with the acceleration of the process of growth in these countries in recent years, this phenomenon has become considerably less evident than it was in the years prior to 1973. It would be useful therefore to review and evaluate recent developments concerned with the various types of regional economic relations.

1. *Labour movement*

As indicated before, Kuwaitis accounted in the 1975 census for only about 47 per cent of the population in Kuwait whereas the remainder comprised 42 per cent other Arabs (of which Jordanians and Palestinians represent about 50 per cent), 4·1 per cent Iranians, 3·2 per cent Indians, 2·3 per cent Pakistanis and 0·8 per cent other nationalities. The labour force figures are even more striking, for Kuwaitis represented in 1975 slightly more than 30 per cent compared with 27 per cent in 1970 and 23 per cent in 1965. The remainder of the labour force, estimated in 1975 at 212,738, is believed to consist almost entirely of Arabs, Iranians, Indians and Pakistanis. While these figures show the extent of Kuwait's dependence on imported labour, they also indicate clearly the benefit accruing to other countries in the region by reducing the numbers of surplus workers in countries like Egypt as well as such non-Arab countries as India and Pakistan. In addition, although there are no reliable estimates on remittances by expatriates to the various labour exporting countries, it is believed that this item has been very significant for such labour exporting countries as Egypt, Jordan, Syria and Pakistan. However, the increased influx of labour to Kuwait and other Arab oil-exporting countries since 1973 has had serious adverse effects on other countries in the region. With the expansion of construction activities in these countries they started to experience serious labour shortages and a rapid escalation of wages and prices. Apart from their effects on growth, it is probable that the economic distortions caused by these developments will take a long time to eliminate. Nevertheless, it should be recognised that regional movement of labour was mutually beneficial for a long time, but now requires some countries to introduce incentives and other domestic measures to check migration and maintain their labour force. In this event, Kuwait may need to seek new sources of supply including, as has already begun, the importation of labour from such countries as

Bangladesh and Korea. A long-term population policy and manpower plan consistent with the country's objectives should be drawn up and more coordination of manpower plans should be developed among the various countries of the region.

2. Capital transfers

In spite of the fact that Kuwait's financial surpluses in the fifties and sixties were only a fraction of what they have become in recent years, Kuwait was always considered a capital-rich country in the region. Kuwaiti investments in date plantations and other activities in Iraq have been noted and there has always been a tradition of investment by Kuwaitis in neighbouring countries as an integral part of its trading network. As will be indicated in Chapters 12 and 13, a sizable proportion of Kuwait's surpluses before and since 1973 have been provided to other countries in the region through concessional and non-concessional flows of resources. Moreover, Kuwaiti private investments in the real estate sectors of such countries as Egypt, Lebanon, Syria and Jordan have been quite significant.[1] Investments in agriculture, industry and tourism have also been made by the government and the private sector in many Arab countries.[2] The benefits accruing from these activities in terms of increased employment and productivity as well as improved balance of payments positions in the recipient countries should not be underestimated.

3. Trade

As indicated earlier, Kuwait relies on the importation of many agricultural and processed foodstuffs from such countries as Jordan, Lebanon, Syria, Iraq and Iran. This is quite natural for a country that has little if any agriculture. Its total imports from the Arab countries increased from KD18·8 million in 1970 to over KD29 million in 1974, but has since declined to about 24 million in 1976. Evidently, these imports have not kept pace with the growth of the country's overall import requirements. With the latter increasing between 1970 and 1976 more than four-fold, the Arab countries' share of Kuwait's total imports decreased between these years from 8·5 per cent to about 2·5 per cent as shown in Table 5.6. The main reason for this trend is believed to be a relatively slow increase in the supply of agricultural products in the Arab exporting countries. By contrast, imports from Asian countries, mainly Japan, have increased from 18·4 per cent to 37·4 per cent; those from Western Europe have declined from over 53

TABLE 5.6 Foreign trade by country groups 1960–76 (Proportionate shares in percentages)

	1960	1965	1970	1971	1972	1973	1974	1975	1976
Imports									
Country groups									
Arab countries	7·6	7·0	8·4	8·1	9·2	7·8	6·5	4·1	2·5
African countries	0·8	1·0	0·8	1·1	1·1	1·1	0·9	0·5	0·2
Asian countries	18·4	23·5	30·8	28·9	31·4	34·9	32·9	29·0	37·4
European Common Market	53·4*	46·5*	35·0	34·7	32·4	30·0	33·2	33·8	32·7
Other Western European countries			3·9	4·5	4·7	4·0	5·9	7·0	5·6
Eastern European countries			4·7	4·8	3·7	4·2	3·8	3·3	3·1
American countries	19·8	22·0	13·9	14·9	14·6	14·9	15·3	19·6	16·0
Others	—	—	2·5	2·9	2·9	2·9	1·6	2·7	2·4
Non-Oil Exports									
Country groups									
Arab countries	56·8	54·0	56·2	61·4	58·3	59·3	50·4	53·2	N/A
African countries	0·2	1·0	0·7	2·8	2·4	1·3	3·4	2·5	N/A
Asian countries	41·5	34·0	30·2	20·6	25·3	30·9	35·3	36·6	N/A
European Common Market	1·2*	6·0*	5·8	9·0	10·8	4·8	4·4	3·5	N/A
Other Western European countries			0·6	0·2	0·2	0·2	2·1	1·6	N/A
Eastern European countries			0·4	0·1	0·3	0·1	—	—	N/A
American countries	0·4	5·0	3·3	3·4	1·5	3·1	4·4	2·5	N/A
Others			2·8	2·4	1·2	0·2	0·1	0·1	N/A

SOURCE: *The Kuwait Annual Statistical Abstract.*
*These figures are totals for the European countries.

per cent to less than 40 per cent, and other groups show little substantial change.

Kuwait's non-oil exports and re-exports to the Arab countries grew from KD14·8 million in 1970 to KD91 million in 1975 and, as shown in Table 5.6, their relative share remained in excess of 50 per cent. This resulted in reversing the Kuwait balance of trade in non-oil products with the other Arab countries from a deficit of about KD4 million in 1970 to a surplus of more than KD60 million in 1975. Although the bulk of this surplus is attributed to re-exports to neighbouring Arab countries, especially Saudi Arabia, Iraq and the UAE, there are indications that the trade balance positions of other Arab countries have become less favourable in recent years as their exports to Kuwait decreased. In addition, trans-shipment of goods to Kuwait via such countries as Lebanon, Syria, Jordan and Iraq which hitherto constituted an important source of foreign exchange earnings for these countries has diminished in recent years as a result of the political disruption in Lebanon. In fact, trans-shipment of goods to Syria and Iraq has become relatively more important. It is clear, therefore, that regional economic cooperation in trade has fallen short of its potential for reasons relating in particular to insufficient support given to agriculture and food production in other countries in the region as well as to such political factors as indicated above. Finally, no particular trend can be discerned in non-oil exports to the non-Arab countries, Asian countries still taking the second largest share.

Regional integration
Many efforts have been made to promote economic cooperation among the Arab countries including the establishment of the Arab Council of Economic Unity and the Arab Common Market. While Kuwait has joined the first, it has not yet ratified the agreement establishing the second. Generally, there has been only limited progress in the promotion of intra-regional trade and the implementation of joint projects. Although most customs duties between member countries of the Arab Common Market have been reduced or completely eliminated, the volume of trade has not increased substantially as yet. As far as joint ventures are concerned, it should be noted that, apart from the Arab Mining Company, the Arab Livestock Company, the Gulf International Bank, the Arab Investment Company and perhaps a few other such enterprises, the major joint companies were initiated by OAPEC and, to a lesser extent, by the Arab Fund. The former instigated four oil-related companies, the latter initiated one;

the Arab Authority for Agricultural Investment and Development. In addition, Kuwait has participated in a number of projects in various Arab countries the aim of which is to bring about greater economic integration in the region; these include the Kenana Sugar Project in the Sudan and the Arab Mining and Industrial Company in Mauritania.

On the other hand, efforts to bring about greater economic cooperation among the Arabian Gulf States have become more earnest in recent years and there are already signs of progress. There is coordination with regard to some economic policies and large-scale industrial projects. There is also strong cooperation in the field of banking and finance which has culminated in the establishment of a number of joint banks. The recent formation of a monetary union and its prospects will be discussed in Chapter 10.

6 Kuwait and World Oil Developments

The last three chapters have described the development of Kuwait since 1946 to the present day and traced its emergence as a modern economy by reference to a number of social indicators and the changes which they presented. Almost exclusively these are directly related to the changing role played by the country's main natural resource, oil. Only when we can understand the intricacy of the rapid evolution of the power of oil on the world stage at the precise time when the control of that power was moving out of the hands of the user countries and into the hands of the producer countries can we understand the significance of many of the changes which have taken place in Kuwait as well as in many other Arab states whose main natural resource is oil.

The peculiar structure of the world oil industry is in many ways the product of the location of its original genesis and the pattern of subsequent further discovery and exploitation. The dominance of America as both the largest producer and consumer of oil led to that country being the dictator of events in the world market in matters of supply, development, exploitation and marketing. The way in which American commercial law controlled home-based companies had vital repercussions on their activities abroad. Legislation concerning price policies at home was immediately translated into exploitation and price policies in foreign markets as domestic and foreign policies of such companies were translated into overall optimising policies for each company as a whole. In 1951 the United States produced 298 of the 580 million tons of oil used in the world. More importantly, the American market was dominated by a few major companies, and these in turn were dominant forces on the world market both as controllers of crude oil and as marketers of the refined products. In 1955 eight companies (Standard Oil New Jersey, Texaco, Gulf Oil Corporation, Standard Oil California, Mobil Oil Corporation, Royal Dutch Shell, British Petroleum and Compagnie Francaise de Petrole) controlled 92 per cent of the world's output of crude oil and the first five of these companies were American (the remainder were British/Dutch, British and French respectively). In 1960 their share had fallen to 84 per cent and in 1965 to 76 per cent.[1] It was the twin factors of the United States' internal market dominating the world market and of the American market being dominated by a few large companies, which themselves controlled most of the rest of the world's output, which gave the world oil market its form and structure.

The way in which a company, faced with alternative sources of production and selling in a number of markets, may arrange its output and distribution to maximise its overall returns is explained in all respectable textbooks on economics and need not concern us here. However, a useful scenario is one in which the price and output policy of a company on the home market is given by a combination of legislative pressure and a policy based on profit maximisation. Even though such companies are supplying the largest home market in the world, if their output is greater than that required at home the remainder is sold on the world market which those companies also dominate. The total market for home production is then delineated by those points at which the home FOB price plus transport is sufficient to absorb such output as is surplus to home requirements. If those companies also control foreign sources of supply then 'price' at foreign sources will be fixed at a level where it is equal to the delineating price less the cost of transport to the edge of the dominated market. As long as exporting takes place from the home market and control of foreign output can be maintained, the maximisation of profit under constraint of home policy requires this type of manipulation. Thus home market adjustments are met by offsetting adjustments in the price and output policy in foreign countries. With a continued output at home from long-established wells, costs continue to rise and profitability falls but, due to political pressures, prices are kept low. To meet increasing demand at home, less is available for exports and the 'watershed point', at which the surplus sold to the rest of the world is exhausted, moves closer to the home country. The paradox now, however, is that such a movement can cause the FOB price paid in the foreign country to fall, especially if prices in the home country are kept artificially low. As supply is regulated to ensure that sufficient is produced to satisfy demand at the new watershed points, the extra freight costs will eat into the final price so that the foreign FOB price might actually be reduced.

A detailed examination, of course, of the post-war years would produce a number of counter hypotheses, of which one is that the pricing system of the immediate post-war years could equally be explained by a competitive equilibrium model as by a cartel. 'Up to this point price and production have evolved according to the competitive scenario, but whether the competition itself has been explained is another matter.'[2]

We are dealing with oil and the balance of political power and, even though reductions in crude prices may be consistent with the competitive model, they are not a sufficient condition to prove its applicability. It is contended that, where the major users are a few major companies with complete control of the home market and dominance on the world market, they are able to influence world crude prices according to their share of the world market and their share of control of foreign output. However, when the amount available for export is reduced due to a fall in home supply or an increase in home demand, or where external competition is increased, the power to influence world price is reduced accordingly. Even if both models are capable of 'explaining' the pricing system in the earlier post-war years, however, it is certain that the sale of Middle Eastern crude oil by concessionaires to their parent companies was not subject to competition. The concessionaires were monopolists in their own concessionary areas, and it was cold comfort to Middle Eastern countries if competition at the consuming end of the market was translated into downward pressure of the crude prices on which they depended.

It can be seen from Table 6.1 that for the fifteen years 1960–74 inclusive United States' production rose from 348 million tons to 432·8 million tons, an increase of less than 25 per cent, but her imports increased from 51·9 to 172·6 million tons in the same period, an increase of over 232 per cent. Her home market developed so that over this period total usage of crude increased by approximately 64 per cent whereas the total used in the world increased by 165 per cent. America's share of world use in 1960 was 38 per cent, whereas in 1974 it was down to 22 per cent. This was still not an inconsiderable proportion, but certainly a clear drop over the fifteen-year period.

One must, of course, guard against the danger of seeing the post-war changes in terms only of changes in the relationships between producer states and American companies. This would be untrue, but it was the fall in the dominance of the American oil influence which in turn affected the relationships of both themselves and others with producer states such as those in the Arabian Gulf. The fall in that dominance left gaps to be filled, and the way in which the number of companies in the industry grew is succintly and very readably described by Tugendhat and Hamilton.[3] The newcomers on the oil scene fell into two categories—independent American companies such as Continental, Marathon, Philips and Signal, and organisations from the consumer

TABLE 6.1 Crude oil production, trade of US, world and trade ratios, 1960–76, and US refinery capacity (Million tons)

	US				World				US Trade to World Trade %	US Refinery Capacity
	Production	Imports	Exports	Trade	Production	Imports	Exports	Trade		
1960	348·0	51·9	0·4	52·3	1052·1	383·0	380·8	763·8	6·8	486·0
1961	354·3	53·1	0·4	53·5	1120·6	427·3	423·1	850·4	6·3	493·8
1962	361·7	57·1	0·2	57·3	1215·6	477·5	477·4	954·9	6·7	495·5
1963	372·0	57·4	0·2	57·6	1304·1	531·9	529·0	1060·9	5·4	493·8
1964	376·6	60·8	0·2	61·0	1407·7	605·7	604·3	1210·0	5·0	508·3
1965	384·9	62·4	0·1	62·5	1509·5	674·4	663·0	1337·4	4·7	513·9
1966	409·2	61·6	0·2	61·8	1639·0	747·2	742·3	2826·9	2·2	512·7
1967	434·6	56·7	3·6	60·3	1760·3	812·7	811·2	1623·9	3·7	525·7
1968	449·9	64·9	0·2	65·2	1922·2	922·9	919·6	1842·5	3·5	560·0
1969	455·6	70·5	0·2	70·7	2069·0	1047·3	1043·5	2090·8	3·4	577·2
1970	475·3	66·2	0·7	66·9	2270·2	1162·0	1162·0	2324·0	2·9	593·0
1971	466·7	83·8	0·1	83·9	2402·3	1103·0	1103·0	2206·0	3·8	634·3
1972	466·9	116·2	0·03	116·2	2531·5	1224·0	1224·6	2448·6	4·7	655·7
1973	452·7	171·3	0·1	171·4	2777·2	1404·0	1404·0	2808·0	6·1	715·0
1974	432·1	179·7	0·2	179·9	2791·4	1386·8	1388·8	2773·6	6·5	745·0
1975	411·4	243·9	0·6	244·5	2706·9	1272·9	1272·9	2545·8	9·6	759·0
1976	400·6	303·8	0·9	304·7	2925·8	1433·8	1433·8	2867·6	10·6	819·0

SOURCES: UN, *World Energy Supplies 1950–74* (UN, 1976).
Petroleum Times, April 1977.
Petroleum Economist, January 1977 Vol. XLIV No. 1.
OECD, *Energy Statistics* (Paris, 1976 and 1978).
BP, *Statistical Review of the World Oil Industry* (London, various years).

TABLE 6.2   Crude petroleum prices, Saudi Arabia (Ras Tanura)
1953–77 in US $/barrel

		1953	1954	1955	1956	1957	1958	1959	1960
		1·93	1·93	1·93	1·93	2·02	2·08	1·92	1·86
1961	1962	1963	1964	1965	1966	1967	1968	1969	1970
1·80	1·80	1·80	1·80	1·80	1·80	1·80	1·80	1·80	1·80
1971	1972	1973	1974	1975	1976	1977			
2·19	2·46	3·29	11·58	11·53	12·38	13·00			

SOURCE: IMF, *International Financial Statistics*, 1977 Supplement
Volume 30 No. 5, May 1977.

countries where demand and general economic prosperity was
developing rapidly. These last were usually backed by the state of the
appropriate consumer country; but to whichever category a newcomer
belonged, the motives were still similar, either to get into the share of
the profits or to establish national control over a vital resource, the
supply of which lay almost exclusively in the hands of a few multi-
national companies based elsewhere. It was not until the second half of
the fifties, however, that these newcomers attempted to secure supplies
in competition with the majors by offering more favourable terms.

The phases of price changes which followed the competition will be
described later, but it is significant that there was a slight increase in
Gulf prices at the same time (see Table 6.2). However, the pressures
placed upon the producer countries by the vagaries in the oil market,
including unilateral reduction by some of the major companies
operating in the Middle East, prompted those countries to resist that
pressure and to seek means to counteract it. The ways in which they did
this brought about many changes and the next paragraphs are devoted
to the formation and early years of their joint organisation, OPEC.

THE ORGANISATION OF PETROLEUM EXPORTING
COUNTRIES (OPEC)

A fixed quantity of reserves implies that a fall in price can only be
countered by an increase in output if revenue is to be maintained, yet
prices of crude oil were fixed without reference to the producing
countries whose well-being vitally depended upon oil receipts. Changes
in the world order, however, with many former colonies achieving

independence and traditional spheres of influence of the major powers being eroded, saw the producer countries more able to join together freely to pursue matters of common cause. One of those matters, of course, was the improvement of their standards of living and, when it is realised that during the late fifties up to 75 per cent of the final price to the consumer of petroleum products in the Western world comprised taxes much of which were devoted to improving social well-being in the generally affluent consumer nations, any pressures on prices affecting the income of the producer nations was particularly irksome. So, faced with the unilateral reductions at the end of the fifties and having a greater number of independents with whom they could negotiate to their advantage, producer countries moved towards a coordination of their efforts. In 1959 the first Arab oil congress was held in Cairo and Iran and Venezuela attended as observers but, after further oil price reductions by the companies, a meeting of producing/exporting countries (Iran, Iraq, Saudi Arabia, Kuwait, Venezuela) formed a permanent organisation to offer a concerted front to the major companies. This was entitled the Organisation of Petroleum Exporting Countries.

The accent was upon the word 'exporting' for it was primarily concerned with the returns to those countries which relied heavily on the price of crude oil for their income rather than on the sale of the finished products. Qatar joined in 1961, Indonesia and Libya in 1962, Abu Dhabi in 1967 and Algeria in 1969. Nigeria joined in 1971 and Ecuador in 1973.

The immediate aims of the founder members in 1960 (and it must be remembered that at that time the five founder members were the source of 85 per cent of oil entering world trade) were relatively limited. They were:

(a) to restore the price of oil to the level immediately preceding the reductions of the late 1950s,

(b) to eliminate quantity discounts whereby concessionaires gave their parent companies 'discounts' for larger quantities ordered, and

(c) to expense royalties i.e. to deduct them as expenses before the calculation of profits, instead of treating them as part of the profit payment. (For example, if receipts were 200 cents per barrel, expenses 80 cents, royalties 20 cents the payment proposed, under a 50 per cent tax take by the producer country would be $50/100 \times (200 - 80 - 20) + 20 = 70$ cents instead of $50/100 \times (200 - 80) = 60$ cents, of which 20 cents royalty would form a part.

Kuwait as a founder member, then as ever, played an important role in OPEC and its membership commenced prior to the cessation of the agreement with Britain. In fact the first secretary of OPEC was a Kuwaiti and development of OPEC with Kuwait as a member was an important aspect of Kuwait's emergence into international politics.

Up to 1967 OPEC had not shown conspicuous success in achieving its aims. They had presented the companies with their demands in 1962 and had asked for royalties to be increased to 20 per cent on the grounds that compensation for depletion of their natural resource base should not depend on fluctuating profits. By 1964 little headway had been made. Many of the larger companies refused to accept the existence of OPEC, but in 1966 efforts were resumed, especially with a view to the elimination of discounts. The major breakthrough did not come until 1970. Iraq, Libya and Algeria agreed to coordinate their efforts in their relationship with the multinationals. At that time the Suez Canal was closed and 95 per cent of crude oil transported in the Mediterranean was from Mediterranean terminals distributing oil from these three countries. Libya led the assault having a very favourable balance of payments position and a very vulnerable independent company, Occidental, operating on concessions within its borders. Occidental had little alternative sources of supply, yet several of the majors were also operating in Libya and it was not policy for them to assist Occidental in resisting pressure from the Libyan government. There is no doubt that the move by Libya could not have taken place without the tacit agreement of OPEC members. In fact, the Kuwait Fund was actively supporting Algeria in petroleum developments (e.g. Sonatrach). Other companies were therefore reticent to assist Occidental, as to do so would not only have endangered their position in Libya, but throughout the whole of OPEC. Libya quickly won an increase in both posted price and the tax take. Other minor companies quickly followed suit so that the majors were forced to follow also. By the end of 1970 Libya's take per barrel had increased by about 27 cents on all oil exported. This success was followed immediately by Iraq who negotiated terms which, although not quite so favourable, were substantially similar after a number of outstanding issues had been resolved with the companies. Further OPEC countries submitted claims, again with success and, with the destruction of the power of the major companies to hold down prices, the power of OPEC members was made evident. The changes of 1970 marked not only the beginning of an era of price rises, but also the end of a period of skirmishing and probing by OPEC members which began in 1966. 1970, in fact, was a culmination of many previous essays by individual members to try out points of strength and weakness in the general relationships between themselves and the companies. At the same time, the significance of 1970 was not lost on governments of the countries in which the majors were based and the struggle was quickly transformed into one between the governments of the industrial and producing countries rather than between companies and the producing countries' governments as hitherto. The problems were now no longer those of prices and profits but problems of international balances of payments and the ramifications of changes in the terms of trade.

While the emergence of OPEC may stem from 1970, however, the era in which its power was really evident was in 1973/4. During much of 1973 there had been discussions with the oil companies concerning an increase in posted prices. These had been resisted and, after a series of meetings in September in Vienna and then Teheran, it was agreed to continue the series in October. However, in view of the outbreak of the Arab/Israeli war, the oil companies decided to postpone their attendance and the OPEC countries decided to proceed unilaterally. They met in Kuwait and on 16 October announced the now famous 'October 73' increases. The Arab members of OPEC held a further meeting on the following day and at this meeting decided on the oil boycott. The commonly held impression that the boycott and the price rises were part of the same package needs correction as the latter were the result of a long series of meetings commencing well before the outbreak of the war including a crucial meeting in Geneva when it was decided to link the price of oil to a basket of currencies because of the fall in the US dollar. The boycott was the result of a decision by Arab members of OPEC only. The decisive influence of the war on oil prices and supplies came later when the boycott showed the extent of the power which the oil producers really held in their grasp.

The establishment and aims of OPEC, however, must not be confused with those of a similarly titled body OAPEC, the Organisation of Arab Petroleum Exporting Countries. This body grew from the work of the Arab League who as long ago as 1952 sponsored a committee of oil experts to coordinate oil policies. Originally oil was envisaged as an instrument of political policy by the League and the Oil Experts Committee was under the aegis of the League's political committee who saw its development as part of military strategy. In 1964 the Oil Experts Committee was transferred to the control of the Economics Committee, as the potential of oil as an instrument for economic development became more and more evident to the member nations. The potential of oil as a political weapon, of course, did not diminish and, as a result of the 1967 war, the reduction in the supply of oil was advocated by some together with the complete suspension of supplies to those nations sympathetic to Israel. This school of thought was led by Algeria and Iraq. However, Saudi Arabia, Kuwait and Libya headed a more moderate school who advocated a more long-term strategy of using revenues from oil to achieve the political and economic aims of the Arab countries. OAPEC was established following those discussions in January 1968 by Kuwait, Libya and Saudi Arabia who sought to alleviate the distress caused by the Arab/Israeli conflict and each pledged substantial support annually to the affected states. Meanwhile, Iraq and Algeria sought to lead a counter group advocating the use of revenues as a weapon in the 'revolutionary struggle'. (When it is remembered that OAPEC's three founder members were monarchies at the time, the seeds of difference were obviously well rooted.)

Kuwait has always played a key role in the coordination of policies of OAPEC members. In fact the OAPEC headquarters are in Kuwait. Many of the rights of membership are covered by the original constitution which guarantees certain powers to the founding members. At the outset the three were essentially traditionalist, finding themselves at odds with some of the other Arab nations who by revolution had divested themselves of their monarchies. However, when the Libyan monarchy was overthrown in 1969 this balance was disturbed and Algeria subsequently joined the organisation. Two organisations were now in existence therefore, OPEC and OAPEC and Kuwait was an important member of both. The power to present a common front with its producer associates to the oil-consuming world, together with the power to coordinate the policies of those Arab countries whose income was derived predominantly from the export of oil, were vital to its future policy. An isolated Kuwait, even though having such a large proportion of the world's oil reserves, would have held an economic power which might have been unable to be exercised if it had been forced by political circumstances to act in economic competition with other producers. Thus, even though the aims of OPEC and OAPEC were essentially different, the important role which Kuwait played in each doubtless enhanced the role which it played in the other and the position enjoyed on the world oil stage by Kuwait undoubtedly derives from the position it enjoys in both these and other bodies.

It was mentioned earlier that once the conflict between the companies and the producer countries had been transformed into one between the consumer and producer countries, the considerations were no longer of prices and profits but of the balance of payments and the terms of trade. It is to this last aspect that we now turn.

TERMS OF TRADE

The values of a country's exports have little meaning except in relation to the imports that such values will finance and changes in the prices of exports are of greater or lesser importance depending upon the changes in prices of imports which take place at the same time. Measures of this relationship are described as the terms of trade: there are a number of these measures which are usually expressed as indices and the most simple is the net barter terms of trade. Quite simply, this is the measure of the relative prices of exports to those of imports.

From Kuwait's point of view, of course, this is effectively the comparison of oil prices with the prices of the goods she needs to import. When, like Kuwait, a country is dependent to a great extent upon imports for its own development, or even in some cases survival, then of course this relationship is of vital importance.

The terms of trade are important too as an indicator of the way in which Kuwait has been able to amass a share of control of the world's productive resources. The amassment of physical capital depends crucially upon the quantity of output which is not consumed and, in Kuwait's case, that part of the value of her exports which is not consumed is available for investment either in physical capital for use at home or in financial capital which is effectively a claim on assets elsewhere. Any change in Kuwait's, or any other nation's income, usually has a more than proportionate effect upon saving so that the terms of trade do not so much affect Kuwait's ability to consume as much as her ability to invest. A fall in oil prices or a change in the price of her imports might see little change in her level of consumption but a large fluctuation in her level of investment. When we discuss Kuwait's terms of trade, therefore, we are really talking about Kuwait's future as this depends vitally upon her ability to command a sufficient share of the world's future productive capacity and the terms of trade help to indicate the direction in which that control is moving.[4]

The net barter terms of trade for Kuwait have been calculated, together with other indices to be discussed, and are shown in Table 6.3. With oil occupying such a dominant role in Kuwait's exports, the price of Kuwait crude was used as the 'price of exports'. The price of crude oil, however, fell from 1958 to 1961 and remained constant to 1970,

TABLE 6.3   Some indices of the terms of trade of Kuwait 1957–77 (1970 = 100)

	Px/Pm Net barter terms of trade[1]	$PxQx/Pm$ Income terms of trade[2]	Rx/Pm Adjusted net barter terms of trade[3]	$RxQx/Pm$ Retained income terms of trade[4]
1957	123·6	53·1	103·8	44·6
1958	132·2	65·3	109·0	53·8
1959	123·5	59·3	110·1	52·8
1960	117·2	65·6	104·9	58·7
1961	113·8	65·4	102·2	58·8
1962	115·1	74·6	103·4	67·0
1963	115·1	79·9	103·4	71·7
1964	112·5	86·9	106·0	81·9
1965	111·2	86·0	106·3	83·9
1966	108·8	92·0	104·6	88·5
1967	107·6	92·1	103·5	88·6
1968	108·8	97·8	105·5	94·8
1969	105·3	100·0	102·3	97·2
1970	100·0	100·0	100·0	100·0
1971	128·8	138·5	139·1	149·5
1972	121·0	137·6	138·6	157·6
1973	141·2	144·9	161·0	165·2
1974	418·8	358·1	519·4	440·1
1975	397·4	275·4	644·5	446·6
1976	418·3	291·1	680·3	473·5
1977	422·0	263·7	686·0	425·8

Px = Index of the export price of oil
Pm = Index of prices of manufactured goods of industrial countries
Qx = Quantity index of Kuwait's oil exports
Rx = Index of Kuwait's share of the price of oil

[1] This index does not reflect Kuwait's relative ability to import by using its oil revenues, as the posted price of oil (Px) is an 'institutional' one used to determine taxes and royalties. It was only these latter which actually accrued to Kuwait and really determined its ability to import.

[2] Apart from the above, this index is affected by the volume of exports and it may rise in spite of a fall in the price of oil due to increased productivity or in spite of a rise in import prices.

[3] This index measures the average oil revenue received by Kuwait relative to the import price index and reflects the increase in oil receipts due to increased participation in the ownership of the oil companies.

[4] This index has a similar problem to the income terms of trade, but reflects more accurately the income retained in the country.

(Apart from the decline in both the 'income' and the 'retained income' terms of trade, there has also been a further deterioration in the net barter terms of trade resulting from the decline in the value of the US dollar which is not reflected in the above indices. To achieve a true picture would require the adjustment of the import index to conform to Kuwait's import pattern from the industrialised world.)

while the price of imports rose over the same period by 13 per cent. Thus the purchasing power of a barrel of Kuwait crude fell by almost 25 per cent over that period. The changes in the price of oil from 1970 onward are only partly reflected in the figures, however, since between 1970 and 1976 import prices rose by over 90 per cent thus almost halving the effect of the oil price rises on the index.

One of the drawbacks of such an index, of course, is that it only measures potential performance if other things remain equal. No account is taken of changes in productivity which might make either imports or exports more competitive. Given the conditions of oil exploitation, however, it is difficult for much change in productivity to be reflected in oil prices. Indeed, it has been shown earlier how prices for so long were administered in such a way that they bore no relation to costs at all. Thus, if one wishes to calculate the way in which Kuwait's ability to import has changed, one must also take account of the actual quantity of exports as well. If export prices fall, then an increase in exports at least compensates for this.

The measure used for this is the 'income terms of trade', expressed as

$$\frac{\text{the price of exports} \times \text{quantity of exports}}{\text{price of imports}} \quad \text{or} \quad \frac{Px \ Qx}{Pm}$$

These also appear in Table 6.3 and the difference is immediately evident from the barter terms of trade. Even though the price of crude fell to 1961 and remained low until 1970, the exports of Kuwait increased so that the actual ability to import would have almost doubled. From 1970 onwards the leap upward due to oil prices was tempered in 1975 and 1976 by a fall in exports as a result of the conservation policy.

Each of the two indices discussed so far have their attributes and drawbacks and the importance of these is directly related to the particular purpose for which the index is required. From the point of view, however, of the oil exporting countries both are subject to major flaws in that not only did the 'official' price of oil vary from the price paid, but the price 'paid' was paid to the extracting companies prior to nationalisation and the amount received by the actual producing country would be but a fraction of this. Consequently, a further measure is necessary to portray this and we have calculated a 'net barter' index adjusted for the proportion of the price of each barrel of oil which accrued to Kuwait. Kuwait's take per barrel of oil did not fall commensurate with the fall in prices up to 1970, so that from 1958 to 1970 her actual command over imports from the income she received from a barrel of oil only fell by around 10 per cent, and not the 25 per cent that would be implied from the unadjusted net barter index. However, the period after 1970 illustrates the combination of increases in both prices and participation leading to full ownership in 1976 so that, in spite of the steep rise in import prices, Kuwait's command over imports per barrel of oil produced increased by almost six times.

For completion, a further measure has also been calculated which is called the 'retained income' terms of trade. This is a further refinement of the adjusted net barter index and includes a term for the quantity of exports also. In fact it represents the way in which Kuwait has been able to increase its power to import over the twenty years covered by the table.

Each of these indices has its uses, but the adjusted net barter index is probably the most important from the present point of view as it shows the power of oil as an agent of change from 1957 to 1970. The imports which the income to Kuwait from a barrel of oil would command gradually fell, but from 1970 onward, due to the factors that have been discussed, it has increased in the manner shown. It is this index which facilitates decisions on such matters as conservation policy—this is reflected in the less steep rise in the retained income index as the output of oil was curtailed after 1973 as part of such a policy.

TAXATION, PRICING AND OIL PAYMENTS IN KUWAIT

This section examines the effect of the country's policies on oil taxation, pricing and payments. It is divided into four periods, each introducing a new stage of development in the government's policies towards oil companies and oil resources. Stage one, 1946–60, outlines the profit sharing arrangements under the original agreements in Kuwait and the introduction of posted prices. Stage two begins with the establishment of OPEC and discusses the resultant activities in its formative years, 1960–70. Stage three extends over the 1970–3 period, during which company–country relations are transformed; and the last stage, 1973 onward, recounts the events leading to the government's control over its oil resources.

1. The Early Oil Period 1946–60
The largest and oldest oil company in Kuwait is the Kuwait Oil Company (KOC) which was owned by two international majors, Anglo-Iranian Oil Company (later BP) with 50 per cent and Gulf, 50 per cent.

Prior to 1954 it was the only company operating in Kuwait. By 1976 its share had dropped to 89·2 per cent of total Kuwait oil production. The original agreement of 1934 gave KOC an exclusive concession to explore, produce and market oil in Kuwait (exclusive of the Neutral Zone) for seventy-five years. The concession was extended by an amendment in 1951 for another seventeen years. Before 1951 the agreement with KOC provided for a fixed money payment of 3 rupees (equivalent to $0·7 in 1951) per long ton of crude in addition to 4 annas (KD0·08) in return for tax exemptions. Thus the payments to Kuwait over 1946–50 totalled $36·5 million for 284·2 billion barrels.

The agreement between Venezuela and the oil companies which provided for a change from fixed payment per barrel to profit-sharing arrangements was applied to the Middle East in 1951, with the exception of Iran who rejected it, and of course during 1951–4 there was an interruption in Iranian supply. A tax law was passed in Kuwait subjecting oil companies to income tax at 50 per cent of profits. Tax on profits meant that KOC had to estimate receipts from oil exports on the basis of transfer prices and, after allowing for outlays, the company was allowed to claim royalty and tax exemptions as a credit against the income tax assessed. As a result of this agreement government revenues rose greatly, and exceeded $60 million in 1953.

The concept of posted prices was introduced in the agreement of 11 October 1955. According to this agreement, imputed tax values of oil exports in 1956–8 were to be assessed on the basis of a 'posted price' per barrel rather than on actual prices received. Companies would post a price in the neighbourhood of what they might realise from the sale of oil, but these prices were employed merely as tax reference prices. Consequently, if oil prices fluctuated, the level of tax would remain unaltered. Royalty payments were changed from Rs. 3 to 12·5 per cent of posted price, but without effecting any change in money payment to the government since royalties continued to be claimed as a credit against the amount of income tax assessed. At the same time, the agreement provided for volume discounts of 8 ⅓ per cent of posted prices on oil sales in excess of 20 million tons per annum valid until the end of 1958.[5] Marketing expenses were set at 2 per cent of posted prices, but were reduced to 1 per cent following the 18 December 1958 agreement, retrospectively effective from 1 April 1957.

During the latter part of the 1950s Kuwait's revenues rose both in per barrel take and total. The per barrel payments as derived by the authors in Table 6.4 are in agreement as to trend with other similar studies, but movements from one year to the other may differ as these figures

TABLE 6.4   Government revenue per barrel of 31° API* crude under 1957–63 conditions (cents, US)

Year	Production in million tons	Average posted prices (1)	Volume discounts (2)	Marketing allowance (3)	Production costs (4)	Revenue: income tax at 50% of 1−(2 + 3 + 4)
1957	67·982	179	10·54	2·237	10·0	78·11
1958	83·324	185	11·73	1·85	10·0	80·11
1959	83·626	170		1·70	10·0	79·15
1960	99·031	164		1·64	8·0	77·18
1961	100·653	159		1·59	7·0	75·20
1962	113·610	159		1·59	7·0	75·20
1963	121·164	159		1·50	7·0	75·20

*API (American Petroleum Institute). The 'degree API' measures the specific gravity of crude oil. The higher the figure, the lighter the crude. Thus, Tia Juana 18° would be a very heavy oil and Zakum (Abu Dhabi) 40° a light oil.

SOURCES: Central Bank of Kuwait, *Annual Reports*; and *Quarterly Statistical Bulletin* (various years)

exclude several non-recurrent items; and also allow for lags in export of oil already produced. But the outstanding fact is that oil companies' per barrel payments to the government rose from around 20 cents per barrel in 1946–50 to 80 cents in 1958–9.

2. 1960 to 1970 and the Establishment of OPEC

Until 1960 oil-producing countries had acted largely individually with the international major companies, whose collective interest dictated a coordinated policy over the company-host country distribution of revenue. OPEC, after its establishment in 1960, succeeded in stopping the decline in oil prices and in stabilising posted prices until early 1970. The establishment of OPEC shifted the subject of conflict from the division of revenues to pricing and production policies[6] and altered the balance of power of antagonists with the inception of a collective front of oil producers.

After two years of drawn out negotiations between OPEC and oil companies, which ended in 1964, the principle of expensing of royalties was introduced with effect from 1 January 1964. According to this principle, royalty on crude oil would be shown as an expense in the same way as production costs in calculating the companies' profits as has been shown earlier in this chapter. But royalty expensing was partially offset by reducing taxable notional profits by discount allowances on posted prices which could vary up to around 8 per cent for heavy crude of 27° API and below, in addition to certain gravity correction allowances for lighter crudes. Marketing expenses were set at ½ cent per barrel in 1964–70.

TABLE 6.5   Tax on Kuwaiti 31° API crude
and government take per barrel under 1964–70
conditions (cents, US)

Year	Average posted price	Goverment take
1964	159	78·93
1965	159	79·96
1966	159	80·49
1967	159	80·49
1968	159	81·17
1969	159	81·34
1970	160·2	84·55

TABLE 6.6   1965 company payments per barrel to Kuwait

	Al-Ahmadi 31° API (cents/barrel)
1. Posted Price	159
2. Less marketing allowance	0·5
3. discount (0·075)	11·925
4. gravity allowance (4 x 0·13235)	0·529
5. production costs	6·0
6. fully expensed royalty at 12·5%	19·875
7. Pro forma profit (line 1 less sum of lines 2 to 6)	120·171
8. Pro forma income tax at 50%	60·086
9. Government take (6 + 8)	79·961

Table 6.5 shows the government take per barrel between 1964 and 1970, while 6.6 illustrates the method of calculation of company payments to the government of Kuwait under 1965 conditions.

The 1966–7 OPEC proposals provided for phasing out discounts by 1973 and were accepted by all OPEC member countries with the exception of Kuwait who delayed ratification of the terms offered and presented its own proposals to reserve the right to raise tax rates, to make claims for back taxes based on pre-1960 posted prices and to contest the claims at a Kuwait court of law. Eventually, however, Kuwait consented to the OPEC proposals with some undisclosed modifications. Thus after the fifteenth OPEC conference on 8 January 1968 companies agreed to phase out the allowable discounts on posted prices.

3. 1970–3

Production, pricing and equity participation remained mostly in the hands of the international majors until early 1970. After prices had remained fixed throughout the sixties Kuwait, in conjunction with Saudi-Arabia and Iran raised both oil prices and income taxes on 14 November 1970. Thus the posted price of Kuwait crude 31° API went up from $1·59 to $1·68 per barrel and income tax on KOC's profits was raised from 50 per cent to 55 per cent. This successful move provided producing countries with the impetus to tighten control over their resources.

Other agreements followed in the early 1970s between OPEC

countries and the international oil companies, notably the ones concluded in Teheran and Geneva. These agreements reflected the buoyant world oil demand and the determination of these countries to protect their oil revenues from fluctuations in the value of the US dollar, the currency in which most prices are quoted. The Teheran agreement of February 1971 fixed the income tax rate at 55 per cent, raised posted prices by 40·5 cents per barrel and adopted a schedule for oil price increases. This agreement was an important turning point in company-host country relations replacing the oil companies' monopoly over price setting 'with a policy of setting prices through negotiations'.[7] The Geneva agreements of January 1972 and June 1973 were intended to prevent the erosion of the real value of oil prices by successive devaluations of the US dollar i.e. against adverse changes in the terms of trade. The first Geneva agreement procured an 8·49 per cent increase in posted prices to recompense for the dollar devaluation of December 1971. The second Geneva agreement, concluded in response to the second dollar devaluation of February 1973, rectified the original agreement in such a way as to accommodate future fluctuations in exchange rates by relating oil prices to a basket of currencies. During this transitional period, the Kuwait government began a conservation policy,[8] in accordance with the agreements in the seventeenth OPEC conference (Baghdad 1968) and in 1972 limited KOC's maximum production to 3 million barrels per day. Production curtailment by Kuwait and other Middle Eastern countries was not only intended to reduce the rate of oil depletion, but to prevent potential worldwide oil surpluses that would depress prices. This reflects the strengthening position of oil-producing countries. The early 1970s, therefore, marked drastic changes in the oil industry. The governments gradually took over from the companies decisions concerning prices, production and marketing, and this was the beginning of a two fold process, in which oil producers first gained control of their resources and their pricing, and later their full ownership. The two have significant differences, for it was not until the latter occurred that producers could really embark upon full-scale developmental planning of their future. This was the period of participation leading to nationalisation and it took the form of an ever-increasing share of the value of oil produced. In Kuwait the original agreement was for a 28 per cent share.

4. 1973 onward

October 1973 saw the opening of the final phase in the transition to the full ownership of oil production by the producing countries in OPEC.

The circumstances surrounding the agreements of that month, in OPEC on prices and among the Arab States on the oil embargo, are dealt with above, but the former included the raising of prices to a level commensurate with $5·119 per barrel, for 34° API crude, i.e. a 70 per cent increase.

By December 1973 the cutback in oil production, which included the embargo, caused a decline in OPEC output of 22 per cent over September 1973. This created a rush on oil purchase on the international oil market, pushing the auction prices of some Libyan and Nigerian crudes to about $20 per barrel. The Teheran conference on 22 December 1973 adopted a compromise price, between the auction price and the October 1973 level, of $11·651. Several factors contributed to the success of these moves, but three are singled out here because of their relevance to this discussion:

1. the moulding of OPEC into a collective front gave it a strong negotiating position with consuming countries;
2. the emergence of the United States in 1973 as a major oil importer and
3. the increasing dependence of world demand on the supply of oil, vis-à-vis production cutbacks.

As a result of a participation agreement with the two companies, effective as from 1 January 1974, KOC was owned 40 per cent by BP and Gulf and 60 per cent by the government. The same agreement had also retroactively provided for a 25 per cent government participation in KOC during 1973 and was, in fact, only reached after long and sometimes heated debates in the National Assembly where earlier proposals for a lower rate of participation had been rejected.

In the latter half of 1974, OPEC countries turned their attention to increasing their take on companies' equity oil (40 per cent share). The net effect was to raise royalties from 12·5 per cent to 20 per cent of posted prices, and income-tax from 55 per cent to 85 per cent.

By the start of 1975 OPEC had adopted a new pricing system under which oil companies should pay a unified price for their crude oil entitlements—equity and buyback. The new price for Kuwait 31° API liftings by BP and Gulf was set at $10·15 per barrel; thus the profit margin for the two companies was reduced to 22 cents per barrel on the $10·37/barrel market price.

On 1 December 1975 Kuwait terminated BP and Gulf's concessions in Kuwait. Since then the company–country relationship became a commercial one. A five-year renewable commercial contract with Gulf and BP provided that the two companies would purchase 950,000

TABLE 6.7   Average posted prices (weighted) and average
government take (weighted) of Kuwaiti crude 31° API,
1971−6 (US dollars)

Year	Weighted average posted price per barrel	Weighted average government take per barrel
1971	2·09	1·23
1972	2·36	1·40
1973	3·11	1·85
1974	11·48	7·47
1975	11·37	10·41
1976	12·09	11·10
1977	−	12·34[a]

SOURCES: 1. Central Bank of Kuwait, *Economic Reports for 1976* (Kuwait, 1977)
2. Central Statistical Office, *Annual Statistical Abstract, 1976* (Kuwait: Ministry of Planning, 1977)
3. Central Bank of Kuwait, *Quarterly Statistical Bulletin* (Kuwait, various)
4. Nasr, Souheil, 'Oil and International economics after the Ramadan War', in *Assasyat Sina't Al-Naft Walgaz* (Fundamentals of Oil and Gas Industry, Vol. II) (Kuwait, OAPEC 1977)
5. Ministry of Oil, *Petroleum Intelligence Weekly* (Kuwait, 1977, various).

NOTES: 1. Agreements were applied retroactively.
2. Government revenue from companies' equity = royalty + income tax. Revenue from government share = market price − production cost. Quality, gravity and geographic location allowances and monthly oil production rates are accounted for in these estimates.
3. By January 1975 two prices were in evidence (a) the market or third parties price normally at 93 per cent of posted price; (b) price to operating, or ex-concessionaire companies, which is at some discount from the market price.
4. KOC's production became fully state-owned with effect from 5 March 1975.

[a] Provisional.

barrels/day of Kuwait crude, at a 15 cents/barrel discount off the market price retroactive to 6 March 1975.

At the time of nationalisation of KOC the government still held a 60 per cent share in Kuwait's half interest in the Arabian Oil Company, which operated off shore of the Neutral Zone, under a participation agreement which came into effect on 1 January 1974. The American Independent Oil Company (Aminoil) which refined its entire production (approximately 81 thousand barrels per day at that time) was not subjected to participation, but the tax rate on its production was raised in line with the tax increases applied to the other two companies. On 19 September 1977 Kuwait announced the termination of Aminoil's concessions, granted on 28 June 1948 and the establishment of Al-Wafra Kuwait Oil Company (a national company) to replace it. In turn, Al-Wafra was split into an operational unit that merged with KOC and a refinery unit that merged with KNPC.

Meanwhile, oil prices were raised by 10 per cent on 1 October 1975 to offset part of the world price inflation. A month later Kuwait and Saudi Arabia adjusted their crude differentials in response to the declining world demand thus reducing the price for Kuwait crude by 10·2 cents/barrel to $11·30/barrel. This price was not changed until 1 June 1976 when it was reduced by 7 cents to $11·23/barrel to allow for gravity differentials under the provisional agreement adopted by OPEC in the Bali conference of May 1976. In OPEC's Doha conference, held on 15 December 1976, Kuwait and ten other members decided to raise the price for their oil by 10 per cent with effect from 1 January 1977 and by a further 5 per cent increment from mid-1977, while Saudi Arabia and the UAE adopted a 5 per cent increase for the whole year.[9] Under a tacit agreement, reached by the eleven-member 'group of maximalists' in Doha, Kuwait reduced the price of its crude 31° API by 5 cents to accommodate for gravity differentials. Thus the price for Kuwait crude 31° API became $12·37/barrel, effective from 1 January 1977. It has remained at this price despite the fall in the US dollar and world inflation. At the OPEC meeting of March 1978 it was confirmed that no price change would take place in 1978.

Table 6.7 illustrates vividly the effect on Kuwait oil prices of the agreements and changes since 1971 which we have listed above.

7 The Structure of the Economy

INTRODUCTION

Although, as has already been indicated, Kuwait shares with other developing countries many of their common properties and problems, the Kuwait economy displays a number of unique characteristics. In order to elucidate these characteristics, it is necessary to examine in detail the structure of the economy as well as the interaction of the various economic sectors, along with their organisation and development in more recent years. This chapter, together with the three that follow, is therefore devoted to a systematic analysis of the domestic economy. However, it differs from the others in that it makes use of an aggregative econometric model in order to portray more rigorously the salient features that warrant emphasis. But firstly an anlysis will be made of the main structural developments which have taken place in recent years, along with an investigation of their causes. The examination of the institutional organisation of the economy, its major production sectors and the local banking and financial structure will be conducted in the following three chapters.

SECTORAL DISTRIBUTION OF ECONOMIC ACTIVITY

One of the properties that Kuwait shares with many developing countries is dependence on the production and export of a single primary commodity. While the share of the oil sector has widely fluctuated with recent changes in prices and output, oil production remains without doubt the dominant sector in the economy. It accounted in 1975/6 for an estimated 70 per cent of GDP compared with 56·5 per cent in 1968/9. As evidenced from Table 7.1, the proportional share of the oil sector sustained three marked increases during the period from 1968/9 to 1975/6. The first occurred in 1970/1 as a result of the combined effect of higher production and prices. Two

TABLE 7.1 Sectoral contribution to GDP, 1968/9–1975/6

Sector	1968/9 (%)	1969/70 (%)	1970/1 (%)	1971/2 (%)	1972/3 (%)	1973/4 (%)	1974/5 (%)	1975/6 (%)
Agriculture and fishing	0·5	0·5	0·4	0·3	0·3	0·2	0·2	0·3
Manufacturing	3·9	3·7	3·9	3·1	3·8	3·6	4·6	5·0
Electricity and water	3·3	3·7	4·1	3·5	2·3	2·0	1·8	2·3
Construction	4·4	4·0	3·5	3·0	1·3	1·0	0·6	0·9
Wholesale and retail trade	8·9	8·6	8·4	6·7	6·8	5·3	4·1	5·8
Transport and communications	3·9	3·5	3·8	3·0	3·8	3·1	1·9	2·6
Banking, insurance and finance	1·8	1·8	2·0	1·6	7·9	6·4	3·3	4·6
Public administation and other services	17·8	17·5	6·0	11·8	13·9	9·9	6·4	8·5
Crude oil and natural gas	56·5	56·7	67·9	67·0	59·9	68·5	77·1	70·0
Total	100·0	100·0	100·0	100·0	100·0	100·0	100·0	100·0

SOURCES: The Planning Board, *The Kuwait Economy 1969/1970*, Kuwait, December 1970.
Ministry of Planning, *An Analytical Study of the National Accounts of the Kuwait Economy, 1970/71–1975/76*, Kuwait, July 1977.

years elapsed before the growth effects could be spread to other sectors
of the economy causing oil's share of GDP to fall from 67·9 per cent in
1970/1 to 59·9 per cent in 1972/3.[1] Following the increase in prices in
October 1973, the share of oil increased again, reaching a level of 68·5
per cent. However, with the continued increase in prices, oil's contribution to GDP reached in 1974/5 a record level of 77·1 per cent.

As for the other sectors, 'services', which includes trade, transport,
communications, banking, finance and public administration,
constitutes a major part of GDP. However, in spite of the remarkably
high growth rate of services (over 30 per cent annually), their proportional share of GDP has decreased from 31·4 per cent in 1968/9 to 21·5
per cent in 1975/6. This has largely resulted from an even greater
growth of the contribution of the oil sector. Among services, trade and
public administration are the most prominent. In the commodity-pro-
ducing sectors, manufacturing, which accounted for 5 per cent of GDP
in 1975/6 ranks first in terms of relative importance. Because of the
effect of the rise in oil prices, the modest increase in the proportional
share of manufacturing does not reflect the true success of the efforts to
promote industrialisation. Construction, on the other hand, has
declined significantly in relative importance over the years 1968/9 to
1975/6. This is mainly due to the fact that the construction boom of the
sixties came to a halt by the end of the decade and the housing crisis of
the last few years is partly attributable to the slow-down of construction
activities during those years.

Finally, it should be noted that the combined value added of the 'non-
oil' sector represents a larger proportion of GNP than of GDP. This is
particularly true for years prior to the nationalisation of the oil companies in 1975. Non-oil sectors accounted in 1968/9 for about 64·5 per
cent of GNP compared with 43·5 per cent of GDP. While both
percentages have gone down in recent years due to the more rapid
increase in income from oil, the difference between them has declined
considerably for reasons that will be explained in the discussion of the
national accounts which follows.

There are five noticeable structural features displayed by Kuwait's
national accounts. Firstly, it will be noted in Table 7.2 the extent to
which the economy is affected by foreign factor payments and receipts.
The difference between factor payments to the foreign oil companies
operating in Kuwait and income from government and private investments abroad accounted for an excess of GDP over GNP of up to 20 per
cent during the years 1968/9–1972/3. However, this excess has been
significantly curtailed over the years since 1972/3 because of the rise in

TABLE 7.2 Kuwait's national accounts for 1968/9–1975/6 (in current prices) (Million KD)

	68/9	69/70	70/1	71/2	72/3	73/4	74/5	75/6
Gross domestic product (in market prices)	951	989	1084	1417	1581	2112	3450	3279
(Less) net factor payments abroad	158	149	175	266	307	342	281	(224)
Gross national product	793	840	909	1151	1274	1770	3169	3503
Private consumption expenditure	297	306	325	340	379	396	423	592
Government consumption expenditure	144	152	160	224	239	308	405	519
Gross private investment	117	108	47	49	52	53	70	116
Gross public investment	54	62	63	72	102	93	113	140
(Less) imports of goods and services	248	286	273	278	271	326	553	737
Exports of goods and services	587	643	762	1010	1080	1588	2992	2650
(Less) net factor payments abroad	158	149	175	266	307	342	281	(244)
Gross national product	793	840	909	1151	1274	1770	3169	3503
(Less) government oil and foreign income	366	321	337	396	588	673	2208	2319
(Less) other government receipts	25	26	46	29	41	42	63	82
(Plus) government transfer payments	35	28	50	54	57	36	143	104
Gross disposable income	437	521	576	780	702	1091	1041	1206
Private consumption expenditure	297	306	325	340	379	396	423	592
Private savings	140	215	251	440	323	695	618	614
Government savings[1]	212	167	173	147	333	371	1723	1778
Gross national savings[2]	352	382	424	587	656	1066	2341	2392
National savings surplus[3] — current account surplus[4]	181	212	314	466	502	920	2158	2136

[1] Government savings = Government oil and foreign income + other government receipts − government transfer payments − government consumption expenditure.

[2] Gross national savings = private savings + government savings.

[3] National savings surplus = Gross national savings − gross national investment.

[4] Current account surplus = Exports of goods and services − imports of goods and services − net factor payments.

Kuwait's share in oil export earnings. In fact, the country has enjoyed net factor receipts from abroad since 1975/6 when the government took full ownership of the Kuwait Oil Company. Hence GNP exceeded GDP by approximately 7 per cent in 1975/6 and the difference is likely to increase with the expansion of government and private investments abroad. Another discernable feature is concerned with the absence of all forms of taxes except for a small custom duty on some imports, an income tax on the oil companies which formed part of government oil revenues and a 5 per cent levy on corporate profits which is devoted to the promotion of technological progress. Two observations relating to this feature will be elaborated later in the book. The first has to do with the government's dependence almost exclusively on oil revenues for the financing of its expenditure with a minimal contribution from the members of the community. The second observation relates to the obvious limitation on the fiscal policy instruments available to the government.

The third feature pertains to the decline in the relative size of disposable income from an estimated proportion of GNP of more than 55 per cent in 1968/9 to a low of approximately 33 per cent in 1974/5. This clearly implies that a substantial part of the increase in GNP has been retained by the government and had not yet found its way into the hands of the people and the business community. The reasons, as will be discussed later, may in large measure be found in the limited absorptive capacity of the country and the government's fear of seriously adding to the inflationary pressures which already existed. The fourth feature is a corallary of the third, i.e. the increase in the proportion of total government expenditure to total private expenditure from 48 per cent in 1968/9 to over 93 per cent in 1975/6. This partly reflects the tendency for expanding the welfare system to which reference was made earlier. As this trend continues the government, even though fully committed to a free enterprise system, may soon become the major spender in the economy.

Lastly, the magnitude of the current account surplus has increased in recent years both in absolute and in relative terms. The country's surplus reached KD1·9 billion in 1975/6 – accounting for about 55 per cent of GNP compared with KD339 million, i.e. 43 per cent of GNP in 1968/9. Similarly, total net savings increased from KD181 million in 1968/9 to approximately KD2·14 billion in 1975/6, resulting in an escalation of the proportion of net national savings to GNP from 23 per cent to over 61 per cent. Apart from their impact on the structure of the economy, these last developments are of considerable importance in themselves. Their effects on the future prospects of the economy have already been emphasised and their implications for Kuwait's role in international finance will be examined in greater detail in Chapter 11.

However, it should be emphasised at this juncture that the presence of such sizable current account surpluses and net savings clearly indicates a level of oil production and exports far in excess of that required merely to meet Kuwait's current and development expenditure on local and imported requirements. This has in part prompted a reduction in the rate of oil extraction in recent years and the adoption of a conservation policy to which reference has already been made. However, reduction in oil output by Kuwait and other exporting countries to levels where these surpluses were minimised would obviously have severe worldwide implications. It is evident that Kuwait's attitude to conservation is tempered by its recognition of its responsibilities in spite of the fact that the current levels of production may not best serve its own interests. This consideration is one of the constraints on Kuwait's choices of allocation of its total assets under the conceptual model which pervades the present work.

A MACRO-ECONOMIC MODEL OF KUWAIT

As pointed out earlier, an income determination model has been formulated to describe the Kuwait economy, to analyse its principal characteristics and to explain the effects of recent phenomena on its development. This model has been estimated using data for the fiscal years 1961/2-1975/6 and consists of four definitional equations and six behavioural equations as well as ten endogenous and ten predetermined variables. The structure of the model and the estimation resuts are discussed below.

The Model

1. $Y_t = Cp_t + Cg_t + Ip_t + Ig_t - M_t + (X-NP)_t$

2. $Yd_t = Y_t - Gr_t - Td_t + Gs_t$

3. $G_t = Cg_t + Ig_t + Gs_t - Td_t$

4. $Gf_t = Gr_t - G_t$

5. $Cp_t = a_1 + b_1 Yd_t + c_1 \Delta P_t$

6. $Ip_t = a_2 + b_2(MO/YD)_t + c_2(Ip + Ig)_{t-1} + d_2 D_t$

7. $M_t = a_3 + b_3 Y_t + c_3 \Delta P_t + d_3(MO/YD)_{t-1}$

8. $Cg_t = a_4 + b_4\,Y_t + c_4\,Gr_{t-1} + d_4\,D_t$

9. $\Delta Mo_t = a_5 + b_5\,G_t + c_5\,R_t$

10. $Td_t = a_6 + b_6\,Y_t$

The endogenous variables are:

Y = gross national product
Cp = private consumption expenditure
Cg = general government expenditure
Ip = gross private investment expenditure
G = net government domestic outlay
Yd = disposable income before deducting depreciation[2]
Td = government domestic revenues
Gf = net increase in government foreign assets
M = total expenditure on imported goods and services
ΔMo = change in the total money supply including quasi-money, i.e. saving plus time deposits

The predetermined variables include seven exogenous variables:

(X − NP) = total exports and re-exports of goods and services minus (plus) net factor payments (receipts) (NP)
Gs = net government subsidies
Ig = gross government investment expenditure
Gr = government oil revenues and income from foreign investment
ΔP = change in the GNP deflator
R = the short-term Euro-dollar interest rate
D = structural shift dummy variable

D = 0 in years 1962/3–1969/70
D = 1 in years 1970/1–1975/6

and the following three lagged variables:

$(I_p + I_g)_{t-1}$ = total gross investment expenditure lagged one year
Gr_{t-1} = government oil revenues and income from foreign investment lagged one year
$(MO/Yd)_{t-1}$ = the lagged ratio of money supply to disposable income

The rationale behind our choice of the exogenous variables lies in the fact that the economy is influenced to a large degree by the inflow of foreign exchange earnings expressed in terms of (X—NP). The justification for considering (X—NP) an exogenous variable is that

Kuwait's oil exports are determined by oil production and the export price of oil. The latter was until 1973 set either by the oil companies alone or through negotiations between them and the government. Since that date, however, they have been decided by OPEC. Factor income transfers by the oil companies are also exogenous because, until 1975, they were based largely on agreements signed with the Kuwait Government as well as on the volume of production and the level of oil prices. As for factor income receipts from foreign assets held by the government and the private sector, it is apparent that they are dependent on the size of Kuwaiti investments abroad and the average yield earned on them. The size and distribution of the former depends on government policies that do not necessarily relate to endogenous considerations, whereas the latter is normally determined by exogenous factors. The rationale for our selection of the other variables is that they are related to government fiscal policies which determine net government subsidies (Gs) and gross government investment expenditure (Ig). The exogenous nature of government oil revenues and income from foreign investments (Gr) was referred to above. In addition, the change in prices, i.e. GNP deflator (ΔP), is considered an exogenous variable because it is partly determined by import prices and partly by local institutional factors and relative liquidity. Attempts to explain domestic price changes in terms of changes in import prices, relative liquidity (Mo/Yd) or changes in the money supply did not prove successful. This was mainly due to the fact that changes in import prices were most prominent and accounted for the major part of the change in the domestic price level. In view of this it was decided to treat the change in the price level as an exogenous variable. The sixth exogenous variable is the short term Euro-dollar interest rate which influences the flow of funds to the rest of the world and is thus designed to explain the change in the money supply. Finally, in view of the apparent structural change that has occurred since the first major increase in oil prices in 1971, a structural shift dummy variable (D) is introduced into the private investment and the general government expenditure equations.

With the inclusion of the three lagged variables the total number of predetermined variables becomes 10, meaning that all the structural equations are overidentified. This aspect has known implications regarding the method to be applied in estimating the model.

The Data

The model has been estimated using data expressed in current prices for the period from 1961/2 to 1975/6 (see Annex I to this chapter regarding data problems). Our decision to use current prices rather than constant prices was based on the following considerations:

1. The lack of adequate price indices that could be used in deflating the appropriate vaviables. Apart from the export price of oil, the only other price index available for the full period under consideration was the GNP deflator.[3]

2. It was considered inappropriate to use a common deflator to deflate all variables, particularly as this would introduce the problem of heteroscedasticity where the variances are proportional to the common deflator. This problem results in inefficient parameter estimates and biased estimates of the standard errors and the t-statistics.

3. The use of constant prices is necessary in cases where there are strong *a priori* reasons to assume that money illusion influences the behaviour of various elements of the economy. Since there is no good *a priori* basis for making this assumption, it was considered justifiable to use current prices.

However it should be noted that the use of current prices encounters two major econometric problems which are mentioned below.

1. Current prices might introduce spurious correlation resulting from common price trends in the variables of the model. This generally leads to spuriously high R^2 values and spuriously low standard errors of the estimates.

2. The presence of the common price trends referred to above also introduces multicollinearity which usually results in imprecise parameter estimates and low t-statistics. In addition this problem makes it difficult to determine the separate effects of the explanatory variables.

Nonetheless, apart from the occasional problem of spurious correlation, the estimates obtained using current prices were generally satisfactory. This was also confirmed by the results obtained through the use of constant prices (see Annex II to this chapter). The two sets of results indicate that economic units in Kuwait generally react to real variables and that the problem of money illusion is minimal. In view of this it was decided to base the analysis and description of Kuwait's economic system on the results obtained with current values of the data.

The Definitional Equations

The gross national product equation indicates that the flow of net foreign exchange earnings into the system equals $(X - NP)$, the difference between export earnings and net factor payments to the rest of the world.

Correspondingly, expenditure on imported goods and services constitutes a major foreign exchange leakage. However, as evidenced from the decrease in the ratio of imports to GNP, the relative importance of this leakage has gradually declined because of the rapid growth of the economy that has been associated with the extraordinary rise in export earnings. Other foreign exchange leakages from the system include:

1. the net increase in government foreign assets which, according to equation (4), is equal to the difference between government foreign exchange income, Gr, and net government domestic outlay G, and

2. the difference between private savings and private investment expenditure.[4]

Both leakages have substantially increased in recent years, but the part attributed to the government has become far greater than its private sector counterpart. However it should be noted that the first item, and to a lesser extent the second, constitute an addition to the country's foreign exchange assets and will in future years increase its income from investments abroad.

The utilisation of foreign exchange earnings can be summarised algebraically by substituting for Y in equation (1) the expression given in equation (2).

$$Yd + Gr + Td - Gs = Cp + Cg + Ip + Ig - M + (X-NP)$$

$$\text{or } (Yd - Cp - Ip) + (Gr + Td - Gs - Cg - Ig) = (X-NP) - M$$

By substituting $-G$ for $(Td-Gs-Cg-Ig)$ as in equation (3), we obtain:

$$(Yd - Cp - Ip) + (Gr - G) = (X - NP) - M$$

Then by noting that private savings $Sp = Yd - Cp$, and government savings $Sg = Gr - G$, we obtain:

$$(Sp - Ip) + Sg + M = (X - NP)$$

and by equation (4) which implies that government savings are invested abroad, we obtain:

$$(Sp - Ip) + Gf + M = (X - NP)$$

This means that export foreign exchange earnings are utilised to finance expenditure on imported goods and services and to acquire foreign assets by the government (Gf) and the private sector (Sp — Ip). This equation conforms essentially to the overall balance of payments condition.

The total leakage from the system includes the full extent of net national savings and imports. These two items combined account for the bulk of GNP with the former representing in 1975/6 approximately 61 per cent of GNP. It should be noted in this respect that the large proportion of total savings represented by government savings is a clear indication not only of the prominence of the public sector but also of the immense resources controlled by the government, the bulk of which is yet to find its way into the domestic economy. This aspect has far-reaching consequences on government policies and the future prospects of the economy.

The Behavioural Equations

The parameters of the six behavioural equations were estimated using two econometric methods:

1. Ordinary Least Squares (OLS): according to this method the structural parameters are estimated by applying the least-squares procedure to the individual behavioural equations.

2. Two-Stage Least-Squares (2SLS): this method involves applying the least-squares procedure to the reduced-form equations and then using the estimates to calculate the values of the endogenous variables. Afterwards, the structural parameters are are estimated by the least-squares method using the observed values of the exogenous variables and the calculated values of all the endogenous variables except the one designated as the dependent variable in this estimation.[5]

The 2SLS method, unlike the OLS method, yields consistent estimates and is particularly useful for estimating the structural parameters in overidentified equations. This makes it possible to assess the appropriateness of the OLS estimates.[6] The estimation results of both methods are as follows (the t-statistics are given in parentheses below the parameter estimates):

(5) Private consumption expenditure:[7]

OLS $Cp_t = 66 \cdot 351 + 0 \cdot 424\ Yd_t - 2 \cdot 856\ \Delta P_t$ $\bar{R}^2 = 0 \cdot 925$
            $(3 \cdot 368)\quad (12 \cdot 283)\qquad (-3 \cdot 143)$ $DW = 1 \cdot 920$

2SLS $Cp_t = 65 \cdot 728 + 0 \cdot 425\ Yd_t - 2 \cdot 875\ \Delta P_t$ $R^2 = 0 \cdot 935$
            $(3 \cdot 327)\quad (12 \cdot 274)\qquad (-3 \cdot 160)$ $DW = 1 \cdot 927$

(6) Private investment expenditure:

$$\text{OLS} \quad Ip_t = -50 \cdot 316 + 116 \cdot 96 \left(\frac{Mo}{Yd}\right)_t + 0 \cdot 482 \, (I_p + I_g)_{t-1} - 33 \cdot 177 \, D_t$$
$$\quad\quad (-1 \cdot 468) \quad (1 \cdot 729) \quad\quad\quad (3 \cdot 797) \quad\quad\quad (-3 \cdot 661)$$
$$\bar{R}^2 = 0 \cdot 709$$
$$DW = 1 \cdot 633$$

$$\text{2SLS} \quad Ip_t = -46 \cdot 733 + 109 \cdot 13 \left(\frac{Mo}{Yd}\right)_t + 0 \cdot 494 \, (Ip + Ig)_{t-1} - 33 \cdot 296 \, D_t$$
$$\quad\quad (1 \cdot 281) \quad (1 \cdot 496) \quad\quad\quad (3 \cdot 101) \quad\quad\quad (-3 \cdot 668)$$
$$R^2 = 0 \cdot 771$$
$$DW = 1 \cdot 597$$

(7) Total imports:

$$\text{OLS} \quad M_t = -101 \cdot 81 + 0 \cdot 172 \, Y_t - 1 \cdot 836 \, \Delta P_t + 303 \cdot 41 \, (Mo/Yd)_{t-1}$$
$$\quad\quad (-1 \cdot 769) \quad (18 \cdot 374) \quad (2 \cdot 366) \quad\quad (3 \cdot 229)$$
$$\bar{R}^2 = 0 \cdot 969$$
$$DW = 1 \cdot 531$$

$$\text{2SLS} \quad M_t = -101 \cdot 65 + 0 \cdot 173 \, Y_t - 1 \cdot 844 \, \Delta Pt + 302 \cdot 80 \, (Mo/Yd)_{t-1}$$
$$\quad\quad (-1 \cdot 766) \quad (18 \cdot 396) \quad (-2 \cdot 376) \quad (3 \cdot 223)$$
$$R^2 = 0 \cdot 975$$
$$DW = 1 \cdot 526$$

(8) General government expenditure:

$$\text{OLS} \quad Cg_t = 41 \cdot 775 + 0 \cdot 095 \, Y_t + 0 \cdot 046 \, Gr_{t-1} + 46 \cdot 567 D_t$$
$$\quad\quad (5 \cdot 865) \quad (8 \cdot 536) \quad (2 \cdot 689) \quad\quad (3 \cdot 600)$$
$$\bar{R}^2 = 0 \cdot 983$$
$$DW = 1 \cdot 999$$

$$\text{2SLS} \quad Cg_t = 41 \cdot 878 + 0 \cdot 095 \, Y_t + 0 \cdot 046 \, Gr_{t-1} + 46 \cdot 780 \, Dt$$
$$\quad\quad (5 \cdot 878) \quad (8 \cdot 501) \quad (2 \cdot 710) \quad\quad (3 \cdot 615)$$
$$R^2 = 0 \cdot 987$$
$$DW = 1 \cdot 995$$

(9) Total money supply:

$$\text{OLS} \quad \Delta Mo_t = -2 \cdot 438 + 0 \cdot 351 \, G_t - 7 \cdot 015 \, R_t \quad\quad \bar{R}^2 = 0 \cdot 789$$
$$\quad\quad (0 \cdot 119) \quad (7 \cdot 028) \quad (-1 \cdot 975) \quad\quad DW = 2 \cdot 826$$

$$\text{2SLS} \quad \Delta MO_t = -2 \cdot 241 + 0 \cdot 351 \, G_t - 6 \cdot 780 \, R_t \quad\quad R^2 = 0 \cdot 819$$
$$\quad\quad (-0 \cdot 109) \quad (6 \cdot 884) \quad (-1 \cdot 906) \quad\quad DW = 2 \cdot 827$$

(10) Government domestic revenues:

OLS $Td_t = 12.550 + 0.018\ Y_t$ $\bar{R}^2 = 0.773$
            (3.20)   (6.982)   DW = 2.327

2SLS $Td_t = 12.459 + 0.018\ Y_t$ $R^2 = 0.789$
            (3.187) (7.011)   DW = 2.328

The results given above clearly indicate that the estimates obtained with the two methods are very similar and that all the regressions are statistically significant with no major problems of serial correlation. The regression coefficients are in most cases also significant and they all have the expected signs. A detailed discussion of the individual behavioural equations is given below.

Private Consumption
The estimated consumption function indicates a relatively low marginal propensity to consume (0.42), which is due in large part to the already high levels of per capita income and private consumption enjoyed by people in Kuwait. The latter is estimated for the year 1975/6 at a per capita rate of KD550 (approximately $1925). The low marginal propensity to consume is also partly due to the existence of a welfare system which enables a large percentage of the population to enjoy, at government cost, many essential goods and services that normally represent major items in family budgets, e.g. health, education and subsidised housing.

There is also a fairly significant negative response to increases in the price level. The relatively low statistical significance of the price effect is due in part to the government price subsidies aimed at softening the effects of inflation in recent years. It is also probably due to the inappropriateness of the GNP deflator in reflecting changes in the prices of consumption goods; hence the difficulty of adequately detecting the effect of price changes on private consumption.

In addition, it should be noted that the structural shift dummy did not prove to be significant. This implies that the extraordinary increase in national income did not result in a significant structural change, either upward or downward, in private consumption.[8] Alternative consumption specifications, including in particular the relative income hypothesis, were tested and found to be statistically non-significant.

Private Investment
Several hypotheses were tested in connection with this function. However only the absorptive capacity hypothesis, and to a lesser extent

that of liquidity, were statistically significant. Lagged gross investment was used as a proxy variable for changes in absorptive capacity and it was found to have a statistically significant positive effect on private investment. This variable not only measures the extent of new investment opportunities created by previous private and public investment expenditure, but also reflects the dynamic features of the absorptive capacity concept.[9] In addition, the magnitude of the regression coefficient (0·48) clearly indicates that private investment has been very responsive to changes in the absorptive capacity constraint. Although this emphasises the importance of this constraint for a small country with abundant capital, it also confirms the widely held views that absorptive capacity can be expanded through increased investment in such fields as infrastructure, housing, manufacturing and manpower which have been prominent throughout most of Kuwait's development.

In order to estimate the effect of liquidity on private investment, the ratio of the expanded money supply, i.e. money plus quasi money, to disposable income was considered the most suitable variable. This is particularly so in view of the absence of such other monetary variables as a freely determined interest rate that would reflect the real scarcity of loanable funds or the actual yield on alternative forms of investment. However, as the results indicate, the response to this variable is of relatively low statistical significance ($t = 1·729$), but it was considered necessary to retain this variable because of the increased role of credit institutions in financing private investment and in order to maintain an effective link between the money and real sectors.

As well as the effects of absorptive capacity and liquidity, the results indicate a strong negative response to the structural shift dummy. The structural change that has taken place since 1971 has shifted the private investment function downwards to the extent of approximately KD33 million. A possible explanation of this is the increased role of government investment associated with the remarkable rise in oil revenues since 1971. Given the absolute absorptive capacity constraint, the amount of private investment that can take place is correspondingly depressed by the amount of the shift. This implies that the dummy variable is a good indication of the absorptive capacity constraint at the date the structural change occurred. The lagged investment variable, referred to above, would account for the effects of changes in the country's absorptive capacity from one year to another.

Finally, it should be indicated that the conventional multiplier or accelerator formulations of the investment function did not give statistically significant results. This finding possibly implies that, given Kuwait's high income level and abundance of capital, the absorptive capacity constraint and changes in relative liquidity are more relevant in determining investment decisions than the level of income or changes in the productive capacity.

Total Imports

In view of the difficulty of separating private from government expenditure on imported goods and services, a total import function was estimated with the gross national product as the main explanatory variable. The response was found to be statistically significant with a relatively low marginal propensity to import of 0·17. This clearly conforms with the low marginal propensity to consume referred to earlier. While the marginal propensity to consume relates to disposable income, the import coefficient relates to GNP. Had the marginal propensity to consume been related to GNP also, it is calculated that the ratio of the import coefficient to this adjusted marginal propensity to consume would have been in the order of 60 per cent, a clear indication of the country's dependence on imports.

The other variable that has a statistically significant effect on imports is monetary liquidity. In view of the important role of the banking system in financing imports, this variable was considered a possible explanatory variable. However, the results showed that imports were influenced significantly more by the lagged liquidity variable than by current liquidity. This seems to conform to a large extent with the procedure applied in financing imports and effecting payment, as in the vast majority of cases the procedure involves opening letters of credit six to twelve months in advance of final delivery of the imported goods and services, i.e. when such imports are actually recorded.

Finally, the results indicate that the change in the price level has, as expected, a negative but less significant effect on imports than is normally the case. This is possibly due to the use of the GNP deflator, instead of an import price index.

General Government Expenditure

Three variables explain over 90 per cent of the variations in general government expenditure; namely GNP, the structural shift dummy and lagged 'government revenues from oil and investments abroad'. The statistically significant response to GNP is mainly due to the fact that the level of government spending on public services is determined by the level of economic activity expressed in terms of GNP. However the magnitude of the coefficient seems relatively small at less than 0·10, possibly because a large proportion of GNP does not relate to the local economy. On the other hand, 'government revenues from oil and overseas investments' was only statistically significant when lagged one period. This is attributable to the lag in the receipt of these revenues. However the small size of the regression coefficient of this variable, along with its relatively low statistical significance are primarily due to the absence of a revenue constraint as far as government current expenditure is concerned. The structural shift dummy, however, has a statistically significant positive effect estimated at approximately KD47 million. This finding confirms a point made earlier regarding the expanded role assumed by the government since 1971 when GNP and the government's share thereof began to increase markedly. Thus, the rise in oil revenues has been clearly associated with increased government participation in the economy and a relative diminution of that of the private sector, particularly as regards investment expenditure.

It should also be indicated that the results clearly show that, apart from these three variables, there is a statistically significant autonomous component of government current expenditure. This component is estimated at approximately KD42 million for the period prior to 1971 and almost KD90 million thereafter. This is in line with the general case where a certain level of government expenditure is regarded as a fixed component that has to be provided, irrespective of the level of economic activity, to cover welfare expenditure and similar items.

Changes in the Money Supply

Monetary authorities in Kuwait have had little influence on changes in the money supply. With the absence of effective monetary instruments such as minimum reserve requirements,[10] 'open market operations' in government securities or periodic changes in the discount rate, the Central Bank has not been able to regulate the size of the money supply. Therefore, the main factors influencing the money supply have been to a large degree independent of monetary policy, namely net government domestic expenditure and the level of short-term interest in major financial centres, i.e. the Euro-dollar lending rate. Regarding the first variable, it may be noted that the Central Bank normally converts to Kuwaiti dinars all government foreign exchange revenues required to pay for net government local outlays. These outlays are approximately equivalent to the difference between net government domestic revenues and government expenditure on directly imported goods and services. However, as it is not possible to make reliable estimates of government imports it was considered preferable not to deduct this component, and

to maintain net government domestic outlays as the main variable determining the change in the money supply.

In addition, no allowance has been made for the effects of hoarding
and the changes in foreign claims in KD due to difficulties of estimation
and the lack of data. Furthermore, the short-term Euro-dollar lending
rate was used as a proxy variable for the outflow of remittances and
private capital transfers, i.e. the magnitude of private funds that form a
leakage from the system. This factor, therefore, is important in determining the effect of the leakage attributable to the private sector on the
initial change in the money supply that would result from an increase in
net government domestic outlays. The two factors are expected *a priori*
to operate in opposite directions.

The estimation results were statistically significant and support the
analysis described above. The response to net government domestic
revenues is positive whereas the effect of the short-term interest rate is
negative. The coefficient of the former, however, is statistically more
significant. Moreover, the results indicate that the autonomous
component of the change in the money supply is not statistically significant. This implies that there is no autonomous or discretionary basis
for the size of the money supply which seems to conform with our
earlier assessment of the role of the Central Bank.

Government Domestic Revenues
These revenues include customs duties, net operating revenues of public
utilities such as electricity, water and ports and profits from government enterprises. The first component is determined by imports
through an institutional relationship whereas the other two are more
related to the general level of economic activity. However, due to the
difficulty of separating the institutional component of government
domestic revenues because of frequent changes in the regulations, it was
decided to keep all revenues aggregated and explain this single variable
in terms of GNP. The results indicate that about 78 per cent of the
variations in government domestic revenues can be explained this way
and the parameter estimates were found statistically significant.
However the small magnitude of the GNP coefficient estimated at less
than 0·02 is a clear indication that this form of leakage from the system
is minimal. This confirms earlier reference to the community's limited
participation in covering the cost of government administration and
social services. The extent of this participation has seldom exceeded 20
per cent; in fact the average for the fiscal years 1970/1–1975/6 was 15
per cent with the remainder financed exclusively from oil revenues and
income from overseas investments.

The Reduced-form System

The impact multiplier coefficients were obtained by applying ordinary least-squares to estimate the reduced-form equations.[11] This method suffers from severe limitations, especially when the number of observations is small compared to that of the predetermined variables. However, as indicated in Table 7.3 below, the estimation results are statistically significant for the overall regressions, although the statistical significance of the individual predetermined variables varies considerably between the different equations.

In the case of the GNP reduced-form, export earnings minus net factor payments abroad (X-NP) was highly significant. However the impact multiplier estimate was rather low at approximately 1·15.[12] This implies that while oil exports and income on assets abroad are of paramount importance as a source of foreign income and government revenues, their income generating effect, measured in terms of the GNP multiplier, is minimal. The same applies to lagged gross investment which reflects changes in the country's relative absorptive capacity. On the other hand, government investment expenditure has a coefficient of 3·89, indicating a strong impact multiplier effect on GNP.

The small multiplier effect of net foreign exchange earnings (X-NP) on GNP is clearly due to its limited effects on the endogenous components of GNP, namely private consumption expenditure Cp, private investment expenditure Ip, total imports M and to a lesser extent general government expenditure Cg. In the same token the relatively more important effects of government investment and relative absorptive capacity can be traced to their significant impact multiplier effects on the same GNP components. This analysis supports certain assertions about the limited role to date of the oil sector in promoting activity in other sectors of the economy. As will be shown later, this is largely attributable to the 'cleavage' nature of the oil sector and the fact that its main role has been confined to a source of foreign income. In this connection it is important to note that government revenues from oil and foreign assets also have weak impact multiplier effects on GNP together with its endogenous components except in the cases of general government expenditure and to a lesser extent, imports.

Regarding the other endogenous variables, the results indicate that the change in the money supply is particularly affected by government foreign income and the short-term Euro-dollar interest rate, whereas government domestic revenues are determined by the relative absorptive capacity and the lagged liquidity variable. However the generally small reduced-form coefficients seem to indicate that there is

TABLE 7.3   Major reduced-form coefficients

Endogenous Variable	Ig	Gs	$(Ip + Ig)_{t-1}$	R	X − NP
GNP	3·893 (4·240)	−0·235 (−0·496)	0·686 (0·944)	*	1·155 (4·058)
Y_D	3·718 (3·244)	0·658 (1·111)	0·219 (0·241)	*	1·072 (3·018)
C_p	1·651 (3·695)	−0·174 (−0·753)	0·676 (1·912)	5·184 (1·071)	−0·080 (−0·573)
I_p	0·671 (2·352)	0·337 (2·286)	0·768 (3·402)	*	−0·031 (−3·49)
M	0·826 (0·968)	0·234 (0·532)	0·727 (1·077)	7·129 (0·771)	−0·135 (−0·510)
C_g	1·360 (4·785)	−0·189 (−1·288)	*	1·371 (0·446)	0·123 (1·396)
Mo	*	0·261 (0·569)	0·269 (0·382)	−0·136 (−1·416)	*
T_D	0·174 (0·744)	0·107 (0·881)	0·467 (2·516)	−1·130 (−0·443)	0·082 (1·135)

( ) Figures in parenthesis are t-statistics   * Negligible coefficients.

a limited degree of interdependence within the economy and that interaction with the exogenous variables is largely confined to the government sector on the one hand and the GNP components on the other.

SUMMARY OF MAIN CHARACTERISTICS

It should be emphasised that the preceding analysis must be regarded as very tentative, particularly in view of the numerous problems and reservations to which attention has been drawn. The main problems relate to the limited availability of reliable data which preclude a more rigorous specification of the model and the difficulties inherent in the method of estimating the reduced-form coefficients. However, it should be reiterated that what has been sought is not an estimated model designed to serve as a basis for projection or prediction, especially in the field of policy, but rather a means of describing and analysing in an orderly manner some of the main features of the Kuwait economy

Dummy	G_R	P	Gr_{t-1}	$(Mo/YD)_{t-1}$	R^{-2}	$D-W$
−30·297 (−0·816)	−0·283 (−0·874)	1·922 (0·804)	0·116 (1·645)	−346·5 (−0·852)	0·999	2·453
−40·737 (−0·878)	−1·188 (−2·937)	2·623 (0·878)	0·112 (1·268)	*	0·983	2·471
36·092 (1·997)	0·050 (0·319)	1·382 (1·188)	0·1226 (3·575)	−88·599 (−0·448)	0·983	2·551
−66·47 (−5·760)	*	1·016 (1·368)	0·034 (1·561)	−100·36 (−0·794)	0·891	2·344
*	0·246 (0·819)	1·537 (0·691)	0·115 (1·754)	120·26 (0·318)	0·971	2·487
*	−0·079 (−0·791)	1·205 (1·628)	0·077 (3·550)	−44·98 (−0·357)	0·995	2·544
−18·770 (−0·522)	0·119 (0·378)	3·117 (1·345)	0·022 (0·325)	*	0·680	2·614
10·440 (1·100)	−0·096 (−1·155)	−70·076 (−1·147)	*	−195·95 (−1·886)	0·842	2·551

according to accepted precepts of economic theory. Therefore, the model has provided us with a far greater insight into the workings of the economy on which much stronger assertions can now be based. Of equal importance, it may be useful for other purposes provided appropriate refinements are made.

The following is a summary of the main characteristics of the Kuwait economy that have been identified:

1. A high national saving ratio: With the national saving ratio to GNP estimated at approximately 50 per cent in 1965 and 67 per cent in 1973, this ratio is considered to be one of the highest in the world.[13] As indicated earlier, this is due in large measure to the high per capita income. This, together with the presence of an absorptive capacity constraint on the utilisation of oil revenues in the domestic economy, also explains the low proportion of savings used to finance domestic investment. With the combined marginal propensity to save of the government and the private sector well above the average, other things being equal, the national saving ratio is expected to rise more with

further increases in the country's foreign income and GNP. However government savings, which constitute the largest portion of national savings (almost 75 per cent in 1975/6), will be increasingly absorbed in financing the expanding social and development programmes and the rising defence expenditure. These developments are likely to check the increase in government surplus funds which have so far been mainly utilised in acquiring assets abroad. Private savings, on the other hand, have become far less important relative to government savings, but, unless appropriate measures are taken to promote domestic investment opportunities, these funds will continue to be used in speculative activities and ultimately find their way abroad through the banking system. In fact, the downward structural shift in the investment function, referred to earlier, may partly explain the speculative tendencies that have developed since 1972.

2. Dependence on the foreign trade sector: Kuwait's dependence on the foreign trade sector is manifested in the high ratio of exports to GDP and the high import component in incremental consumption and investment expenditure. The former, which averaged approximately 75 per cent during the years 1974/6, is considered among the world's highest ratios.[14] Dependence on the foreign sector becomes more intense if net factor income receipts from abroad are taken into account.

On the other hand, although the ratio of imports to GNP is relatively low, averaging less than 25 per cent during the years 1965–73,[15] the country is obviously greatly dependent on imports to satisfy its consumption and investment requirements. This is evident from the ratio of imports to total domestic expenditure on consumption and investment which averaged approximately 45 per cent during the years 1972–6. More important in this respect is the ratio of incremental imports to incremental domestic expenditure. Deduced from the structural coefficients of the model, this ratio, as indicated earlier, is estimated to be in the order of 60 per cent, meaning that the ratio of imports to domestic expenditure will escalate as the latter continues to increase. Therefore, the economy's dependence on the foreign trade sector, in respect of exports and imports, is well established. Its vulnerability to international economic fluctuations has obviously been a source of increasing concern to the Kuwaiti authorities. Consequently, efforts to augment the country's productive capacity, broaden its base, expand the range of products produced domestically and develop other sources of foreign income are being given high priority. Assessment of these efforts and the future prospects of diversification will later be made.

3. Increased government role: In view of the welfare orientation of the economy and the fact that the oil industry now belongs exclusively to the government, it is inevitable that the government has assumed a dominant role in the economy and, as indicated by the structural estimates, it has become more prominent both in terms of general expenditure and investment. This is obviously due to the government's control of the country's major source of income. It is however feared that, in view of the relatively lower degree of efficiency of government agencies and enterprises, a continuation of this trend might circumvent development efforts and restrain the country's growth.

4. Limited role of the oil sector: A great proportion of the value added derived from oil is via its export. Therefore, the oil sector can be regarded to a large degree merely as an income component of GNP and a source of foreign exchange earnings. This view is supported by the small magnitude of the reduced-form coefficients of the GNP components in relation to net foreign exchange earnings. Consequently, the gradual substitution of oil export earnings by income from foreign investments may take place without impairing the growth of the economy or causing major structural problems. However, the infrastructural role played by oil and gas in the provision of electricity and water is obviously crucial.

Annex I to Chapter 7. Data Used in Estimating the Model

Due to limited data availability, the model was estimated for the years 1961/2—1975/6 only. It should also be indicated that, while the data's quality and degree of reliability were generally satisfactory, there were particular problems with regard to the consistency of the time series obtained from different sources regarding private consumption expenditure for years after 1969/70, government oil revenues and income on foreign assets for the years 1966/7–1973/4 and the national account estimates of 1973/4. Attempting to reconcile the time series obtained from different sources was a major problem and in certain cases it proved impossible. Therefore, it was decided to rely as much as possible on one source for each series.

TABLE 7.4   Data used in estimating the model
(Million KD)

	60/1	61/2	62/3	63/4	64/5	65/6	66/7	67/8
GDP(MP)[1]	–	613	653	679	740	749	854	872
NP	–	−199	−193	−179	−198	−158	−172	−138
GNP	–	414	460	500	542	591	682	734
CP	–	183	188	192	200	198	232	280
Cg	–	78	80	89	102	99	118	135
Ip	48	50	52	50	52	70	101	118
Ig	27	30	33	45	47	43	50	68
M	–	107	122	141	141	173	208	248
X	–	379	422	444	480	507	561	519
Gr	172	180	189	215	226	247	259	291
Td	–	14	17	17	16	20	20	50
Gs	–	65	52	39	43	90	108	48
Mo[2]	117	146	176	178	205	258	305	322
R(%)	–	5·13	4·18	3·95	4·32	4·81	6·12	5·46
P (index)	101.4	106·9	102·1	100·7	100·0	99·3	107·7	109·1

[1] In market prices
[2] End of calendar year, e.g. 1961 for 1961/2

The following are the major sources of the data reproduced in this annex.

National Accounts:	World Bank, *World Tables*, 1976. The Johns Hopkins University Press, 1976, for the years 1961/2–1972/3.
	Ministry of Planning, for the years 1973/4–1975/6.
Government Finance:	*Kuwait Annual Statistical Abstract*, 1975 and 1976.
Money Supply:	*International Financial Statistics* (various issues) for the years 1960–70.
	The Central Bank Economic Reports (various issues) for the years 1971–5.

68/9	*69/70*	*70/1*	*71/2*	*72/3*	*73/4*	*74/5*	*75/6*
951	989	1084	1417	1581	2112	3450	3279
−158	−149	−175	−266	−307	−342	−281	224
793	840	909	1151	1274	1770	3169	3503
297	306	325	340	379	396	423	592
144	152	160	224	239	308	405	519
117	108	47	49	52	53	70	116
54	62	63	72	102	93	113	140
248	286	273	278	271	326	553	737
587	643	762	1010	1080	1588	2992	2650
366	321	337	396	588	673	2208	2319
25	26	46	29	41	42	63	82
35	28	50	54	57	36	143	104
386	379	362	456	524	572	720	891
	6·36	9·76	8·52	6·58	5·46	9·24	4·01	6·99
112·3	110·2	115·4	143·3	151·5	176·8	204·5	201·6

Annex II to Chapter 7. Model Estimation Results with Constant Prices

The following are the results obtained by estimating the model using real values. It should be noted that while the coefficients of determination in this case are lower than their counterparts in the case of the current values, the regression coefficients are generally consistent in respect of their signs and orders of magnitude.

(5) Private consumption expenditure:

$$\text{(OLS)} \quad Cp_t = 83 \cdot 436 + 0 \cdot 360 \, Yd_t - 1 \cdot 993 \, \Delta P_t$$
$$\phantom{\text{(OLS)} \quad Cp_t = } (2 \cdot 957) \quad (5 \cdot 422) \quad (-3 \cdot 189)$$

$\bar{R}^2 = 0 \cdot 644$
$DW = 1 \cdot 395$

$$\text{(2SLS)} \quad Cp_t = 82 \cdot 377 + 0 \cdot 363 \, Yd_t - 2 \cdot 050 \, \Delta P_t$$
$$\phantom{\text{(2SLS)} \quad Cp_t = } (2 \cdot 886) \quad (5 \cdot 394) \quad (-3 \cdot 198)$$

$R^2 = 0 \cdot 712$
$DW = 1 \cdot 410$

(6) Private investment expenditure:

$$\text{(OLS)} \quad Ip_t = -39 \cdot 582 + 116 \cdot 77 \left(\frac{Mo}{Yd}\right)_t + 0 \cdot 368(Ip + Ig)_{t-1} - 36 \cdot 057 \, D_t$$
$$\phantom{\text{(OLS)} \quad Ip_t = } (-1 \cdot 639) \quad (2 \cdot 763) \quad\quad (3 \cdot 351) \quad\quad\quad (-5 \cdot 658)$$

$\bar{R}^2 = 0 \cdot 826$
$DW = 1 \cdot 702$

$$\text{(2SLS)} \quad Ip_t = -37 \cdot 603 + 112 \cdot 82 \left(\frac{Mo}{Yd}\right)_t + 0 \cdot 373(Ip + Ig)_{t-1} - 35 \cdot 897 \, D_t$$
$$\phantom{\text{(2SLS)} \quad Ip_t = } (-1 \cdot 471) \quad (2 \cdot 482) \quad\quad (3 \cdot 340) \quad\quad\quad (-5 \cdot 599)$$

$R^2 = 0 \cdot 864$
$DW = 1 \cdot 658$

(7) Total imports:

(OLS) $M_t = -58 \cdot 263 + 0 \cdot 146\, Y_t - 1 \cdot 442\, P_t + 243 \cdot 00 \left(\dfrac{Mo}{Yd}\right)_{t-1}$
          $(-1 \cdot 129)$ $(6 \cdot 751)$ $(2 \cdot 089)$ $(2 \cdot 770)$

$$\bar{R}^2 = 0 \cdot 842$$
$$DW = 1 \cdot 482$$

(2SLS) $M_t = -58 \cdot 181 + 0 \cdot 147\, Y_t - 1 \cdot 447\, P_t + 242 \cdot 40 \left(\dfrac{Mo}{Yd}\right)_{t-1}$
          $(-1 \cdot 127)$ $(6 \cdot 765)$ $(-2 \cdot 096)$ $(2 \cdot 763)$

$$R^2 = 0 \cdot 876$$
$$DW = 1 \cdot 476$$

(8) General government expenditure:

(OLS) $Cg_t = 47 \cdot 504 + 0 \cdot 080\, Yt + 0 \cdot 048\, Gr_{t-1} + 21 \cdot 677 D_t$
          $(5 \cdot 753)$ $(4 \cdot 284)$ $(1 \cdot 816)$ $(2 \cdot 447)$

$$\bar{R}^2 = 0 \cdot 945$$
$$DW = 1 \cdot 227$$

(2SLS) $Cg_t = 47 \cdot 877 + 0 \cdot 079\, Yt + 0 \cdot 049\, Gr_{t-1} + 21 \cdot 980\, D_t$
          $(5 \cdot 788)$ $(4 \cdot 214)$ $(1 \cdot 858)$ $(2 \cdot 478)$

$$R^2 = 0 \cdot 957$$
$$DW = 1 \cdot 216$$

(9) Total money supply:

(OLS) $\Delta Mo_t = -10 \cdot 726 + 0 \cdot 447\, G_t - 9 \cdot 293\, R_t$ $\bar{R}^2 = 0 \cdot 458$
              $(-0 \cdot 412)$ $(3 \cdot 348)$ $(-3 \cdot 018)$

(2SLS) $\Delta Mo_t = -10 \cdot 419 + 0 \cdot 444\, G_t - 9 \cdot 268\, R_t$ $R^2 = 0 \cdot 535$
              $(-0 \cdot 397)$ $(3 \cdot 277)$ $(-2 \cdot 999)$ $DW = 1 \cdot 648$

(10) Government domestic revenues:

(OLS) $Td_t = 12 \cdot 837 + 0 \cdot 015\, Y_t$ $\bar{R}^2 = 0 \cdot 290$
          $(2 \cdot 474)$ $(2 \cdot 587)$ $DW = 2 \cdot 412$

(2SLS) $Td_t = 12 \cdot 709 + 0 \cdot 0154\, Yt$ $R^2 = 0 \cdot 340$
          $(2 \cdot 448)$ $(2 \cdot 613)$ $DW = 2 \cdot 263$

8 Organisation of the Economy

UNDERLYING PHILOSOPHY OF THE SYSTEM

The organisation of the national economy of Kuwait may be examined from several aspects. An overview of the existing structure of its institutions will tell much; an examination of the national accounts, with the division of the national product, either by source or by end use, or an analysis of the labour market and the distribution of labour between the public and private sector will tell more. However, without understanding the basic philosophy underlying the state's activity which has brought these structures into being, such analysis would be essentially sterile and it would not be possible either to explain the evolution of its existing structure or to make any meaningful criticism of its performance. In one sense, an organisation is a manifestation of a strategy, no matter how it has evolved, and that strategy is a series of policy measures designed to attain certain goals which, in turn, are derived from the underlying philosophy of the state. Without knowledge of this, and the goals or aspirations which it implies, no measure of performance is possible.

Probably the most frequently quoted statement of aims of the Kuwait economic strategy is derived from the First Five Year Plan, 1967/8–1971/2.[1] Briefly, these aims are:

1. to raise the per capita income
2. to achieve a more equitable distribution of total income
3. to obtain a greater diversification of the economy
4. to train indigenous skills, and
5. to coordinate the work of development with that of other Arab countries in order to achieve greater economic integration of the Arab world.

However, even these aims, while making quantitative evaluation of economic performance possible, still require some statement of a social philosophy against which a qualitative assessment may be made. Thus, if a measure of state participation is undertaken, it could be part of a conscious effort to achieve greater socialisation or to reduce the overall level of risk in the economy and thereby encourage private investment. These alternative aims, diametrically opposed, would not be ascertainable from a mere examination of tables or graphs and these latter would not provide a measure of performance without knowledge of those aims.

In brief, the economic aims of the Kuwait government form part of an overall social strategy and the ultimate measurement of the economic strategy, as evidenced by its resulting economic structure and performance, must be according to criteria derived from the social strategy of which it forms a part. The social strategy of establishing a future Kuwait, in which the aspirations of individual Kuwaitis may be fulfilled and the Kuwaiti character and culture of Kuwait enhanced, is drawn from the underlying adherence to private initiative and enterprise coupled with a national degree of paternalism which is evidenced in Kuwait's development to date; individual economic policy measures are formulated against that historic background. Thus, when discussing the Kuwait economy more than any other we are, perhaps unconsciously, discussing in reality a socio-economic structure or organisation rather than a purely economic entity.

So often Kuwait is described as a combination of a welfare state with the free enterprise system and in one sense this is unique for a developing country. The development of the welfare services are described elsewhere (see Chapter 3) but the real difference between Kuwait and most other developing countries is that while the latter are generally prevented from achieving even their basic aspirations in the welfare field due to a low per capita income, the transfer of the proceeds of the development of its oil resources to its own benefit, and the increase in prices due to combined efforts with its OPEC partners, have removed this constraint from Kuwait's development. Consequently the state is able to achieve that which so many others desire, but find unattainable, at great speed.

The removal of the capital constraint, however, brings its own problems.[2] So many of the principles of planning derived from economic theory presume a basic shortage of capital and therefore concentrate on capital allocation. This leads almost inevitably to a central direction of planning in order that the scarce resource of capital may be allocated with maximum efficiency. The achievement of so many social objectives is seen as conditional upon the rate of economic growth which that capital allocation is held to determine. But, in the case of capital surplus economies, accent upon capital allocation according to principles derived from conventional theory is useless and any judgement of performance based upon those principles would be misleading. Thus, whereas the proportions of the national product allocated to investment and consumption are of paramout importance, in Kuwait's case the way in which the product is distributed and the manner in which it is enjoyed are the twin determinants of overall development.

Many of the policies of the Kuwait government may be seen, in fact, as being aimed at income distribution. These include not only the more obvious policies of land purchase and sale, but the policies of joint participation in industry between the government and the private sector. This encourages individual enterprise by the lessening of risk. Other policies facilitate the creation of the infrastructure for enterprise, or provide health and other social services: all have the effect not only of distributing existing income, but of making more equal participation in future development possible.[3]

Investment in activities which provide employment, or even the creation of employment itself, not only distributes income, but also has an educative role. The raising of income levels makes saving possible by a greater number and therefore spreads the ownership of capital and its claims on future benefits. The concentration of public expenditure on employment (approximately 75 per cent of the Kuwaiti workforce is in the public sector) further indicates the emphasis on the distributional aspect of government policies, and perhaps also shows an underlying preference for maintenance of the work/reward relationship which a completely paternalistic distribution by social services and subsidies tends to destroy. Thus, 'the formation and administration of economic policy (in Kuwait) is concerned with the location of economic power, which determines the pattern of overall development and its shape rather than the direction of its development by centralised planning.'[4]

In previous chapters it has been noted that government activity, both via social services and economic participation, is designed to support rather than supplant free enterprise. However, since 1973 the balance between government and private roles in the economy has been altered due to the escalation in oil income. Efforts by the government to introduce this into the local economy to restore the balance inevitably imply an increase in government activity which, in the short-run, creates the apparent contradiction of a government increasing its proportion of total national activity while professing to encourage private enterprise. This is borne out by findings reported in the preceding chapter when it was indicated that, due to a productive capacity constraint at any particular time, increases in government investment following a rise in revenues from 1973 onward appear to have been accompanied by a contraction in private investment, but this should not be interpreted as being self-defeating; in the long run it is intended to result in expanding the overall absorptive capacity. In the meantime the government has alternative means available, via promotions through the joint sector, which ought now to be given greater priority, as will be emphasised later in this chapter. In view of the implications of increasing income from foreign investments, and the eventual need to raise finance via taxation which will restrict the private sector, this problem has become one of added urgency.

It also poses a special problem in view of the narrow power base in Kuwaiti society and the restricted sources from which political leadership is drawn. This may be inevitable if Kuwait is to remain in command of its own destiny, but, as the process of dissemination of political power is inevitably gradual, it is difficult to achieve any meaningful spread of economic power by the spread of wealth alone.

ECONOMIC SECTORS

If we adopt the usual classification of the Kuwait economy according to sectors, then in effect we are not only labelling those sectors according to who controls them, but are also giving some indication of the form of that control and the rationale according to which it is exercised. Indeed, such a classification is most useful as it will help to differentiate between the methods of control exercised in each and from this to draw some inferences of the efficiency of the Kuwait economic system as a whole in attaining the multiplicity of economic and socio-economic goals of Kuwaiti society.

The four sectors that have evolved in Kuwait are: the government sector, the private sector, the joint sector and the co-operative sector. We shall discuss below the role and activities of each.

The Government Sector
We have indicated previously the importance of the government sector in the Kuwait economy and have drawn attention to the enormous increase in GDP since 1971, which was due almost entirely to the change in ownership and in world prices of Kuwait oil. An additional consequence of this increase was the structural change in the system which has been emphasised. However it should be noted that, before

1971, the Kuwait Government was already a major operator in the economy. It almost matched the private sector in the level of final expenditure, was rapidly approaching the level of the private sector in gross capital formation and controlled the country's increasing investments abroad. In 1970/1 government accounted for some 48 per cent of the local expenditure component of GDP and by 1974/5 this proportion had reached approximately 60 per cent. However government prominence is even more marked when it is realised that the excess of oil revenues over imports is controlled largely, if not wholly, by government direction. Thus the relative role of government in overall GDP accounted for up to 70 per cent in 1970/1 and 87 per cent in 1974/5.

In view of this the decision-making process is of extreme importance and it is significant that the National Assembly (the Kuwait Parliament) was very active in its interest in economic matters and developments, being frequently at odds with the government. Created in 1963, elections were to be held every four years based on male suffrage of Kuwaiti citizens by birth. Always a lively body, it frequently refused to sanction legislation. In 1973 it rejected proposals for a 25 per cent share in the Kuwait Oil Company which the government had concluded on the Saudi Arabian model, and had forced the percentage up to 60 per cent by the time of the final agreement in 1974. After the 1975 elections the National Assembly continued its important influence in oil and economic affairs. However, the Government felt that the Assembly was becoming more responsive to pressure groups to the detriment of urgent national problems and that delays in important legislation could be attributed to this cause. Consequently the Prime Minister and his Cabinet offered their resignation in August 1976, on the grounds that government had become impossible due to obstruction by the National Assembly. The Assembly was suspended by the Amir pending the drafting of amendments to the constitution and a new government was formed.

The Prime Minister has always assumed a supervisory role of all financial activities, and since 1976 control has been exercised through a committee of the Ministers of Finance, Oil, Commerce and Industry, and Planning. Since the dissolution of the Assembly this control is much more direct. The Ministry of Finance has a very important role in that it controls the country's foreign investments as well as the internal receipts and expenditures of the government. It works in close coordination with the Central Bank, and also participates actively in the joint sector of the economy. The Ministry of Oil also exerts a direct influence, being in control of the country's main, almost sole, source of physical wealth.

As indicated in Chapter 7, the Government's receipts, and to a lesser extent its expenditure, reflect directly the changes in the oil sector.

As will be seen in Table 8.1 the government's total receipts increased almost eight-fold between 1971/2 and 1976/7. Investment income also increased by roughly similar proportions, but 'other receipts' (taxation and levies, etc.) barely quadrupled. The effect of the oil receipts is so immense that any attempt to interpret the table would be extremely hazardous. However, it should be noted that, while the oil income increases were due both to increased participation (up to outright national ownership) and to the price increases, the trend through these years can in no way be regarded as long-term for the future. Only the price element is capable of adjustment upward. However, the income from investments can be expected to continue to grow; for, as long as the Government's current income is sufficient to cover its expenditure, the effect from investments will be cumulative. Addition to foreign investments made possible by further surpluses will obviously have an accelerating effect. Consequently the ratio of oil and non-oil receipts is a matter of importance for future development prospects. (See Annex to Chapter 9.)

TABLE 8.1   Summary of government revenues and expenditure*
(Million KD)

	1971/2	1972/3	1973/4	1974/5	1975/6	1976/7
Receipts	424·0	597·7	675·3	2271·4	2838·3	3224·7
Oil receipts	354·1	506·0	543·9	2056·4	2509·7	2800·8
Investment Income	42·3	50·8	89·1	152·2	265·1	317·0
Others	27·6	40·9	42·3	63·0	68·5	106·9
Expenditures	346·9	396·9	536·7	1085·2	779·9	1031·8
Current*	276·3	313·3	438·4	821·5	554·1	678·0
Development	50·7	60·2	73·2	128·7	165·4	304·9
Land Purchase	19·9	23·2	25·1	135·0	60·4	48·9
Surplus	77·1	201·0	138·6	1186·2	2058·4	2192·3
*Includes transfers abroad	(32·9)	(43·5)	(153·2)	(332·0)	(57·1)	(70·5)

SOURCE: *Kuwait Annual Statistical Abstracts.*
*Some of these figures may differ slightly from those used in the preceding chapter due to different methods of compilation.

TABLE 8.2   Government oil and non-oil receipts
             (% of total receipts)

	1971/2	1972/3	1973/4	1974/5	1975/6	1976/7
Oil	83·5	84·8	80·5	90·5	88·3	86·8
Non-oil	16·5	15·2	19·5	9·5	11·7	13·2
	100·0	100·0	100·0	100·0	100·0	100·0

The increased share of non-oil receipts was interrupted by the extreme changes of 1974 / 5, but continued on its upward path thereafter, and the fact that the base on which the percentages were calculated took such a large upward leap in that year has cloaked the growing absolute importance of the non-oil sector. Further evidence of the growing importance of non-oil receipts is provided in Table 8.3 which illustrates that the growth rate of these receipts reached a height of 64 per cent in 1974 / 5.

On the other hand, total government expenditure has shown a general upward trend as evidenced by Table 8.1 with an increase over the period from 1971 / 2 to 1976 / 7 of almost 200 per cent. The relevant per capita figures given in Table 8.4 indicate that average total expenditure per head of population more than doubled during the years 1971/2–1976/7, reaching a level of KD901·4 by the end of the period. This contrasts with comparable figures for 1976 of KD480 in the US, KD427 in the UK, and KD316 in Germany. The growth of development expenditure, however, is even more striking, rising over the same period by more than six-fold. The corresponding per capita figures in Table 8.4 show an overall increase of 340 per cent. This clearly supports the hypothesis that Kuwait's investment in infrastructure and social developmental services has been receiving prior consideration in order to increase the national absorptive capacity and promote diversification.

The Government land purchases shown in Table 8.1 are needless to say subject to wide fluctuations and merely reflect the Government's intention in each year of its policy to transfer some of the oil wealth received into the hands of the people by this method. This has already been discussed, and its consequences analysed, in Chapter 4.

TABLE 8.3   Percentage year to year increases in government receipts
             from non-oil sources

71/2–72/3	72/3–73/4	73/4–74/5	74/5–75/6	75/6–76/7
31%	43%	64%	55%	27%

TABLE 8.4   Government expenditure per capita (KD)

	1971/2	1972/3	1973/4	1974/5	1975/6	1976/7
Total expenditure (less transfers abroad)	402·2	428·1	439·0	814·2	726·6	901·4
Development expenditure	64·9	72·9	83·8	139·2	166·3	286·0
(Development expenditure per capita, Kuwaiti population)	139·6	158·9	177·1	311·3	350·4	607·0

As far as the Government's current expenditure is concerned a substantial amount is spent on the social services and the per capita expenditure on selected social services is shown in Table 8.5.

However the social services are not available equally to all residents in Kuwait and care needs to be exercised in any interpretation of these statistics. For example, publicly provided education is essentially available for Kuwaiti citizens only, while private schools, attended by non-Kuwaitis as well as Kuwaitis, are supported by subsidies. The age structure of the Kuwaiti population would show a greater proportion in the low-age groups than the non-Kuwaiti population and this is where the immediate results of that expenditure would be most felt.

As mentioned previously, public expenditure is financed almost entirely from oil revenues so that the national budget is concerned with the distribution, rather than the redistribution, of a substantial part of the national product. This is in marked contrast to the more usual situation where government expenditure is financed by a reduction in incomes by taxation or borrowing. In the absence of any form of personal income tax and with a trivial *ad valorem* tax of 4 per cent on

TABLE 8.5   Per capita expenditure on selected social services (KD)

	Social welfare	Public health	Education
1971/2	8·3	22·2	48·4
1972/3	8·2	24·1	56·5
1973/4	8·1	25·2	55·2
1974/5	8·7	28·5	59·3

SOURCE: *Kuwait Annual Statistical Abstract*, 1977.

most imports, and a levy of 5 per cent on corporate profits to support
scientific research, the government has no need to weigh the pros of its
expenditure against the cons occasioned by its taxes. Apart from the
fact that this reduces the government's power to influence the economy
by fiscal means, it also encourages a completely different attitude
toward its welfare activities, both by itself and by its citizens. The
government, even when the National Assembly is in operation, is not
inhibited by public attitudes to the incidence of taxes. The lack of this
constraint encourages pressure from the general population for ever-
increasing expenditure on subsidies and the social services. When the
alternative use of funds is investment abroad or foreign aid, it is often
difficult to resist such pressure.

The importance of government activity in the economy, however,
cannot be judged solely by reference to operations via public finance.
Its policies relating to other sectors, to their relationships with each
other and to the relationships of the economy with the world at large are
all important indicators of its attitude. Of overriding importance, is its
policy toward the supreme source of its wealth, oil. Its attainment of
complete ownership and control of the country's oil has been described
in Chapter 6. This was achieved with the aim of ultimate control of its
own destiny. Consequently, its attitude toward oil since its assumption
of control has shown a marked change from when it was the government of an area of land from which the supply of a natural resource was
drawn to be processed by others. Now it can view oil in all its processes,
from extraction to consumption, as a possible source of benefit to its
people. Ever more importantly, as oil is a finite resource, it can adopt a
policy on extraction which it calculates will allow oil to make its
maximum contribution to long-term development and well-being.

The formulation and control of its policy is in the hands of the
Supreme Petroleum Council. This consists of the Prime Minister as
Chairman, the Ministers of Oil, Finance, Foreign Affairs, Commerce
and Industry and the Minister of State for Cabinet Affairs. The
composition of this committee is an excellent indication of the
importance of oil to the country and also its importance to Kuwait's
position in the world.

One of its first actions since assuming control was the formulation of
a conservation policy. This has to be undertaken in the light not only of
its own requirements, but also in conjunction with its partners in
OPEC. Furthermore, because of Kuwait's importance in the world
supply spectrum, it must have regard to the way in which its own
actions will affect the world economy and therefore its own future as
part of the world community.

With its newly acquired freedom to interest itself in the whole process of oil extraction, transformation and marketing, the government has quickly evolved policies for the training of Kuwaitis to take their place in these various activities. It has also become directly involved in exploration activities and services relating to oil production and also in many of the downstream operations. As well as refining for its home consumption, there is also a growing export trade in refined products and derivatives. It should be borne in mind, too, that while the 'oil crisis' of recent years has laid stress on the importance of oil as a fuel for transport, a large proportion of value added is derived from non-fuel sources and Kuwait is actively interested in investigating and furthering its activities in the 'non-fuel' side of the oil industry. One of its first diversification efforts was in seagoing oil transport and the Kuwait tanker fleet now has a capacity of over 2 million tons. Kuwait has invested in pipeline capacity elsewhere in the world and, while these investments may be primarily for the benefit of the recipient countries, it would be idle to pretend that Kuwait has no interest in their operation and their effect on world oil distribution, e.g. the Sumed pipeline from the Gulf of Suez to the Mediterranean. The details of both home and overseas diversifications will be noted in later chapters, but one of the biggest problems facing the government is the need to ensure that diversification in order to obtain the maximum value added from oil production is harmonised with a programme of diversification in non-oil activities to secure the country's future when oil is exhausted. Even though oil is the dominant force in the economy, other industrial activities are being actively encouraged.

There are now about ten government agencies charged with the development of industry, ranging from the Ministry of Planning (which replaced the Planning Board in 1974) to the Industrial Bank and the specialised departments in the Ministry of Commerce and Industry, which include a joint office with UNIDO charged with promotion of industrial projects and provision of technical advice.

Both the World Bank Mission on the 'Promotion of Manufacturing in Kuwait' (1971) and a special report commissioned by the Industrial Bank in 1974 drew attention to the apparent lack of coordination between these various agencies. Such a feature is common under conditions of rapid change, but there may well be a more deep-seated cause, namely the lack of an explicit, coherent policy on development and diversification within which such agencies can work. At the highest level, where policies are at the most general, there is no lack of government or ministerial statements. At the operational level there is certainly no lack of will; but, until general policy statements are translated into general policy measures, these agencies do not have sufficient guidelines within which to formulate their own detailed operational programmes. Coordination is the harmonious inter-relation of activities in the pursuit of common objectives. But when common objectives were detailed in, for example, a national plan, these were never given full approval. Until the national objectives are specified in such detail as a plan provides, no set of operational objectives can be generated by the executive departments and agencies which will focus their attention, and of those in government, on the need for coordination.

By contrast, the government's trade policy is quite explicit, at least on the foreign side. It is one of minimum intervention. On the home market, however, the benefits of this policy from the consumer's point of view is blunted by the lack of competition among major distributors. This has arisen by common usage and because of the phenomenal growth of an economy that was until recently small and closely-knit rather than as a matter of policy, and there are signs that this is giving way as those of entrepreneurial ability emerge and are exposed to opportunity by the country's development. Realising the trade potential of the country, particularly in the field of re-export which is gaining in importance, the government has sought to encourage industrialisation through such direct measures as the provision of soft loans, cheap land and services in the industrial areas. While this policy is meeting with some success there is need for a more explicit order of priorities to guide these types of development.

As well as by its trade and development policies, the government plays a vital role in the economy via its budgetary and monetary policies. Both of these, however, have been constrained by the lack of many of the traditional instruments that have evolved in the developed countries and, far from easing the burden on government, the lack of a national debt and of an income tax make direction and control of the economy more difficult. This problem will be dealt with in more detail in Chapter 10.

With regard to budgetary policy, the aims of Kuwait are:
1. To rationalise public expenditure
2. To stimulate the growth of domestic economic activity and to ensure its smooth operation
3. To improve income distribution
4. To build reserves for future generations
5. To develop other sources of income—primarily foreign income from government investment abroad.

We see immediately that, while these may have a common goal in the overall development of the country, they are at the same time in conflict with each other in that they all make demands on government expenditure. Even though the Government may be spared the problem of raising revenue by fiscal means, this conceptual framework of competing ends still requires a systematic mechanism for the allocation of the country's revenue no matter how this is raised. It is obvious from ministerial statements and recent policies that the need to conserve the country's oil as a source of revenue is being given urgent attention, but in keeping with the general theme it is stressed here that, for this to be effective in ensuring the country's future, the conservation and budgetary policy needs to be seen as a single allocative process of which the allocation of revenue forms only a part.

As for income distribution, this cannot be restricted to budgetary policy alone. A whole set of government policies on almost all economic matters has a bearing on income distribution. In particular, expenditure on social and other services and the provision of cheap concessions, such as electricity and water or loans for housing, have a distributional component and the actual distribution of government expenditure, through employment in the government service, is as much a part of distribution policy as of employment policy.

As for monetary policy, the government seems to have even less room for manoeuvre than in the field of budgetary policy. As already mentioned, there are very limited means in Kuwait of controlling the money supply by the usual methods. As monetary problems will be dealt with in greater detail in Chapter 10, however, it is sufficient to remark on the government's difficulty and the urgent need to form new instruments of control. This need is obviously recognised.

As well as the aspects of economic policy so far discussed, population policy must also be considered. At first sight this may seem a strange assertion, but, with the small initial base of the Kuwaiti population, economic development and expansion has necessitated the importation of labour and specialised skills on a large scale. A naturalisation policy has been evolving by general usage, but there has been no explicit population policy recorded which derives from an overall policy designed to fashion Kuwait's economic future. A policy of industrialisation and diversification will have important consequences for the size and structure of the future population, and yet any decision on the desired size and structure of the future population has equally important implications for industrialisation and diversification. Economic policy and population policy in Kuwait, therefore, are very interdependent and the one cannot be formulated without regard for its implications on the other. The population increase over the past eighteen years from 1957, and the way in which its composition has changed, was shown in Table 4.1. Although the natural growth of the Kuwaiti population has been very high, it appears that the rapid increase of Kuwaitis has been caused in the main by the policy of naturalisation. As for the non-Kuwaiti population, its growth and structure has already been remarked upon in Chapter 4 and it was noted especially that an increasing proportion of this group aspires to have a more permanent and secure status than hitherto. These considerations, together with the rapidly changing conditions in the region, increase the urgent need for an explicit population policy to be formulated. Furthermore, given the high per capita expenditure on welfare services, the rate of population increase has enormous consequences for other government policies as well as industrialisation. Industrial or other development cannot take place without regard to these consequences. However, there is growing evidence of the awareness of this problem in some policy areas, notably in construction activities. Certain contracts are undertaken to include the importation of the labour force, which departs on completion. This is particularly important where the construction labour force is much greater than that required for subsequent operations.

The Private Sector

The importance of the private sector in the Kuwait economy cannot be stressed too highly. As explained in the historical review in Chapter 2, the country has developed on a basis of private enterprise and has based its past, pre-oil prosperity on trade with the outside world, an activity which invariably requires that flexibility and quickness of response which a free enterprise, decentralised economic system can encompass. It is not accidental that this should be so, for, in as much as the free enterprise system developed in its present form in the Christian Protestant countries, the similarity of the regard in which individual achievement is held both in Protestantism and in Islam is most marked. Added to this, the necessity for self-reliance embodied in desert life, and the shortage of resources which forced Kuwaitis throughout their history to seek outside opportunities, bred a particularly venturesome society. There is no doubt that history has been a rigorous sifting process, for many of the current leaders in Kuwait, whether in commerce or politics, have, with their families, survived this process and thereby prospered. This may be in marked contrast to some of its neighbours, where society, being based on agriculture, provides less room for individuality and different social patterns have evolved.

In encouraging the free enterprise system, the state sees its duty as protecting individual rights and facilitating their exercise. The problem of such a state as Kuwait however, with the prospect of rapid development, is to ensure that the developments which do take place do not endanger its own safety and are not harmful to particular sections of society. With such a growing market, small population and narrow economic base, a completely free economy would see the establishment at will of firms controlled by outsiders, attracted by the prospect of high profit, available capital and low local competition. Thus, without at least some restrictions, the Kuwait economy could pass once more into the hands of outsiders. These restrictions are designed to restrict entry by non-Kuwaitis into strategic sectors of the economy, but there has been little attempt to offset these restrictions by greater competition in the local market, particularly at the wholesale level.

The first duty of any government is to its citizens. To protect the rights of Kuwaitis in the sudden developments which became possible as a result of oil, Kuwait instituted a series of measures designed to restrict the activities and rights of outsiders in the Kuwait economy, while at the same time promoting Kuwaiti interests. In 1965 the Industrial Development Committee was formed, charged with the duty of promoting industry and also of licensing private enterprise developments in the non-oil sector. All industrial firms must be at least 51 per cent Kuwaiti owned, and the IDC is responsible for ensuring this and issuing the necessary development licences. As the term 'industrial firm' covers almost all activities from transformation of raw materials to retailing, this control is quite wide and is universally applied.

Such a policy also operates in banking and financial institutions, and Kuwait has succeeded in keeping these exclusively in the hands of its citizens to safeguard the interests of the state and also to promote the interests of other sectors of the economy.

The success of the state's policies regarding the private sector are difficult to gauge in the face of the tremendous progress of oil and the way in which it focuses attention on the public sector. It is important, therefore, not to overlook the importance of the private sector and its considerable achievements, especially in areas such as trade, contracting, banking, insurance and other financial activities. As has been shown, the concentration of Kuwaiti activities throughout history has been in these areas, so it is hardly surprising that these were where the first developments would take place, and where enterprise was most likely to succeed. In fact, occasions have arisen where developments in the private sector have gone ahead at such speed that the service provision by the public sector has been unable to keep pace.

The Kuwaiti propensity for self-employment is evident from the most cursory examination of the annual Abstracts of Statistics, or any other appropriate publications. In 1973 (the latest census for which data is available), there were approximately 11,800 Kuwaitis in gainful employment in the private sector, 2660 were employers, 6620 were self-employed and 2520 were employees. There is little doubt, however, that these are underestimates. A large number of Kuwaitis in trade and commerce are not included. Of 123,300 non-Kuwaitis in the private sector, 15,600 were employers, 23,800 were self-employed and 83,900 were employees. The composition of the total labour force is not recorded for that year, but it must have included about 81,000 Kuwaitis. Thus it can be seen that only a small proportion of Kuwaitis enter the private sector. Attention has already been drawn to this, of course, in previous chapters in remarking on the preference of the younger Kuwaitis to enter the Civil Service. As a source of total employment, however, the importance of the private sector is still important, for in 1973 it employed 135,100 from a total labour force of about 515,000. Furthermore, all evidence indicates that its importance has been increasing since then. Unfortunately, due to the lack of data, no assessment of the sector's importance as a contributor to GNP can be made.

TABLE 8.6   Forms of business organisation and their distribution, 1973*

	Number
Individual Proprietorship	14553
Partnership	211
De facto company	3593
Joint stock company	30
Limited liability partnership	1
Limited liability company	745
Shareholding company	95
Co-operative Society	49
Non profit-making society	80
Total	19357

*The latest census year for which data is available.

Forms of Organisation within the Private Sector

The organisational forms within the private sector are varied and exhibit most of the elements to be found in industrialised, Western economies, although the distribution between the differing forms of organisation might vary. In 1973, a total of 19,357 establishments were reported, as shown in Table 8.6. Many of these had more than one branch, however, and, including branches, there were 21,695 establishments distributed among various forms of activity as shown in Table 8.7.

The concentration of the private sector in trade and financial activities is vividly illustrated in Table 8.7, with 77 per cent of the total establishments in these two activities. Care, however, should be taken in the interpretation of Tables 8.6 and 8.7, as it would appear that some of the businesses reported should validly be allocated to the 'joint sector', which will be the subject of other sections of this chapter.

By the end of 1977, there were a total of forty-two public shareholding companies of which two were by then fully owned by the government. Of the remaining forty, eighteen were really in the joint sector, with government participation ranging from 18·5 per cent to 80 per cent with an average participation of 47·5 per cent per company jointly owned. Of these, however, the government owned controlling interest in four and 50 per cent in a further three. The market value of the thirty-four companies quoted on the exchange (i.e. after deducting six companies not yet being traded) stood at approximately KD2.1 billion on 29 December 1977. Of these thirty-four companies, twenty-nine declared profits in 1976 totalling over KD20 million. Although the 1977 figures are not yet available, the ratio of the 1977 market value to

TABLE 8.7   Establishments classified by form of economic activity, 1973

	Number
Agriculture, hunting, fishing	508
Mining and Quarrying	24
Manufacturing industry	3084
Electricity, gas and water	19
Construction	402
Wholesale and retail trade	12638
Transport, communications and storage	284
Financial, insurance, real estate	596
Services	4140
Total	21695

the 1976 profits clearly indicate the extent to which these companies were overvalued, and as we shall later explain this is due to the relatively restricted supply of alternative investment availability and also to speculation.

Up to July 1977, 122 private shareholding companies had also been established. The first dated from June 1963, but no less than forty-four had been established since 1 January 1976.

There was foreign participation in forty-seven of these companies with the maximum foreign participation allowable, 49 per cent, in twenty-seven of them. The trend towards foreign participation has fallen, however, with thirty of the forty-four companies established since January 1976 being wholly locally owned. Twelve of the total companies also had some government participation and one, the Kuwait Oil Company, was wholly government-owned. These thirteen, therefore, are again not strictly part of the private sector, but in as much as the first twelve represent the government's interest in stimulating activity in the private sector, they give an added insight into government policy. The companies in which participation is practised range from paper production, tourism, agriculture and construction, to industrial banking. (The Kuwait Oil Company appears in this total for historical reasons, having been established as a private company into which the government entered later as a participant and then assumed complete control.)

As may be deduced from the foregoing paragraphs, joint activity between government and private enterprise forms an important part of total activity in Kuwait. That is why a separate section is devoted to the joint sector.

The Joint Sector
The joint sector can better be described as a concept or an experiment rather than a sector of industrial activity which might appear separately in the national accounts. Politically, it is regarded as one of the most important steps taken in the development of the country and marks one of its major attempts to transform the low income, narrow-based economy of pre-oil years into an economy able to take its place among the modern industrial states and to hold its own on equal terms with its rivals. It is also one more important indicator of Kuwait's attitude towards industry and private enterprise in that the need for rapid industrialisation is often given as the excuse for national enterprise undertakings on the grounds that private enterprise is too slow to respond or is unwilling to take the necessary risk. The joint sector in

Kuwait is an alternative to this argument in that enterprises conducted on the joint sector principle are intended as instigators of private participation, and the government participation is seen as a means of overcoming private reluctance to invest in certain activities which are thought nationally desirable. Government participation reduces the risk of the private entrepreneur as well as indicating the government's commitment to the industry which is the recipient of the investment. As stated by the Minister of Finance and Oil in 1974:

The incentive for private investment in industrial and service development was still insufficient and the initial role of the joint sector system was to encourage private involvement in areas considered valuable to Kuwait's long term development but which possessed the deterrent elements of being capital intensive or having a protracted pay-off.

It must also be borne in mind however that rapid development requires rapid social changes, many of which are the result of industrial and economic change, yet the private sector only responds to market signals such as profits, prices and interest rates. An involvement by the government can be justified when there is a difference in the social and economic pay-off of any particular enterprise and this too has been a major factor in the promotion of activity in Kuwait by government involvement. Through the joint sector the government has the power to influence the direction of investment and also the development of joint stock activities without in fact controlling them and thereby stultifying the benefits which flow from individual initiative and enterprise. This influence is exercised through the appointment of directors by the government; and their role was described by the Prime Minister in 1974 in the following words:

They should act as normal commercial directors but should direct the policy of the company in accordance with strategic goals laid down by the government as and when found necessary.

It is this dual social and economic role which makes the justification of joint sector activity something more than merely the assistance of infant industries. When these have matured and are able to exist unaided, it is generally held that a government should relinquish its holdings if only to make more capital available to other industries which may still need it. In the case of Kuwait, it is recognised that the prospect of profit alone may not result in the fulfilment of some of the state's social and political aims, so that government involvement in joint enterprises will probably remain permanent in most cases and will be a further example of Kuwait's adherence to the private enterprise principle in economic activity while at the same time attempting to control the country's destiny by securing its social and economic base within the Arab world. This problem of control is important when it is remembered that with hardly any taxation and no national debt Kuwait has a limited ability to direct its economy and the joint sector is one of the few tools available to it.

Up to the late sixties public involvement in the joint sector was haphazard but in the early seventies the government began to draw conclusions as to the future role which the sector should play and to consider how additional development should be undertaken to facilitate the operations of the sector. While a cohesive strategy has not been made explicit, the Planning Board expressed the objectives of the Joint Sector to be:

1. To encourage the private sector to increase its role in development, especially in industries requiring capital beyond the means of the private sector.
2. To encourage the private sector to undertake investment in industries in which government takes the initiative, and then invites private participation.
3. To achieve social and socio-economic goals which may not be achieved by the private sector operating alone.
4. To support the private sector by undertaking necessary activities for its operation, but which might not be undertaken on their own initiative (e.g. infrastructural activities which may require economies of scale, or where the pay-off might be very far into the future).
5. To achieve political ends, e.g. security of supply, or to safeguard against monopoly.

The contribution of the joint sector to the economy is again difficult to judge, and it would certainly be more difficult to analyse its contribution to the attainment of the objectives set out above after so short a time. However, it appears from a recent study that the return on government investment in the joint sector has been increasing, although the study concluded that the performance of management in both managerial and technical positions is low (see table 8.8).

Altogether, there were twenty-six public and private companies in the joint sector in June 1977, with government participation in the range from 8 per cent to 80 per cent.

The Cooperative Sector
This is an interesting phenomenon in Kuwait business activity, and has developed entirely in the consumer market. In contrast to most

TABLE 8.8   Index of returns to government
investment in the joint sector

	Investment	Returns
1968/9	100	100
1969/70	111	200
1970/1	123	400
1971/2	138	733
1972/3	165	833

SOURCE: M. A. Hamouda 'Auditing of Joint
Sector Companies'. Paper presented to the Third
Seminar on High Management, Arab Planning
Institute, January 1977.

developing countries, where co-operation is usually encouraged in production in order to promote the spread of mechanisation, to mobilise savings or to maintain the maximum of value added in the hands of the producers, the Kuwaiti co-ops are to ensure that the consumer benefits as much as possible from his consumption expenditure. In this it resembles the early consumer co-ops of Britain which grew up in the 1840s and developed in order to allow consumers to benefit from bulk buying, not by cheaper prices but by receiving a share of profits based on the levels of their expenditure rather than on their holding of capital. The movement commenced in the early sixties, and the Co-operative Union received its own charter in 1971. Membership of individual co-ops is entirely open to Kuwaiti citizens and is established by share purchase. Return on shares is limited to a maximum of 1 per cent, and surpluses declared are distributed annually to shareholders on the basis of their purchases for the year.

As shown in Table 8.9, the total sales have almost tripled in four years and must now represent a very significant part of total consumer

TABLE 8.9   Growth of co-operative outlets, membership and sales
1973–6

	31.12.73	31.12.74	31.12.75	31.12.76
Number of Co-operatives	18	30	21	22
Membership	26855	35815	50607	52021
Total sales (KD'000)	13183	19553	32691	34426

SOURCE: *Annual Report of the Consumers' Co-operative Union*
31.12.1976.

expenditure in Kuwait. In 1976 sales were about 10 per cent of total private consumption and, in view of the nature of the sales patterns, the co-ops accounted for about 50 per cent of total expenditure on foodstuffs in that year. It should also be noted that the co-ops have undoubtedly facilitated the provision and distribution of foodstuffs throughout the country and it is a movement which will undoubtedly grow in importance still further. It will be interesting to see whether the movement will reach back into manufacturing or importing, or even into housing, in response to the needs of its members, as has happened with similar movements in other countries, but there is no evidence of any trend in this direction yet. One criticism that is levelled, however, is that the restriction of membership to Kuwaiti citizens implies that a substantial profit is made from non-Kuwaitis which is passed on to the restricted membership. This could encourage a tendency to benefit from co-operation, not from lower prices, but from distribution of higher surpluses. Again, however, there seems no evidence to support these fears and it is obvious from the growth of the co-operative movement that the current accent is on development and expansion.

This completes the review of the organisation of the Kuwait economy, and the next chapter will contain an analysis of the economy's major production activities.

9 Absorptive Capacity and Major Production Sectors

Hitherto the growth of production in developing economies has tended to follow fixed paths, with certain key sectors expanding at predictable rates as per capita income increases. In fact the predictability of such rates is sufficiently accurate for elasticities to be computed from historical data which illustrate the percentage change in the proportion of the national product arising from each sector of the economy for given percentage changes in per capita income.[1] These data, however, are usually related to economies which have followed the accepted modes of development, with each economy starting from a low level and over time increasing its capital, this increase in capital being accomplished either by borrowing or saving. As income increases consumption patterns change to match the increased income and output patterns change to correspond to that changing demand spectrum. Such elasticities have been derived from cross-section studies of groups of economies in varying stages of development in the same way as the quoted work by Chenery. One of the main determinants of growth in most economies has been the speed at which capital can be mobilised.[2] Indeed much of the activity of the world's organisations devoted to assisting development is concerned with aid in providing capital in order to break the cycle between low income–low saving with low consumption–low investment–low income. Without increased incomes, increased savings are rarely possible. Only recently has there been a tendency to examine other constraints on the speed of development.

If the supply of capital were no problem, then inevitably there must be a limit at which an economy finds itself able to absorb that capital and one of the problems at present receiving much attention is that of the 'absorptive capacity' of developing economies. This is usually the second constraint affecting any state whose growth is not restricted by the supply of capital. It is, however, much more complicated and difficult to define than the straightforward capital shortage. Briefly it implies a lack of some or all of the skills and services necessary to enable

133

the economy to use the capital available to its maximum advantage. It implies a lack of appropriate education of the general population, lack of technical and administrative skills or an inability to replace traditional outlooks with those more suitable to the growing economy. Equally, it implies the lack of a basic infrastructure on which development may take place. But the level of absorptive capacity may be influenced as much by bottlenecks in specific sectors as by the lack of general availability of some or all of those requirements. These bottlenecks may be in the form of a shortage of essential skills or key provisions of infrastructure which make other skills or provisions under-utilised.

As far as many of the oil-exporting states are concerned, the problem of capital for indigenous development has suddenly been dispelled and the problem of absorptive capacity has become paramount among those states which aspire to become as industrialised as some countries in the West. However, there are a few problems of especial importance which have hitherto hardly ever arisen and yet have important consequences for these states and their future. Firstly, most are dependent upon the single resource of oil. It is not a case, as in that of so many of the other developing countries, of using capital to build an economy on the development of natural resources. The very source of capital in the oil-exporting countries is that single natural resource and, while it can be argued that capital should be devoted to the development and processing of oil in order to maximise the value added accruing to the producing state, the lack of other resources limits the indigenous possibility of diversification. The climate and topography of so many of these states is such that it is the exploitation of that resource for use by others that at present sustains the current high standard of living, and this resource is finite. Secondly, notwithstanding their high purchasing power, the size of many of these states in terms of population, and in some cases area also, is small. The prospect of diversification and balanced self-sustaining growth, even if all other impediments were not present, could be remote in many instances since some form of specialisation would be necessary. The most important problem arises because the amount of the capital which is available is such that states are able to make some choice concerning their path of development. This creates the necessity of ensuring that the amount of monetary capital which is surplus to requirements at any one time is used in order that the returns yielded are maximised consistent with maintaining a spectrum of liquidity and diversification that will (a) allow sufficient funds to be available to be transformed into physical capital as the country's development strategy proceeds and (b) ensure that the value of investments are safeguarded for future generations.

The mention of a strategy implies planning, and the ability to choose a plan or strategy in the face of such a large availability of capital is a factor unique to most of the oil-exporting countries as has already been mentioned. Effectively they are more able to choose their 'desired end state' and to plan for development to reach that state than other countries who are forced to adopt a more on-going planning process where each step is conditional upon the one before having generated sufficient capital to enable development to continue. This freedom permits countries such as Kuwait to take a much longer view of their planning and to evaluate the benefits and drawbacks of alternative end states and their required strategies in a manner different from that which would be required under conditions of capital shortage. They no longer view the aim of planning merely to raise the standard of living of the indigenous population over a period of time by ensuring that capital generated is deployed optimally. They are experiencing a major shift of the ownership of productive capital, largely via the medium of financial assets, to themselves from other nations. Their aim must thus also be to ensure that a maximum share of the world's productive capacity is retained in their hands when oil is exhausted. If a shift of existing capital ownership takes place merely for this to be sold back to the original owners in exchange for consumption goods this would not provide the conditions necessary for self-sustaining development, even though the high standard of living is being maintained in the meantime. On the other hand, if industrialisation implies the development of industries which can only survive by continuous subsidy due to lack of comparative advantage or require a level of in-migration which is not socially acceptable, then the investment of capital abroad must be managed so that it will provide sufficient returns for the country to maintain its high level of consumption in the post-oil era and to generate sufficient reinvestment for this flow to be continued indefinitely.

It may be seen at once that under these conditions the optimum level of oil extraction in each oil-producing country may be different. It will depend upon the level of population, the current level of income, the possibility of alternative resource development and, perhaps most importantly, the level of oil reserves. Also it is unlikely that the optimum rate of extraction from the country's point of view will be the optimum rate from the point of view of the world. Many of the recent models forecasting doom and collapse unless the world conserves its resources and has regard to the need for future generations completely miss the point that decisions on resource extraction are not made in the world context. Furthermore, if the rates of extraction crucially determine the level of world capital accumulation, then even a world optimum level will depend upon the rate at which capital can substitute for resources and technology can combat shortages. But where decisions on extraction rates are taken by countries whose aim is not only to maximise its own capital accumulation but also its share of the world's total capital, these rates may bear no relationship whatever to any world optimum. It is salutary to note that it is only since countries who own many of the natural resources of the earth have gained control of them that the imbalance of the distribution of the results of the exploitation of those resources has been emphasised. Many of the oil price increases of recent years were attempts to redress that imbalance. Yet only after the world has come to the end of an era in which it was neglectful of the gross imbalance of the inter-regional distribution of the fruits of the world's total output are we being exhorted to have regard to the inter-generational distribution of resources, while the inter-regional problems inherited from the era which has just closed remain still largely unsolved.

In theoretical terms an optimising policy for a country like Kuwait would be such that the extraction rate of oil and the disposition of the proceeds of its sales would ensure that the rate of increase in the value of its oil reserves is equal to the marginal return on productive capital at home, and that both are equal to the return on capital invested on the world's monetary markets. Put another way, at any given time Kuwait is able, by extracting more from its oil reserves, to devote the results either to monetary or to real investment. Its choice of action will be based upon its view of how its future income flow from all sources (future oil sales, home production, foreign investments, etc.) will be affected. If oil values are expected to rise more than the rate of return expected from investments, then it is better to leave oil where it is. If anticipated returns from investments are greater than the expected increase in oil values, then it would be beneficial to increase oil output and devote the results to increased investment. Once Kuwait has the option of extracting or not extracting oil it is choosing the form in which it will hold its capital in exactly the same way as any businessman or industrialist would look at a portfolio of investments and decide upon its structure. In fact the model that we propose would see oil as an asset in an investment portfolio, with other assets in that same portfolio being in the form of indigenous investment or investment in financial or other assets abroad.

This is of course a counsel of perfection which ignores many other factors such as:

1. The extraction rate which would satisfy the optimisation conditions stated above may be substantially below that which is required by industrial nations. This of course is a matter for political consideration but undoubtedly it has loomed large in the minds of the oil-exporting countries during recent years.

2. The investment of funds abroad may follow a non-optimal path, for it may be that to do otherwise may have serious repercussions on the world economy. Not all these repercussions might be adverse to oil producing states, however, but they may be viewed within the context of world responsibility. Again this is a political problem which impinges upon the economic model in that the maintenance of the world's productive activity might be in Kuwait's interest in non-economic ways.[3]

3. Different degrees of uncertainty are attached to each of the options which will undoubtedly offset decisions of choice between the alternatives open. Investment abroad may be more profitable than at home but control over investments at home may be more certain. Oil, when in the ground, is guaranteed its safety, but its price may vary suddenly if substitutes are found or the world market conditions alter.

Implicit in this model is an objective function that would embody the maximisation of long-term returns from the country's total resources of oil, foreign assets and domestic investments. The realisation of this objective is expressed in terms of the optimisation conditions outlined earlier. A more rigorous development of this model is possible and, while it should ideally embody political and other constraints, a simplified diagramatic analysis of major aspects relating to it is carried out in the annex to this chapter. In its conceptual form it is considered to be most useful at its present state of refinement as a means of approaching the allocative problems facing Kuwait, as well as a vehicle to guide investigations. Much greater information on the constraints and on the objective function would be necessary, together with more detailed data, before any conclusions could be drawn from a refined analysis.

It is against this background that Kuwait's industrialisation strategy is viewed. With the limited resources of oil and the specialisation of indigenous skills which have been forced upon the country by its history and geographical position, Kuwait has to carve for herself a future which is secure and that future must extend beyond the oil period. Furthermore, it should be the type of future that Kuwaitis desire.

The rest of this chapter is devoted to two parts of the conceptual model, the oil industry and industrial development. Foreign investment is dealt with in Chapter 11 while Chapter 10 deals with local banking and finance covering the essential link, or the operational infrastructure, by which the financial resources, which both enable and stimulate the allocative process, are handled.

INDUSTRIAL INFRASTRUCTURE

One of the first concerns of the Kuwaiti government after independence in 1961 was with the creation of an infrastructure which would facilitate industrial development and in 1964 the Shuaiba Industrial Area was established. In 1970 this was put under the control of the Shuaiba Area Authority which was responsible to the then Ministry of Finance and Oil[4] which provided its financing. The main purpose of the Area has been to provide basic infrastructure so that those industries which would be attracted by the availability of cheap power, natural gas or oil may be given every encouragement. The Area is about 50 km south of the city on the coast.[5] It has a small port and oil pier as well as good communications with the city and the sources of oil and natural gas. The types of industries which would find the cheap facilities attractive are almost wholly large and medium-scale and the Area provides for them. The Authority has very extensive powers in choice of industry and their control over industrial operations. It also provides cheap services, e.g. fresh water, 250 fils ($0·85) per thousand gallons; electricity, 1 fils (less than ½ cent) per kW; natural gas, 14 fils (5 cents) per thousand cu. ft; land, 50 fils (17 cents) per annum per sq. metre.

To date the industries located here include power and water desalination, the KNPC oil refinery, petrochemicals, fertilisers, cement, drilling mud, plastics, sulphur and oxygen. A liquid natural gas plant producing for export will shortly be commissioned.

By the nature of the cheap provisions, and indeed in accordance with the original intention of the Area's establishment, the industries are rather specialised but form a very useful function of utilising so much of the hitherto unused by-products from petroleum production. In this way some diversification at least is taking place and of course there is an addition to total value added. The industries located in Area may be seen not so much as examples of industrialisation itself but as basic prerequisites for the industrialisation process. They provide so much of what would be necessary in the event of manufacturing industries wishing to establish in Kuwait, besides providing a diversification of

Kuwait's exports and increasing the value added in the latter from the Kuwait point of view. This is again only the start of the process. For example, to manufacture plastics is an advance on exporting the feedstock, but to transform the plastics into finished products would be the next stage which is now facilitated by the establishment of the plastics plant.

The Shuwaikh Industrial Area, by contrast with the Shuaiba Area, is on the edge of the city and is administered by the municipality in conjunction with the Department of Industrial Affairs of the Ministry of Commerce and Industry. The provision of utilities (water, sewerage, roads, etc.) is the responsibility of the municipality. The Area, like Shuaiba has tended to become dominated by large-scale activity rather than the medium-scale such as one would expect to find in an area similar to the trading estates on the edge of a large town in other economies. Kuwait Metal Pipes, Kuwait Prefabricated Buildings, Kuwait Flour Mills, Kuwait Transport, Kuwait Shipping Company and the United Fisheries of Kuwait all have factories or appropriate establishments there; later entrants, mostly of a smaller expanding scale, have not therefore had sufficient room for establishment. Consequently, the municipality designated a further site for industrial development on the edge of the city in 1973 and allocations to the area are now being made.

THE OIL INDUSTRY

Although the infrastructural developments may be addressed mainly to non-oil activities, the oil industry occupies such importance in the economy, and other industrial activities depend upon it to such a degree, that it will be discussed in the paragraphs that follow before discussion of other industries ensues.

The role of oil in the economy as a store of national wealth has already been stressed. Consequently, it would be a fundamental error in the analysis of the industrial structure of Kuwait to treat oil production as a sub-sector of the industrial sector. It is realised that, under the existing systems of national accounting in general use, it is difficult to make a distinction between other industrial activities, but reserves in any country of a given quantity of oil or so much natural gas are really part of that country's balance sheet. When the national income and expenditure figures for that country are prepared these are the equivalent of the 'profit and loss' account of a firm in private industry and the reduction in the nation's assets should be shown as depreciation in the same way as a firm would enter depreciation of its capital against its gross profit. In this way, only the net value added would be the contribution to the nation's 'profit and loss' account and the national balance sheet would give a true reflection of the national productive capacity each year.

In the description earlier of a simple optimising model where physical, monetary and oil assets were deployed in order to maximise their social value in the contribution they make to national wealth, it is the balance sheet that would describe these assets, in their quantity and form at any point in time, while the national income and expenditure accounts would show how the use of these assets over the accounting period has resulted in the flow of goods and services. Ideally, such data should also show how these flows have altered the state of the national assets and just as any business accounting period opens and closes with a balance sheet, so ought the national 'profit and loss' over the year to be reflected in the changes in the structure of the balance sheet.

The neglect of resource depletion in the generally accepted forms of national accounting is not merely an important omission from the point of view of the oil-producing country wishing to use its national accounts as part of its information flow. It also gives a serious distortion to the figures on national income when compared with those, for example, of the industrial countries. In the latter, the sale of a physical asset, such as a building or a factory, to a foreign owner would appear in the capital accounts and the use of such assets would be offset in the accounts by depreciation before figures on the national product are calculated. For a resource-based economy, however, the value of the natural resources would appear as part of the flow which would make up the national product for the year. Such a distortion gives a totally false view of the comparative incomes of oil-producing countries and some adjustment in methods of national accounting is urgently required, both from the point of view of the producing countries involved who are deciding on an extraction and development policy, and the world at large where misleading comparisons are at present being made.[6]

If national accounts are to be the basic data on which allocative policy decisions are made, then some form of accounting as we advocate is vitally necessary to facilitate decision-making according to the conceptual model described.

The proven oil reserves of Kuwait are vast by any standards, comprising about one-eighth of the free world's proven total. The

Greater Burgan field alone holds reserves estimated to equal the total reserves of the United States. Changes in both the world situation and those of Kuwait give a constantly changing picture of Kuwait's relative position, but the changes never alter the basic fact of her importance.

The relationship between output and reserves is of crucial importance for the formulation of a development strategy, and the IBRD report mentioned in Table 9.1 made various forecasts of this relationship based upon a series of assumptions concerning the growth in output and the level of new discoveries. The report was viewed with alarm in many quarters since, on the assumption that reserves remained constant, the growth in production of a constant 6 per cent per annum would imply exhaustion of Kuwait's total reserves by 1998 and as that was the rate at which output had been increasing in the period immediately preceding 1971, it was not an unreasonable assumption given Kuwait's lack of control of its own resources. If output had increased by 8 per cent per annum, then depletion would have been complete by 1994. Other forecasts based on percentage increases in new discoveries gave a somewhat more optimistic picture, but the report gave impetus to the need for Kuwait not only to be able to maximise its income from the production of oil, but also to be able to control its extraction so that its flow could be harmonised with the needs of its development. Pressure was brought to bear upon the oil companies and the annual lift of oil was reduced as from 1973. Meanwhile, the revenue take from oil underwent a number of increases as shown in Chapter 6, and, with the assumption of complete control of the KOC in 1976 the increase in take was completed and a nationally determined extraction policy could be formulated. Up to its suspension in 1976, the National Assembly had been loud in its demand for a reduction in output to 1·5

TABLE 9.1   Annual production and reserves

	1946	1950	1953	1960	1965	1970	1977
			(millions of US Barrels)				
Reserves	4000	11,000	30,000	65,000	68,700	80,000	80,000
Annual production as % of reserves	0·15	1·14	1·34	0·95	1·25	1·36	0·9

SOURCE: IBRD, *Report on Production and Manufacturing in Kuwait*, 1974
          Kuwait Oil Company *Annual Reports*

million barrels per day but 'the production ceiling in Kuwait is 2.0 million barrels per day as an annual average'.[7] While there is no doubt that this level will vary as policy unfolds, it is a significant statement of intent on conservation policy.

The production of oil in Kuwait is undertaken by three companies, the Arabian Oil Company (a Japanese Company with offshore concessions), Al Wafra Oil Co. (formerly Aminoil operating in the Neutral Zone and in which Kuwait has a part interest together with Saudi Arabia) and KOC (the Kuwait Oil Company) which is by far the greatest of the three. Table 9.2 shows the output levels for selected years of each and the total national output. It is obvious that production is 'on target' if the industry is working within the limits stated by the Minister of Oil.

Of further interest, too, is the quantity and proportion of output which is utilised locally as refinery feedstock for subsequent local consumption or export. Table 9.3 shows how the refined exports have been maintained in spite of the drop in extraction. Thus the proportion of value added to output has been rising and the fall in world demand has been absorbed by the fall in crude oil exports where value added is minimal. This may have important consequences for the world oil industry elsewhere, for if refined exports from Kuwait and other OPEC

TABLE 9.2   Kuwait oil production (Thousand barrels)

	Kuwait Oil Co.	Aminoil*	Arabian Oil Co.	Total
1946–53	1,077,291	–	–	1,077,291
1954–60	3,170,249	89,119	–	3,259,368
1961	600,226	29,284	3,551	633,061
1965	791,903	36,515	32,846	861,264
1970	998,110	29,860	62,636	1,090,606
1971	1,067,795	33,269	65,296	1,166,360
1972	1,097,719	28,890	74,987	1,201,596
1973	1,004,781	25,772	71,912	1,102,465
1974	830,580	30,033	68,729	929,342
1975	670,918	30,356	59,455	760,729
1976	699,900	29,700	55,400	785,000
1977	650,500	33,000	34,500	718,000

SOURCES: *Kuwait Annual Statistical Abstract*, 1976 and 1977
Central Bank of Kuwait, *Quarterly Statistical Bulletin*, July–December 1977
*From 1977, renamed Al Wafra Oil Co.

TABLE 9.3   Crude oil production and export of refined products
(Million barrels or equivalent)

	Production	Crude oil exports	Exports of refined products	Refined exports as % of production
1970	1090·6	941·7	154·6	14·2
1971	1116·4	1008·9	155·0	13·9
1972	1201·6	1070·6	146·5	12·2
1973	1102·5	966·0	148·9	13·5
1974	929·4	804·8	132·7	14·3
1975	760·7	652·5	106·8	14·0
1976	785·0	655·4	147·1	18·7
1977	718·0	572·3	134·6	18·7

countries are to go on increasing while conservation reduces crude oil output, then the supply of crude to the non-oil producers' refineries from current sources will be reduced both by the conservation measures and the demand of the new refining capacity of the producer countries. Low cost producers like Kuwait will have a steadily increasing advantage if they are able to increase their own income by refining, but at the same time force up costs of their rivals in the non-producing but refining countries who will be forced to look elsewhere for their refining feedstock.

The nationalisation of the oil industry in 1976, although conducted in a gradual manner which had commenced a few years previously, has naturally required fundamental changes in its attitude and role, much more so, in fact, than in its actual structure. An early move after nationalisation was to establish the Kuwait Oil, Gas and Energy Corporation (KOGEC) but this was dissolved when the Ministry of Finance and Oil was divided into two. In many ways the new Ministry of Oil was to undertake the functions that were originally assigned to KOGEC, but it set about nationalising the relationships between the various companies involved in oil activities rather than completely re-orientating them to conform with the structure of the proposed Corporation. Significantly, the Kuwait National Petroleum Company emerged as the main government instrument, with divisions for petro-chemicals, marketing and transportation control. The KOC, for long the most important company while crude oil output was the source of the country's wealth, was superceded in importance as the government sought to increase the country's wealth through the value added by oil related downstream activities.

The output of oil and its importance in the national budget has been touched on in Chapter 4 and elsewhere, but the changes in oil output in recent years have been swamped in their effect on the national income by the contemporaneous changes in prices as discussed in Chapter 5. The marketing agreements with the former concessionary companies provided that Gulf would lift 500,000 barrels per day on average, and BP 450,000 as against their total lift of 1·3 million barrels immediately prior to takeover. The minimum agreed lift was 800,000 barrels daily. (KOC had lifted 1·83 million daily in 1975 and 2·27 million in 1974.) With other contracts (Shell 310,000 b/d and a number of smaller contracts), and refining requirements (500,000 b/d), Kuwait commenced the independent control of its resources with agreements to cover an amount approaching the 'ceiling' of 2 million b/d quoted by the Minister for Oil. If the aim on takeover was one of conservation, the age of the known reserves at this rate is well in excess of eighty years, a comfortable prospect for a state the size of Kuwait and, with an income per capita at that level of extraction, at least as conventionally measured, among the highest in the world.

Conservation is a means to an end, like any other policy, and the Government also has the stated aim of diversification in the sources of national income while, at the same time, increasing the relative contribution of the non-oil sectors of the economy. However, the greatest scope for this so far has been within the oil industry rather than outside it and, while this may widen the spectrum of opportunities available to Kuwaitis, it does nothing to lessen the country's reliance on oil and to provide a wider base for the economy.

It may be mentioned, too, that diversification both within and outside the oil industry will lessen the country's reliance on the international market and at the same time increase the proportion of value added accruing to Kuwait. This would undoubtedly lessen problems created by fluctuation in the terms of trade and increase the self-reliance of the country. Additionally, with the increase in the proportion of value added, Kuwait moves nearer to the consumer in the production process and, with her interest in promoting development among the less developed countries, her entry into the production process, perhaps eventually in direct contact with consuming countries, is almost a prerequisite to the development of new sets of marketing relationships which will lessen the dependence of the LDC's on the established industrial economies.

THE INDUSTRIAL SECTOR

An overview of the national statistics of output and employment gives a useful description of the current state of Kuwait industrialisation, and an illustration of some of the problems mentioned earlier.

MANUFACTURING

From Table 9.4 it can be seen that the manufacturing activities in Kuwait comprise a small proportion of the total number of establishments. Furthermore, many of those manufacturing establishments operate on a small scale, with about 75 per cent employing less than five people. This may seem a little surprising in view of the foregoing description, but it is entirely in keeping with a developing country where there is a great deal of industrial initiative which finds expression in what is sometimes known as the 'informal sector'. This sector is closely linked to the services and wholesale and retail sectors and consists of establishments which provide repair facilities, the manufacture of small items from a mixture of resources which may be available and so on. A high proportion of that 75 per cent will be found in the informal sector which has an essential function to perform in development as it offers an instant response to market demand which could not be met by central planning, allows the expression of individual inititative and is part of an essential process for the sifting of the population in order to produce the entrepreneurs necessary for the future.

The employment levels in the second half of the table show the way in which the small-scale activities give a much smaller fraction of total employment even though they dominate the number of establishments. In manufacturing they provide 25 per cent of employment while the twenty-six establishments which form less than 10 per cent of the total provide over 32 per cent of manufacturing employment. If we examine Table 9.5, value added for the years 1971–4, we may also gain further insight into the structure of manufacturing in the country. The first impression is of the major dominance of oil, which in 1974 accounted for about 93 per cent of the total value added in the economy. The price increases gave oil a tremendous boost between 1973 and 1974, when oil income went up from just under KD1000 million to over KD3000 million. Yet, interestingly enough, the proportion of value added attributable to oil hardly changed over the two years. An examination

TABLE 9.4 Operating establishments by size and economic activity, 1973

Employment Groups	Total	Services	Financial, insurance and real estate	Transport, storage and communications	Wholesale and retail trade	Electricity, gas and water	Construction	Manufacturing	Mining and quarrying	Agriculture, hunting and fishing
Number of Establishments										
0	432	29	3	3	337	1	24	33	1	1
1–4	17,895	3559	369	134	10,925	15	198	2309	5	381
5–9	2115	322	145	78	971	1	77	431	6	84
10–14 / 15–19	722	130	46	39	276	–	30	164	3	34
20–49	321	65	17	13	97	–	30	95	2	2
50–99	102	17	7	9	26	1	14	26	–	2
100–199	62	15	3	4	3	1	16	16	2	2
200–499	35	3	6	2	3	–	10	8	3	–
500+	11	–	–	2	–	–	3	2	2	2
Total	21,695	4140	596	284	12,638	19	402	3084	24	508
Number of Employees										
1–4	34,341	6806	831	325	19,488	20	423	5665	15	768
5–9	13,078	1978	958	487	5979	7	496	2614	42	517
10–14 / 15–19	9436	1695	585	500	3540	–	429	2193	49	445
20–49	9642	1926	519	380	2944	–	969	2766	63	75
50–99	6848	1159	476	534	1715	91	990	1757	–	126
100–199	8606	1907	401	585	429	111	2223	2325	304	321
200–499	11,296	1015	1521	708	895	–	3195	2827	1135	–
500+	11,432	–	–	2734	–	–	2880	1943	2431	1444
Total	104,679	16,486	5291	6253	34,990	229	11,605	22,090	4039	3696

SOURCE: *Kuwait Annual Abstract of Statistics*, 1977

TABLE 9.5   Value added by major groups of industrial activity (Thousand KD)

	1971	*1972*	*1973*	*1974*
Fishing	17,088	1320	1135	1638
Crude petroleum and gas	856,381	922,275	999,263	3,024,807
Quarrying	1204	1091	3000	2900
Food and beverages	6366	7340	9279	5949
Textiles, clothing and footwear	4045	5470	8227	7392
Woodwork and furniture	5806	2986	5277	5421
Paper and printing	1555	2455	2273	2078
Chemicals	4203	7969	14,358	37,282
Petroleum refining	83,891	30,131	27,963	95,763
Rubber, plastics and glass products	46	5230	7009	8723
Iron and steel products	606	912	1170	1983
Fabricated metals	1974	2088	6130	6073
Machinery and electrical	1579	1671	2181	3237
Other	682	826	1036	1780
Totals	989,905	994,793	1,088,299	3,207,025

of the table shows that many other industries also increased their outputs, notably industrial chemicals and petroleum refining, where the increase in value added likewise more than tripled. This is in keeping with the country's emphasis on diversification within the oil industry to improve the retained value added from oil, but the table shows little sign of diversification into the non-oil sectors to establish an alternative economic base.

The imbalance in the industrial structure is obvious and, even in the absence of oil, this would have been true. Furthermore given the size and geographical location of Kuwait, it is probable that some imbalance will always remain. A detailed examination of the data, however, from which these tables were drawn indicates vividly the very few linkages which exist between industrial activities in the country and it is undoubtedly possible that many other activities are capable of development around those which have already commenced.

However, these figures terminate in 1974 and any observer of the Kuwait scene will have noted the rapid developments since that date. The new airport is nearing completion, extensions to the port have greatly relieved congestion and there is no doubt that infrastructural provisions generally are occupying the government's attention at present in order to establish more fertile ground for industry in the future.

NATURAL GAS PRODUCTION

One of the earliest diversification activities has been the utilisation of natural gas. This commenced as the common-sense use of a valuable input which was formerly going to waste. Its use in production of electricity and water has long been practised in Kuwait. Water is supplied to residents at a price little above the cost of transport and electricity too is provided at low cost. These services are provided to industry at a very low price to encourage industrial development, as mentioned in the discussion on industrial areas.

The production of natural gas is directly dependent upon the output of oil, since almost all that is used is 'associated gas' and is not found independently. Consequently, fluctuations in oil production in Kuwait imply fluctuation in gas supply also. As for utilisation, Kuwait has one of the highest levels of utilisation to output ratios in the Middle East. Table 9.6 illustrates total production and, although oil and the world energy problem may have dominated discussion over recent years, the development and use of her gas production for purposes of social and industrial improvements is one of the most striking of all Kuwait's achievements. The projects and plans for improvement and diversification of gas utilisation are vast, with some KD1 billion committed to this area of development. One of the greatest developments is an LPG plant, to produce for industrial use and export, which when fully used, would require the level of oil production to reach 3 million barrels per day.

By mid 1977 over 68 per cent of the natural gas produced with the petroleum was being utilised as fuel or feedstock or was being reinjected into the wells. Current plans well in hand should soon ensure that this resource is completely utilised mainly for liquified petroleum gas export or as petrochemical feedstock.

The possibility of maximum utilisation of gas and consequent competing demands raises the important problem of costing. As long as gas which is used would otherwise go to waste, the only costs attributable to its use are the costs of preparation and transport. As soon as there are alternative uses which are deprived of satisfaction because of the use of gas elsewhere, however, the cost incurred should be measured by the value of the alternatives foregone. Thus, if at full

TABLE 9.6   Natural gas production and utilisation

	1970	1971	1972	1973	1974	1975	1976	1977
1. Natural gas production*	570·4	643·7	647·8	581·1	466·9	382·4	395·8	373·0
2. Natural gas utilisation	188·0	227·5	246·8	265·1	251·4	266·0	243·8	246·0
2 as % of 1	33·0	35·3	38·1	45·6	53·8	59·1	61·6	65·9

*in billions of cubic feet

TABLE 9.7   Allocation of natural gas by user (Million cu. ft)

	1967	1970	1973	1976
Public utilities	23·082	52·707	85·098	107·537
% of total	(19·0)	(28·0)	(32·1)	(44·1)
Injection in oil wells	27·043	45·342	79·043	46·655
% of total	(22·2)	(24·1)	(29·8)	(19·1)
By oil companies	71·410	89·999	100·947	89·562
Total	121·535	188·048	265·088	243·754

utilisation the government continues to provide cheap power based upon petroleum gas and is unable to meet the demand for gas for say petrochemicals, then the cost to Kuwait would be the opportunity to produce the amount of petrochemicals which it has foregone, after allowing for differences in the associated costs of production. The difference between this opportunity cost and the price charged is in reality a further subsidy, even though no money actually passes. Furthermore, this type of subsidy distorts the market forces and may prevent Kuwait developing in those areas where possibly other factors of production might enjoy a natural advantage.

In addition, there is always the need for explicit planning. Without a conceptual framework such as that advocated, both policy-makers and those who implement the policies have no means of either setting a correct price for gas or judging whether existing prices should be altered. The adherence of Kuwait to a free enterprise economy makes such an exercise more rather than less imperative because the artificial prices set for commodities such as gas and water act as the attractions for other industries; yet if that pricing system is not integrated into an overall mechanism of industrial planning, development may well take a different direction from the one intended. That is why, when discussing the planning process in the last chapter, it was suggested that one of the roles to which planning should address itself should be the pricing of the services of public utilities.

TABLE 9.8   Production of electricity and potable water

	1970	1972	1974	1976
Potable water (mn gallons)	6635	8584	10,031	14,385
Electricity (mn kWh)	2213	3295	4092	5202

Power is used to a large measure for domestic purposes as well as by industry and Table 9.7 shows the comparative allocation of utilised gas in selected years.

While injection and use by oil companies fluctuates with oil production, the use by public utilities shows a constant upward trend, due in part at least to the increase in population and urban provision. Planning decisions need, therefore, to take this extra dimension into consideration and forecasts of sustained and rapid population growth, if fulfilled, may make future conservation policy difficult to apply according to purely economic criteria. The production and use of both electricity and potable water, which rely crucially on oil production for gas or oil itself as a fuel, are shown in Table 9.8.

PETROCHEMICAL INDUSTRIES

The government, in keeping with its policy of controlling the development of the country's main resource and maximising the value added in its transportation which accrued to Kuwait, bought complete control of the Petrochemical Industries Company (PIC) in 1976. Apart from natural gas exploitation, Kuwait's earlier petrochemical developments centered on fertilisers and were formerly controlled by the Kuwait Chemical Fertilizer Company, now part of PIC.

The general increase in the figures given in Table 9.9 is self-evident, but the increased use at home and the development of exports are both important indicators of Kuwait's potential in this field. Between 1971

TABLE 9.9   Production for selected years of fertilisers and chemical products (metric tons)

		1968	*1970*	*1972*	*1974*	*1976*
Sulphuric acid	Production	57,194	57,821	79,000	98,000	4,825
	Export	69	4305	3300	7000	3355
Ammonium hydroxide	Production	75,161	119,608	386,999	508,000	513,776
	Export	55	260	37,396	139,000	180,138
Ammonium sulphate	Production	73,593	71,198	92,179	126,286	–
	Export	87,268	64,187	80,701	102,597	4724
Urea	Production	85,364	162,294	514,249	516,590	530,591
	Export	82,537	159,474	482,537	553,232	524,643

SOURCE: *Kuwait Annual Statistical Abstract*, 1977

and 1975 the value of chemical exports alone increased over ten-fold from KD6·50 million to KD65·90 million.

As for future developments, current indications and investment projects in hand suggest that the production of ethylene and certain of the aromatics essential for the production of plastics will figure highly. The long-term trend is likely to be toward the production of plastics and perhaps their subsequent manufacture into finished products. The tendency appears to be, however, for Kuwait to 'move downstream' in an orderly fashion, developing expertise in each level before it proceeds to the next. There is no doubt that the scope for downstream development in oil is vast and the scope for both employment creation and profit increases in the downstream direction. There are, however, further areas within the oil industry where diversification is possible but which do not imply processing. A notable example in Kuwait is oil and oil products transportation, but since shipping and maritime transport is so important as a growing sector in Kuwait's industrial development, this will be dealt with separately.

OTHER MANUFACTURING INDUSTRIES

Other manufacturing industries are few in Kuwait, as may be noted from Tables 9.4 and 9.5, although the government is committed to expansion and diversification into non-oil industries. The Kuwait Flour Mills Company, established in 1962, has doubled its output of flour to 108,000 tons since 1967. While primarily for home consumption, export of all commodities is undertaken on a limited scale.

As well as the fertiliser industry mentioned previously, production of salt and chlorine-based chemicals has been developed as by-products of de-salination, 6000 tons of caustic soda and 5000 tons of chlorine being produced during 1973. Cement production has been developed to meet the needs of the building industry and for export; between 1972 and 1976 annual production increased from 97,590 tons to 351,000 tons. Plans are in hand to increase capacity to around a million tons per annum. However the relative smallness of the figures in so many industries indicates their share in output rather than importance. Many are young and capable of development and given the market stimulus this will no doubt be forthcoming.

BUILDING AND CONSTRUCTION

Building and construction is the other industry which spans the oil and non-oil sector. Intimately related with infrastructural development, it is one of the keys to the overall development of the country at large. One of the major problems with large-scale development requiring initial, rapid construction activity is that the labour required is far in excess of that subsequently needed when the plant or establishment is in operation and a completely different set of skills is usually involved. In a mature economy construction is usually the most fluctuating activity due to the gearing between general economic activity and investment, but, with a 'rolling' construction programme, such economies absorb the fluctuations reluctantly as part of economic life. In economies such as Kuwait, however, the development is proceeding at such a rapid rate that it cannot be sustained by construction forces derived from within the country and a substantial part of the construction activity is serviced from outside, both for the provision of expertise and labour. As far as expertise is concerned this is an accepted part of the development process and increasingly contracts are being undertaken by locally-based firms. As for labour, however, this presents an entirely different problem. The importation of masses of unskilled labour places a heavy strain on local infrastructure and services which is 'external' to the contract made between the client and contractor. The unskilled labour especially is itinerant, usually from neighbouring Gulf countries. With the acute population problem and the necessity for Kuwait to adopt some form of population policy, increasing concern has been expressed at the continued influx and changes in policy have been reflected in changes in contract structures. Contractors may be required to provide adequate accommodation for the work force and to adhere to a policy of 'local labour first' in their recruitment. Alternatively, some may bring the whole labour force with them and guarantee its removal on completion. Prefabrication is another innovation which reduces labour demand on site and many parts for local constructions are prefabricated in existing Kuwaiti factories.

In spite of these reservations, however, Kuwait still places the major emphasis of its current Five Year Plan on housing for, with the pressure on living space and the planned increase in population of some 6·5 per cent per annum, the housing problem will remain acute for a long time to come. Total investment under the Plan is KD4·441 billion, of which over 30 per cent is to be allocated to housing. The current lack of housing, at all income levels, is one of the major bottlenecks in the economy, and the increase in supply relative to demand would give a much needed increase to the absorptive capacity of the economy and also help to correct the market distortions occasioned by the inordinately high rents.

SHIPPING

Kuwait's maritime background has influenced its attitude toward shipping and sea transport as a possible area for diversification of her economic activity and, even though oil transport may be classified as oil-related diversification, the diversification of her activity into general cargo transport is equally important. Indeed, its long-term implications may be more significant since, given the development of new markets in the Indian Ocean and South-East Asian developing countries and Kuwait's active interest in their industrial development and in financial cooperation with them, sea transport would undoubtedly be an expanding area, while oil transport may be rather stultified by conservation, pipe-line developments and off-shore oil developments nearer the points of use.

Dealing with oil transport first, the Kuwait Oil Tanker Company is one of the oldest public shareholding companies in Kuwait, having been established in 1957. It is a 'joint sector' company, with government participation of 49 per cent, which was achieved by doubling its capital to allow government participation in 1976. In the same year it agreed to charter five of its six tankers, with a total capacity of 300,000 tons, to Gulf and BP for five years. At that time, three further tankers were reported to be on order with a projected total of eleven ships and a capacity of 2·1 million tons. Owing to the fall off in tanker demand in recent years, any plans for expansion have been shelved, but at least the agreement on the full take-over of oil by the state from the two concessionaries (Gulf and BP) contained a clause ensuring that Kuwait ships would be used for the transport of Kuwait oil. This, coupled with the charter agreement, at least secures the base of the tanker carrying industry in Kuwait at the present time, although of course the future of the world's tanker fleets are very precarious.

As well as oil transport, Kuwait has recently moved into the transport of liquified gas and refined products. The Kuwait National Petroleum Company recently made arrangements for the leasing of tankers for this purpose from the K.O.T.C. and deliveries have commenced from orders for a number of LPG tankers placed prior to reorganisation. The state-owned company has expressed the intention of handling some 60 per cent of future exports of natural gas and, while initial indications were that the additions to the fleet might consist of charters or purchase of second-hand ships available at low prices due to the depression in shipping, this may be a long-term aim. This is another area of downstream activity in which Kuwait is qualified by experience to exploit. It is one of the vital links in a chain, too, of an alternative strand of development strategy for, if Kuwait decides to increase its investments in developing countries in petrochemical industries, the supply of feedstock and transport in her own ships would make good business sense. Kuwait is proceeding slowly in these shipping developments, therefore, and is more likely to respond to the market than to make any major moves on assumptions of future trends.

Lastly, Kuwait's involvement in general shipping is a form of non-oil related diversification of her economic base which is of extreme importance. The Kuwait Shipping Company was established in 1965, and on 31 December 1976 it was 77 per cent government-owned, with a nominal capital of KD 21 million. The build-up in the fleet has been rapid in recent years. Four ships were reported to have been ordered in June 1974 to bring the fleet to thirty-two ships and in November of the same year orders were reported to have been placed for a further ten. By the beginning of 1976, the fleet existing or on order consisted of forty-seven ships with a carrying capacity of around one million dead weight tons. This, together with the modernity of most of its fleet, put it in the top flight of general cargo carriers. In 1976, however, plans were made to transfer the whole of the fleet to the United Arab Shipping Company, a new group to be based on the KSC, but with participation by five other Gulf States — Qatar, Bahrain, Saudi Arabia, Iraq and the UAE. The new capital value was KD 500 million and the other partners 'bought in' on a cash basis, only Iraq providing ships. With the planned expansion, the new line could become the major dry cargo line in the world, with over two million tons dead weight capacity. This intriguing development is indicative of how the growth of Kuwait's leadership in shipping activities of the Arab world was transformed into cooperation leading to substantial Arab influence in general world shipping. It is a model of what might well be achieved in other spheres among the Arab states.

Throughout this chapter, while attempting to provide an overview of general industrial activity, an effort has been made to use descriptions to illustrate the theme which has been developing throughout this work so far. That is, the need for a different approach to the allocation of resources in a country not bound by capital shortage to that which is adopted in other types of economies. Thus the internal economy, and especially domestic industrial development, needs to be seen as part of a wider national economy which includes foreign investments and natural resources yet to be utilised. Oil and home industry has been examined in this chapter. The Kuwait financial system, which not only plays a vital part in home development but is that link by which home and overseas activities may be viewed as a single unit under the approach already outlined, will be considered in following chapters.

Annex to Chapter 9

We have discussed in this chapter a conceptual model for Kuwait whereby the government would be deploying its resources in such a way that its growth and income levels are maximised and maintained through and beyond the period when the oil resources are depleted. In theoretical terms this is accomplished by ensuring that the marginal returns from each of the three alternative forms of holding the country's assets (oil reserves, domestic capital and foreign investments) are equalised. These are ideal conditions, and in practice, matters such as the domestic absorptive capacity, instability of exchange rates and other constraints need to be considered. In view of this, much government expenditure is devoted to the alleviation of the first of these constraints. Given the current source of government income this implies the use of other assets (oil revenues or financial assets) for this purpose, thereby reducing income from these sources for the future. There must be a level therefore at which the development of the three forms of assets would result in an optimum growth path being followed by the economy which would correspond with the theoretical condition which has been outlined.

This analysis is designed to examine some current aspects of government policy and in particular to explore the conditions necessary for them to be consistent with the objective of optimum growth. The analysis may be simplified by making the following assumptions:

1. Constant prices are assumed throughout the analysis.
2. The country's national foreign exchange reserves are assumed to include all government and private sector holdings of foreign assets and are entirely deployed for the purpose of generating the income necessary to replace oil receipts.
3. A positive real yield on foreign assets, i.e. the rate of return exceeds the rate of inflation.
4. The net foreign exchange requirements are determined by the difference between the sum of imports for consumption and investment purposes together with remittances minus non-oil exports.

The problem this analysis will try to resolve may be stated as determining the level at which earnings of foreign exchange can be utilised while at the same time permitting an accumulation of foreign assets in the face of a depleting oil resource so that the income flow from foreign earnings can be maintained at a level consistent with the optimum growth condition.

The following diagram illustrates the build-up of income on foreign assets over time in the face of constant or falling foreign revenues from oil and their relationship with alternative levels of foreign exchange requirements.

Figure 1 to Annexe to Chapter 9

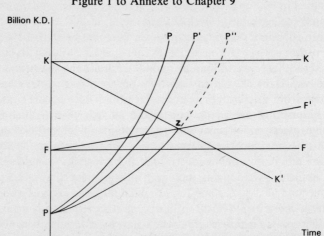

In the diagram KK represents the annual oil revenues in constant terms while FF is the annual net foreign exchange requirements referred to earlier. The third line PP is the real income generated from the national reserves at each point in time. It is immediately apparent that as long as FF lies below KK, the reserves grow not only by a compound rate annually, but also are supplemented by the difference between KK and FF each year. Under these circumstances there is clearly no problem since income from foreign assets will never be needed to cover the country's foreign exchange requirements and thus GNP would be ever-increasing.

A more realistic situation, however, would assume falling oil revenues denoted by KK'. This would result in a diminishing addition to foreign assets from the oil source for the period when KK' is above FF. This diminution causes a flattening of PP to PP'. However, as long as the rate of reduction in KK' is less than the rate of increase in PP', the level of GNP will go on increasing in real terms at a steadily rising rate but that rate would be below the one in the previous case. On the other hand, if KK′ falls at a rate faster than the rate of increase of PP′, the prospects for future GNP would depend on whether the two curves would intersect above or below the FF line. As long as the intersection point is above the FF line foreign exchange earnings are in a position to supplant oil revenues and at the same time to allow a net surplus to augment foreign assets, hence GNP would continue to grow. If the point of intersection is below the FF line, the level of GNP could not be sustained in the long-run without structural alterations in the domestic economy to reduce the level of FF.

Both PP and PP′ were drawn under the assumption of constant FF, but variations in FF would clearly cause variations in both curves. If FF were to be upward sloping as in FF′, under the conditions of KK′ there would be a further flattening of the curve corresponding to income from foreign investment as in PP″. All three curves as drawn now intersect at one point. This would indicate that the income from foreign assets is sufficient just to supplant oil revenues. Thus there would be no surplus over and above requirements, i.e. no further accumulation of foreign assets, but the country's foreign exchange requirements would always be satisfied. However, beyond the point of intersection (Z), the income from foreign assets would grow according to this analysis at a rate just sufficient to satisfy the net foreign exchange requirements. Therefore, ZP″ would not exist beyond that point and the remainder of that curve would now coincide with FF′. In this case, GNP would be rising beyond (Z) at a rate of growth equivalent to that of FF′ under our assumptions.

Using KK*, PP* and FF* to imply a given KK, PP and FF, the diagram gives an insight into some of the problems which face many of the oil-exporting states. If it is considered that the government aims at maintaining a balanced growth path for the economy, this would imply a steadily increasing level of consumption as a constant proportion of GNP. Thus, we could presume an upward sloping FF*. Also, given a restriction of home development during early years caused by the lack of absorptive capacity, this may be lifted by calling on foreign exchange for home investment in the same way. For any given oil extraction policy and oil price structure KK* is also determined. This would imply that the curve PP*, given the rates of return on foreign investments, is determined by FF*.

This being so, however, the intersections of both PP* and FF* curves with KK* are also determined by FF* and therefore a coincidence of their intersection at Z is a matter which may be decided by policies on foreign exchange utilisation and, if the three curves do not intersect at the same point, then these policies, or conservation policies, or both, are non-optimal.

If PP* crossed KK* above its intersection with FF*, then the accumulation of foreign reserves will go on increasing beyond this point at a rate greater than that required to replace the declining income generated by oil exports. GNP will be increasing, but non-optimally, as consumption will not grow commensurately. If the point of intersection of KK* and PP* is below that of KK* and FF* then the FF* line can only be maintained by drawing on foreign earnings at a rate greater than that which will permit their growth to be maintained at an optional rate. In fact, beyond th point of intersection of FF* with KK*, the PP* line alters its shape in such a way that it will never reach FF*, and might eventually turn down, i.e. if the PP* intersection with KK* is below the FF* intersection, GNP growth will eventually slacken and then decline.

The intersection of all three curves at one point, Z, however, is an optimal situation in that beyond that point the receipts from oil exports are no longer sufficient to maintain the requirements of FF* and these have to be supplemented from foreign investment earnings, but the intersection of PP* at Z also indicates that foreign investments have already reached that level where they are generating sufficient to take over from oil as the foreign exchange earner and to provide funds which regenerate themselves. In fact, beyond Z, PP* would coincide with FF* under conditions of optimal growth, for we must assume that the total foreign exchange income will be enough and only just enough to provide for FF*, otherwise growth will be non optimal. Further, the slope of PP* at any one time is dictated by levels of FF* and KK* in the past. Thus, current policies not only influence the point of intersection Z, but also the slope of PP* beyond it, which implies that current policies not only decide whether the intersection will be made at Z, but also will determine its slope and therefore the rate of growth which can be sustained in the long-run.

Here the dynamic aspects of the conceptual model that have been discussed in the main part of the chapter are being considered. At any point in time it may be tested whether the disposition of Kuwait's assets between oil, domestic investment and foreign assets is optimal in the static sense, in that the optimum distribution will yield the maximum return. The dynamic problem is concerned with how that yield is distributed between consumption, home investment and increasing foreign assets so that a maximum rate of sustainable growth is achieved.

To perform a simple test of some of the problems raised above current known figures were used to estimate whether the rate of growth in the earnings of government foreign investments might reasonably be expected to be sufficient to ensure the replacement of oil earnings before the time which would be signified by Z.

Working in constant prices, we took the current level of government foreign reserves at KD5 billion, and assumed a real rate of return of 2 per cent on foreign investments.[8] Assuming that under current policies of conservation the income from oil will remain constant for a fairly long period, the foreign investments will also grow according to the difference between current requirements (KD1·3 billion) and oil earnings (KD2·8 billion) at present the equivalent of KD1·5 billion annually.

Under these assumptions, the time required to generate enough funds to cover total oil earnings and to maintain the reserves at that constant level would be forty-six years. However this includes the KD1·5 billion addition to requirements which is added to the reserves annually. If the intention is merely to cover the current requirements of foreign earnings, then this would be accomplished in twenty-seven years. Given an anticipated life of Kuwait's oil reserves at upwards of eighty years, then either solution is 'feasible' in that the aims could be altered. Whether the policies are optimal however requires much more detailed analysis and more information than is available at present. In particular, in the absence of well-defined policies on many issues which should be reflected in a more detailed analysis, especially on population, it is impossible to do much more than has been done. Even from such a simple analysis, however, it can be seen that the rate at which the domestic economy grows relative to the accumulation of foreign reserves is an essential element in achieving optimality and this is a matter which should concern policy-makers now. Given the assumption of an eventually declining income from oil, then more and more of this investment needs to be in the non-oil sectors of the economy.

10 Local Banking and Finance

INTRODUCTION

The financial sector assumes an important role in Kuwait, particularly because of the openness of the economy and the absence of major restrictions on dealing in foreign exchange, outflow of remittances and movement of private capital. Thus, many of the international monetary fluctuations are transmitted to the local economy through the financial sector. In addition, the rising importance of the financial sector is reflected in the eight-fold increase in its contribution to GDP over the years 1970/1–1975/6. In spite of the rapid increase in oil exports, the proportional share of this sector increased from about 2 per cent in the early seventies to 5 per cent in more recent years.

Due to the lack of effective monetary tools, fiscal policy decisions, especially changes in government expenditure, tend to work themselves through the economy almost completely unabated by monetary policy. This, coupled with the extraordinary increase in net domestic government expenditure in recent years and the relative decline in the outflow of private capital, has caused growing concern about the role of the financial sector. The effects of recent monetary developments on inflation, speculation and the general attitude of the private sector is indeed alarming. Hence the role of the financial sector has become of greater consequence.

This chapter is intended to review the historical background of the monetary sector. Following this, the organisational structure of the broader financial sector, of which the monetary system forms a subset, will be discussed. Recent monetary developments in Kuwait, the financial conditions of its banking system and those of other financial institutions will also be discussed.

HISTORICAL BACKGROUND

Kuwait's monetary system did not become fully independent until the Currency Board was established and the Kuwaiti dinar was put into circulation on 1 April 1961, replacing the Indian rupee. Prior to that, the Indian rupee was the circulating medium throughout the Gulf area including Kuwait. The Kuwait government was able to obtain rupees to finance local expenditure by selling pounds sterling to the Reserve Bank of India and the Kuwaiti banks were able to convert their holdings of excess rupees into sterling through the same channel. However, as large amounts of rupees obtained by Kuwaiti merchants by selling gold in India were also being presented to the Reserve Bank of India to be converted into sterling, the Indian government became concerned about the effect of this on its foreign exchange reserves. Therefore the Indian rupee was replaced in May 1959 with a special 'Gulf' Indian rupee which, while fully convertible into sterling through the Reserve Bank of India, could not be obtained by selling gold in India.[1] This new policy partly succeeded in suppressing the gold trade and helped in putting an end to the drain on India's foreign exchange reserves during the years 1959–61.

At the time of independence in 1961 the Kuwait Government decided that, in order to have full control over the monetary sector and the country's increasing foreign exchange reserves, it should issue its own currency through a newly established Currency Board. Between the time the Kuwaiti dinar was put into circulation on the first of April and the end of the exchange period on 17 May 1961 a total of 341·9 million rupees (equivalent to $72·7 million) was exchanged and ultimately presented to the Reserve Bank of India for conversion. It was also agreed at that time that India would settle its corresponding sterling obligations to Kuwait over a period of eleven years.

The Currency Board continued to perform its primary function of issuing currency until 1968 when the Central Bank was established. In addition to the Currency Board, the financial system evolved during the period from 1961 to 1968 to include four commercial banks, three insurance companies, two investment companies and one specialised bank.[2] However the role of the monetary sector was limited and the size of the money supply was being largely determined by the fiscal authorities which would arrange through the Currency Board to convert into Kuwaiti dinars the equivalent amount of foreign currencies needed to meet government domestic expenditure. This expenditure was the primary source of funds to the local economy and was used to finance net imports of goods and services and accumulation of money. The remainder was transferred abroad both as remittances by expatriates and as foreign investments by Kuwaitis.[3] Lending by the banking system also helped increase the accumulation of money by the private sector; hence more funds were available for private transfers abroad.[4] Government foreign exchange deposits with the banking system were thus used to finance the foreign currency required for imports, remittances and private capital transfers.

THE ORGANISATION OF THE FINANCIAL SYSTEM

Kuwait's financial system has had a remarkable expansion record since 1970, both in terms of the number of institutions and size of its resources. This is due mainly to the private sector's entrepreneurial ability and traditional interest in the field of finance being greatly enhanced by the substantial wealth acquired through government policy. This included banning the operation of foreign banks on its soil and concentrating on 'developing large and powerful national financial institutions which will handle the placing and investment of its own enormous funds abroad, and will be able to stand by themselves as a major force in the international market'.[5] The government has largely achieved this objective by adopting a policy of using Kuwaiti banks and investment companies for a large part of its Euro-bond purchases and real estate investments in the Arab world. The result has been the emergence of the present financial system which is considered by far the largest and most developed in this region and which has the potential for Kuwait to evolve into one of the world's important financial centres.

Apart from the Central Bank, Kuwait's financial system now includes six commercial banks, three specialised banks, seventeen investment companies, several insurance companies,[6] and a number of exchange dealers and stock brokers and the recently formed Social Security Authority. The six commercial banks are the National Bank of Kuwait (established in 1952), Commercial Bank of Kuwait (1960), Gulf Bank (1960), Al-Ahli Bank (1967), Bank of Kuwait and the Middle East (1971)[7] and Burgan Bank (1975). The first four are fully owned by the private sector, while the last two are owned jointly with the government. The commercial banking system also consists of a network of approximately 100 branches with an average number of inhabitants per branch in the order of 11,000. Unlike the other Gulf states, where foreign banks are allowed to operate, the expansion of the banking system has come about through local initiatives. However, the law has been amended recently to admit banks which are at least 50 per cent owned by Kuwaiti financial institutions, and one has already commenced operations (Bank of Bahrain and Kuwait). In addition, major foreign banks are assisting in the management of a number of Kuwaiti banks. Also, some foreign banks have been allowed to hold sizable stakes in Kuwaiti investment companies and other financial institutions.[8]

The rapid expansion of Kuwait's banking system is clearly reflected in the growth of their consolidated assets which have more than tripled since 1971, reaching by the end of 1977 about KD2·6 billion (approximately $9:3 billion). Considering their individual assets, five of the six banks rank near the top of the list of the biggest banks in the Arab world, and the sixth, the Burgan Bank became operative in 1977. The capitalisation of the commercial banks has increased from KD36 million in 1971 to over KD 198 million (approximately $700 million) by the end of 1977. In addition, the Kuwaiti banks have participated in establishing banks in many Gulf states and other Arab countries, as well as in the setting-up of a London-based commercial bank and a number of joint-venture banks in major European cities.

Of the three specialised banks, the Credit and Saving Bank which is fully owned by the government is the oldest and has been predominantly engaged in extending soft term real estate and social loans. The second, the Real Estate Bank of Kuwait, is privately owned and its lending operations are directed mainly to the financing of large real estate projects. The third specialised bank, the Industrial Bank of Kuwait, is owned jointly by the government and the private sector and its purpose is to 'contribute to the development of the Kuwait economy and diversify its structure of production through the promotion of new industries and the support of established ones'.[9] To achieve its objectives, the Bank's activities cover a wide spectrum, including the identification of new investment opportunities in industry, providing financial assistance to industrial projects and extending technical advice to private enterprises and the promotion of a capital market in Kuwait. These three specialised banks have had varying effects on the financial and economic activities in Kuwait as will be discussed in greater detail later.

The rapid institutional development of Kuwait's financial sector is reflected mostly in the substantial increase in the number and resources of the investment companies-cum-merchant banks. Until mid-1973 there were only two investment companies, Kuwait Investment Company (established in 1961) and Kuwait Foreign Trading, Contracting and Investment Company (1964), respectively 50 per cent and 80 per cent government owned. Since 1973, a total of fifteen new investment companies have been established all with exclusive private ownership except one.[10] As indicated earlier, the government was instrumental in the growth of the Kuwaiti investment companies, particularly the first two, which have been used by the Ministry of Finance to invest in the Euro-bond market. However, the government's role in promoting the activities of the investment companies is becoming less crucial as private wealth percolates wider and individual investors become more sophisticated.[11] Thus, the leading Kuwaiti investment companies no longer need to rely entirely on the Ministry of Finance for their placing power in the Euro-bond market. Meanwhile, the smaller investment companies have been gradually stepping up their activities. A number of financial institutions, which have foreign banks among their share-holders, have made considerable efforts to develop the retail side of the bond market. Many of Kuwait's investment companies are increasingly offering the broad range of services normally performed by merchant banks, including the arranging of syndicated loans, underwriting, managing private portfolios and trusts, giving financial advice to clients, carrying out project feasibility studies and a range of other financial intermediation services. Another sign of the increased role of the investment companies and the growing maturity of the Kuwaiti financial market is the establishment of a new company (Arab Corpora-tion for Trading Securities) aimed at developing the secondary market for KD and other bonds floated in Kuwait. However, and perhaps in part because of these favourable developments, Kuwait's financial sector still faces many serious obstacles including shortage of qualified personnel, relatively narrow customer base, insufficient world know-ledge of the Kuwaiti dinar and its prospects, as well as the occasional resistance to the participation of Kuwaiti financial institutions in under-writing some international bond issues.[12]

The insurance sector in Kuwait is considered relatively more com-petitive since, in addition to the four Kuwaiti insurance companies, there are several foreign firms that operate through local agents. Of the four insurance companies only one is partly owned by the government and the rest are fully owned by the private sector. The financial system also consists of exchange dealers, some of whom are non-Kuwaitis, who perform many banking transactions, particularly those relating to the remittance business. Lastly, there are stockbrokers who handle the exchange of local company shares and, unofficially, shares of companies established elsewhere in the Gulf which have heavy Kuwaiti participation. A formal stock exchange has been established recently using a temporary building as a market place. Foreign brokerage houses are also allowed to operate in Kuwait in foreign securities through branch offices sponsored by local businessmen.

In addition to the financial system outlined above, there is the Ministry of Finance which, either directly or through the financial institutions it controls, has exerted a great influence over Kuwait's monetary and financial sectors. Its most obvious and significant role is reflected through its influence on the operations of the monetary sector, as is shown below.

THE OPERATIONS OF THE MONETARY SECTOR

Given the constraints on the monetary authorities referred to earlier, namely the 7 per cent ceiling on interest rates until 16 February 1977, the absence of minimum reserve requirements and the non-existence of an active short-term money market, the actual operation of the monetary sector has not changed significantly from the situation that preceded the establishment of the Central Bank which we have already described. Net government domestic expenditure from oil receipts and income from foreign investments remains the major factor that determines the change in the money supply, with the Central Bank having very limited control over this change. However, a part of net government domestic expenditure and private expenditure on consumption and investment, less non-oil exports and re-exports, flows out of the economy in the form of expenditure on imported goods and services. Also, there is the influence of private capital movements between Kuwait and the rest of the world and remittances by expatriates working in Kuwait. While both of these variables are determined in large measure by the amount of surplus private savings, the latter is also determined by such international factors as changes in interest rates in the principal foreign money markets and the relative stability of major foreign exchange currencies. The pattern of influences on the money supply envisaged here may be illustrated with the flow diagram shown on p. 168:[13]

The flow diagram consists of the following items:
1. Part of government foreign exchange revenues are exchanged for Kuwaiti dinars at the Central Bank.

FLOW DIAGRAM

Factors affecting changes in the money supply

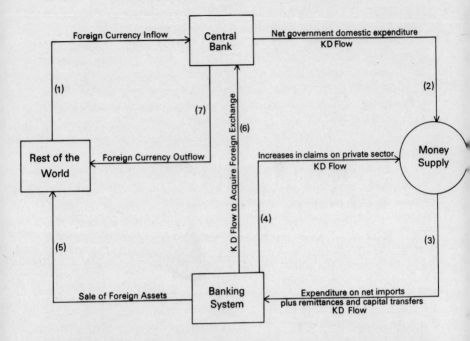

2. Government uses Kuwaiti dinars obtained from the Central Bank to cover net government domestic expenditure leading to an increase in the money supply.
3. The private sector uses KD balances to pay via the banking system for net expenditure (i.e. after deducting earnings from non-oil exports, re-exports and income from private investments abroad) on imports, remittances and net private capital transfers.
4. The banking system contributes to the expansion of the money supply through increased claims on the private sector.
5. The banking system draws on its foreign assets to finance part of imports, remittances and capital transfers paid for by reducing private deposits, money in circulation or by increasing its claims on the private sector.
6. The banking system turns back to the Central Bank Kuwaiti dinars required to pay the remainder of the import bill, remittances and private capital transfers.

7. Central Bank transfers abroad part of its foreign exchange holdings required for item (6).

There are two approaches for determining the change in the money supply which the Central Bank refers to as the traditional approach and the alternative approach. Using the notation of the flow diagram the former would be expressed essentially as $(1 - 5 - 7 + 4)$ and the latter as $(2 - 3 + 4)$.[14] As illustrated in Table 10.1 below and verified later in the annex, the two approaches yield identical results.

Based on the above analysis, it can be concluded that the balance of payments for the 'local economy,' as opposed to the overall balance of payments, would be in disequilibrium if credit expansion and government domestic expenditure were to cause expenditure on net imports, remittances and private capital transfers to exceed the foreign exchange made available through the inflow of government foreign revenues and the liquidation of foreign assets held by the banks. This obviously assumes that government capital transfers are financed directly by other government foreign revenues and therefore do not enter this analysis.

MAJOR MONETARY DEVELOPMENTS

A number of important developments have occurred in the monetary sector in recent years, some of which are highlighted in the sections below.

OVERALL MONETARY POSITION

As indicated earlier the growth of Kuwait's monetary sector has been most remarkable; the consolidated assets of the Central Bank and the commercial banking system almost quadrupled between 1971 and end of 1977. The greatest increase has taken place in claims on the private sector. As shown in Table 10.2 the ratio of this item to net foreign assets has increased from 34 per cent in 1971 to almost 102 per cent in 1977, which is mainly attributed to increased financial activity in the local economy and a growing interest among commercial banks in domestic lending. The latter represents a major change in position on the part of the directors of commercial banks in Kuwait who had generally preferred holding foreign assets to lending in the local market. However,

TABLE 10.1   Factors affecting changes in the money supply (Million KD)

	1973	1974	1975	1976	1977
Traditional Approach					
(a) Domestic assets (net)	88·4	171·9	50·4	361·8	28·1
1. Claims on private sector[1]	78·9	95·6	144·8	427·6	308·0
2. Government deposits (increase)	−20·0	−207·2	−72·5	17·0	−98·2
3. Other items (net)	−10·5	−60·3	−21·9	−82·8	−181·7
(b) Foreign assets (net)	−40·3	320·5	120·3	−32·7	320·3
1. Central Bank	26·6	245·5	92·9	61·9	268·5
2. Commercial banks	−66·9	75·0	27·4	−94·6	51·8
Change in money supply[2]	48·1	148·6	170·7	329·1	348·4
Alternative Approach					
(a) Net government domestic expenditure[3]	288·3	463·7	586·7	821·5	1089·5*
(b) Increase in claims on private sector	78·9	95·6	144·8	427·6	308·0
(c) Private sector balance of payments deficit[4]	−308·6	−350·4	−538·9	−837·2	−867·4*
(d) Change in other items (net)	−10·5	−60·3	−21·9	−82·8	−181·7

SOURCE: The Central Bank of Kuwait, *Quarterly Statistical Bulletin*, October—December 1977.
* Provisional estimates.
[1] Including claims on specialized banks.
[2] Consists of currency in circulation outside commercial banks, KD private deposits and KD deposits of specialised banks at commercial banks and Central Bank.
[3] Consists of general government expenditure plus government investment and domestic transfer payments, less government domestic revenues, less government purchases from abroad.
[4] Residual item.

TABLE 10.2   An overview of the monetary sector (Million KD)

	1971	1972	1973	1974	1975	1976	1977
Assets							
Foreign assets (net)	470·4	531·5	491·2	811·7	932·0	899·3	1219·6
Claims on private sector	161·4	187·4	266·3	361·9	506·7	934·3	1242·3
Total	631·8	718·9	757·5	1173·6	1438·7	1833·6	2461·9
Liabilities							
Money	111·3	145·8	174·7	199·5	290·3	393·8	490·6
Quasi-money	344·5	377·9	397·2	521·0	600·9	826·5	1078·1
Government deposits	102·5	99·1	79·1	286·3	358·9	341·8	440·0
Other (net)	73·5	96·1	106·5	166·8	188·7	271·5	453·2
Total	631·8	718·9	757·5	1173·6	1438·7	1833·6	2461·9
Monetary Ratios							
Claims on private sector/ foreign assets (%)	34·4	35·3	54·2	44·6	54·4	103·9	101·9
Foreign assets/money supply (%)	103·2	101·5	85·9	113·7	104·6	73·7	77·8
Money supply/disposable income (%)	58·5	74·6	52·4	72·5	73·9	87·3*	89·6*

SOURCE: The Central Bank of Kuwait, *Quarterly Statistical Bulletin*, October–December, 1977.
* Provisional estimates.

with the relative decline in foreign interest rates since 1974 and the increased instability in the foreign exchange markets, there has been an obvious change in attitude on the part of Kuwait's banking system. Table 10.2 shows that the expansion of domestic credit has contributed to a very sharp increase in liquidity, particularly since 1974. As will be discussed later, the rise in domestic prices has, therefore, been far greater than that which could be justified on the basis of the increase in world prices alone. In addition, the expanded credit has been directed mainly into such non-productive activities as speculation in company shares and real estate. This prompted the Central Bank, and more recently the government, to draw the banks' attention to the adverse consequences of this policy and to call for greater emphasis on providing finance to more productive sectors.[15] The repercussions of this policy on the pursuit of the country's objectives of growth, diversification and price stability are obviously a source of major concern. Serious efforts are being made to rectify the situation before a permanent adverse change in the private sector's attitude develops.

One comforting aspect regarding the above-mentioned credit expansion policy, however, is the maintenance of a relatively high ratio of foreign assets to the money supply (including quasi-money). Although this ratio decreased in 1975 and 1976, it is still in excess of 70 per cent, which is evidently among the highest even in comparison with other oil-producing countries. Thus, credit expansion at home is not expected to create major pressures on the value of the Kuwaiti dinar in foreign exchange markets.

THE CENTRAL BANK

Established in 1968 to replace the Currency Board, the Central Bank commenced operations on 1 April 1969, concentrating its efforts primarily on acquiring greater insight into the operations of the commercial banks, monitoring their activities and collecting data to assess their performance and role in the financial sector. In more recent years, the Bank has aimed at influencing the credit policies of the local banks. However, as indicated earlier, given the ceiling on interest rates and the non-existence of appropriate short term monetary instruments, the Central Bank was left with few tools to apply. Moral persuasion was to a large extent the only device available to the Bank to influence the credit policies of the commercial banks. Occasionally, the Bank also gave directives to the banks such as upper limits on credit facilities provided for the purpose of subscription in shareholding companies, and issued instructions to the banks pertaining to the observation of sound banking practices in financing domestic stock purchases.[16] However, due to the expansion of government expenditure and the shortage of adequate local investment outlets, the banking system's accumulation of surplus funds substantially increased in 1972 and 1973. Therefore, in order to curtail credit expansion, the Central Bank decided to accept from commercial banks time deposits at an interest rate half per cent above the rate paid by these banks on savings deposits. The Bank's role has become somewhat more active in recent years with the introduction of such measures as a 25 per cent mandatory liquidity ratio in 1974 and the opening of a rediscount window in February 1975.

Due to the comparative inability of the Central Bank to influence credit policies and the limitation on its role in determining the money supply, the above measures were insufficient. The rapid escalation in the money supply and in credit expansion referred to earlier, as well as the serious shift in the pattern of credit that will be discussed in the next section, clearly indicate that the Central Bank was constrained in its ability to affect the policies of the banking system. The spread of speculation and the accelerated rate of inflation required more effective measures and a greater degree of coordination with the country's fiscal authorities. Thus, the resulting increase in prices through its significant effect on expenditure as mentioned in Chapter 7, brought about a slowdown in economic activity in more recent years.

As regards its financial position, the Central Bank has experienced a remarkable rate of growth. The eight-fold increase in its assets since 1971 is mainly attributed to the rise in foreign exchange purchases from the government against Kuwaiti dinars needed to finance its domestic expenditure.[17] The other factor contributing to the Bank's foreign assets is the transfer of foreign exchange funds from the Ministry of Finance to the Central Bank to cover the latter's participation in the International Monetary Fund's Oil Facility in 1974 and 1975.[18] Thus, the Bank's assets consist almost exclusively of foreign assets obtained from the government. On the liabilities side, the largest item is government deposits which constitute approximately 40 per cent of the Bank's resources. Until 1976, the second item in relative importance was currency (25 per cent), followed by commercial banks' deposits (16 per cent), with the remainder (9 per cent) consisting of the Bank's capital and reserves and other liabilities. However, commercial banks' deposits increased markedly during 1977, accounting by the end of the year for 32 per cent of the Bank's liabilities.

The substantial rise in commercial banks' deposits is mainly due to the Bank's policy of siphoning away surplus funds from the banking system. While this represents an important element in the Bank's policy, its effectiveness in checking the expansion of credit seems to have been relatively limited as has been already indicated.[19] Apart from increasing the mandatory liquidity ratio, it would have been useful for the Bank to consider raising the interest rate on banks' deposits, particularly in view of the non-existence of other measures of mitigating credit expansion. More important, however, is the need for greater coordination between the Ministry of Finance and the Central Bank as regards government domestic expenditure, since this represents in the final analysis the main factor that triggers monetary expansion in Kuwait. While welfare policy considerations and the financing of government development expenditure weigh heavily in determining the amount of government domestic expenditure, there is need also to take into account the effects of this expenditure on the price level. This is particularly so in an economy where the supply of many critical items is relatively inelastic and where, as shown in Chapter 7, absorptive capacity is a major constraint on investment and real growth.[20] Moreover, given the high correlation between government expenditure and credit expansion the above-mentioned coordination becomes, of course, more pertinent.

A point that should be noted, however, is that the Kuwait situation regarding the limited availability of monetary instruments is not entirely unique, but certainly it is new. Kuwait not only realises the problems, but exhibits the inadequacy of conventional models and methods of economic and monetary control when adapted to such a situation as its own. The accepted methods of the Western economies evolved over very many years as governments responded to changes in their economies and fashioned instruments of control from the practices that developed in their own private sectors. The whole structure of discount houses, underwriting practices, commercial papers, discount rates, banks and stock exchanges, all grew in response to the needs of the private sector and governments only entered this system gradually as excesses evolved into crises which could not be solved by the automatic workings of the system existing at any particular time. The Kuwait economy, however, has not so far exhibited the need for many of the instruments available elsewhere, as these normally developed in response to shortages of funds in the face of a broad local production base requiring such financial facilities.[21] Kuwait, therefore, is faced with the difficult problem of operating in a world in which the established methods of control evolved in response to stimuli which it has not experienced, yet, in order to maintain monetary stability and to take part in world economic activities on a scale which its wealth and circumstances justify, it has either to copy the methods in common use and establish them artificially, or to forge new methods which may be more suited to its needs but remain compatible with those of the world in which it operates. This calls for imagination and flare by the financial sector in the face of opportunities for experimentation.

THE COMMERCIAL BANKS

Kuwait's commercial banking system, which consists now of six banks and a network of about 100 branches, has experienced a number of major developments since 1971. Apart from the rapid growth of their activities, there have been a number of important changes in the composition of the banks' assets and liabilities, in the policies they apply and in the increased interdependence within the system.

In the utilisation of their resources, the banks' foreign exchange assets have significantly decreased in relative importance. As a percentage of total assets, net foreign assets have declined from over 50 per cent in 1971 to less than 16 per cent in 1977. This development, as indicated earlier, is mainly due to increased local demand for credit and the instability displayed by the international financial markets. However, the bulk (76 per cent) of the banks' foreign assets still consist of deposits with foreign banks and short-term negotiable certificates of deposit. Medium and long-term foreign bonds, a large part of them in KD, and direct investments abroad, mostly in joint-venture banks, represented approximately 14 per cent of the banks' foreign assets in 1977. The remaining part (about 10 per cent) consists of advances and discounts to non-residents which are primarily expressed in Kuwaiti dinars. The banks' policy of sacrificing higher yields in favour of greater flexibility, i.e. liquidity, is dictated by their need to safeguard the value of foreign assets against possible currency fluctuations. With the relatively large size of their foreign assets, a 10 per cent reduction in their value is sufficient to wipe out a major part of the banks' capital and reserves. This also explains the growing preference on the part of the banking system for maintaining an increasing proportion of their assets in local currency either in local credit operations or in rapidly rising deposits with the Central Bank.

Apart from the rapid expansion of credit that has resulted since 1971 in a two-fold increase in the proportion of claims on the private sector to total assets, there has been a significant shift in the distribution of such claims among the various economic activities, particularly in recent years. Personal loans increased during the years 1972–7 from KD30 million to over KD212 million, with their relative share increasing from approximately 16 per cent to 20 per cent. With the main part of these credits being utilised in speculation in company shares and real estate, there has understandably been a growing concern over the implications of the banks' credit policies. Although some improvements have already taken place, it is believed that these policies have seriously affected the pattern of investment in recent years.

Developments on the liabilities side include the rapid increase in private deposits which historically account for more than 65 per cent of the banks' resources and the extraordinary rise in their foreign liabilities. The latter resulted from two factors, (1) increased participation of the Kuwaiti banks in the Euro-dollar market through short-term borrowing and reinvesting for matching maturities, and (2) escalated foreign borrowing to finance the expansion of local credit in 1975 and 1976. Finally, the banking system's capital and reserves have also been sharply augmented in 1976 and 1977, as required by the rapid expansion of credit and the rise in private deposits in order to maintain a sound financial position.

Table 10.3 summarises developments in the consolidated financial position of the commercial banking system and changes in the major financial indicators.

As shown in Table 10.3 the reserve position of the banking system improved considerably in 1974 following the Central Bank's measure imposing a mandatory liquidity ratio according to which the commercial banks are required to maintain not less than 25 per cent of their total deposits in liquid assets with at least 7·5 per cent thereof to be kept in Kuwaiti dinars. The latter remains well over 7·5 per cent even after the inclusion of government deposits. The sum of the first and fourth ratios in the table indicates that even though the liquidity position of the banking system has declined considerably, it is well over the 25 per cent limit set by the Central Bank. However, in spite of the high liquidity position of the commercial banks, it is clear from the second ratio (claims on private sector to private deposits) and the fourth ratio (claims on private sector to net foreign assets) that the banks' credit expansion has been quite substantial. Claims on the private sector represented by the end of 1977 more than 87 per cent of private deposits in comparison with only 40 per cent in 1971. There also seems to have been an inordinate increase in the commercial banks' local utilisation of their

TABLE 10.3 Consolidated balance sheet of commercial banks (Million KD)

	1971	1972	1973	1974	1975	1976	1977
Assets	679·8	736·7	803·4	1037·6	1300·7	1839·0	2595·7
Reserves	8·5	13·8	26·9	58·0	67·2	92·4	271·0
Cash	(5·6)	(4·5)	(4·7)	(5·3)	(6·1)	(7·9)	(10·4)
Balances with Central Bank	(2·9)	(9·3)	(22·2)	(52·7)	(61·1)	(84·5)	(260·6)
Claims on private sector	161·4	187·4	286·3	361·9	506·7	934·3	1242·3
Foreign assets	477·9	513·5	479·1	561·4	614·4	674·9	822·4
Other assets	32·0	22·0	31·1	56·3	112·4	137·4	260·0
Liabilities	679·8	736·7	803·4	1037·6	1300·7	1839·0	2595·7
Capital and reserves	36·4	40·8	45·5	51·0	63·8	89·2	198·4
Private deposits	405·4	466·6	500·8	638·9	789·5	1091·2	1417·8
Demand deposits	(60·9)	(88·7)	(103·6)	(117·9)	(188·6)	(264·7)	(339·7)
Quasi-money	(344·5)	(377·9)	(397·2)	(521·0)	(600·9)	(826·5)	(1078·1)
Government deposits	71·6	62·5	50·7	73·2	87·3	71·0	114·9
Foreign liabilities	104·2	103·6	136·1	143·4	169·0	324·1	419·8
Other liabilities	62·2	63·2	70·3	131·1	191·1	263·5	445·8
Financial Ratios							
1. Cash reserves/private deposits (%)	2·1	3·0	5·4	9·1	8·5	8·5	19·1
2. Claims on private sector/private deposits (%)	39·6	40·2	53·2	56·6	64·2	85·6	87·6
3. Capital and reserves/total liabilities (%)	5·4	5·6	5·7	4·9	4·9	4·9	7·6
4. Claims on private sector/net foreign assets	43·2	45·7	77·6	86·6	113·8	153·1	308·6
5. Net foreign assets/private deposits (%)	92·2	87·8	65·8	65·4	56·4	32·2	28·4

SOURCE: The Central Bank of Kuwait, *Quarterly Statistical Bulletin*, October–December 1977.

resources with claims on the private sector increasing by the end of 1977 to over three times net foreign assets compared with less than 50 per cent in 1971. Finally, it is important to note that there has been a significant rise in the profitability of commercial banks since 1973 that could be explained by the above-mentioned increase in available resources, the reorientation of their activities and, more recently, the change in the interest rate structure.

INTER-BANK OPERATIONS

The increased maturity of Kuwait's financial sector has been reflected in the phenomenal growth of inter-bank deposits since 1973. The size of inter-commercial bank deposits increased from KD6·6 million in 1973 to more than KD193 million in 1977. This development is mainly due to the Central Bank's decision in 1974, referred to above, in connection with the mandatory liquidity ratio imposed on commercial banks.[22] On the other hand, the expansion of the banking system following the establishment of two new specialised banks also helped to increase the overall volume of inter-bank operations. This is evident from the rise in commercial banks' balances with the three specialised banking institutions fróm KD6·6 million in 1974 to KD155·7 million in 1977. In the same period, deposits of specialised banks with the commercial banking system reached KD126·3 million in 1977 compared with KD25 million in 1974. Furthermore, there has been a substantial growth in the Kuwaiti dinar short-term inter-bank market at the regional level. This has resulted mainly from the increased participation of Kuwaiti banks in joint-venture banking institutions in Bahrain and other parts of the Gulf as well as the ceiling on interest rates imposed locally. The growth of the KD short-term regional market has been a positive development in spite of the obvious shortcomings of the institutional restriction on the rate of interest and its effect on the smooth operation of the local financial sector.

SPECIALISED BANKS

The three specialised banks operating in Kuwait are: the Credit and Saving Bank, the Kuwait Real Estate Bank and the Industrial Bank of Kuwait. Of these, the first two are confined mainly to the housing and real estate sector, whereas the third is designed to promote industrial development. While these banks are not permitted to accept demand deposits, they are authorised to accept time and savings deposits from the public. In addition, as part of its efforts to develop Kuwait's financial market, the Industrial Bank of Kuwait has issued medium-term KD bonds and certificates of deposit. Apart from this, the main operations of these banks consist of extending medium and long-term loans for the construction of personal housing in the case of the Credit and Saving Bank and for the implementation of large real estate development projects in the case of the Kuwait Real Estate Bank. The Industrial Bank, on the other hand, is concerned with extending long-term loans to industrial projects and in providing equity funds to newly-created projects, particularly those identified through its own efforts. The lending terms of the Credit and Saving Bank and the Kuwait Industrial Bank are concessionary which is mainly due to government ownership in the case of the former and to a large government soft-term loan in the case of the latter. The loans of the Kuwait Real Estate Bank are generally extended on market terms for a period of less than ten years. In view of this, there have been calls for the establishment of a mortgage bank that would be able to fill the gap regarding the provision of more suitable finance for real estate projects. The Real Estate Bank and the Industrial Bank are also active in providing technical assistance to their clients and assume an important advisory role in their respective fields of operation. They normally require detailed feasibility studies on projects submitted for financing and apply rigorous techniques of project evaluation.

The consolidated balance sheet of these banks shows total assets as at the end 1977 of approximately KD705 million compared with KD137·5 million in 1974. Local loans amount in 1977 to KD301·7 million, representing almost 43 per cent of their total assets, of which 65 per cent were extended to housing and real-estate projects. Foreign assets are the second largest item totalling approximately KD196·2 million, followed by deposits with commercial banks in the order of KD126 million. They represented, respectively, 28 per cent and 18 per cent of the banks' consolidated assets. On the liabilities side, local deposits reached by the end of 1977 a total of KD234 million followed by capital and reserves of KD206 million. These two items constitute respectively 33 per cent and 29 per cent of the banks' consolidated resources. The remainder of their resources consists of long-term obligations to local and foreign banks. Moreover, these banks have experienced in recent years a remarkable growth in their resources due mainly to a three-fold increase in their equity and local deposits. For example, in its efforts to alleviate the housing problem, the government raised in 1976 the capital of the Credit and Saving Bank from KD120 million to KD320 million.

In spite of their rapid increase, local loans still account for only 45 per cent of the total resources of these banks, which partly explains the relatively high proportion of foreign assets they hold. Their loan commitments, however, are believed to be substantial but require a period of two or three years to be disbursed. In addition, the Industrial Bank, which commenced operations in 1974, was until recently still concentrating on identifying suitable industrial projects. As emphasised before, there should be an intensification of project identification efforts because this role is considered to be of greater importance in a capital surplus country than the role of financial provision.

INVESTMENT COMPANIES

The expansion of Kuwait's financial sector is also reflected in the establishment of a large number of investment companies. Fourteen new investment companies were created during the years 1974–7, bringing the present total to seventeen with assets totalling, by the end of 1977, approximately KD420 million. The three largest institutions whose assets represent about 92 per cent of the global assets of the investment companies are public shareholding companies whereas all the rest except one are closed companies. The resources of the three major companies almost quadrupled during the years 1974–7. Of the 1977 total of KD388 million, capital and reserves constitute about 20 per cent, local deposists and borrowed funds 34 per cent and foreign liabilities 25 per cent. The role of these companies in foreign investment is reflected in the high ratio of foreign assets (approximately 60 per cent) to their total resources. This is partly due to the relatively higher foreign interest rates earned on deposits and their desire to diversify into foreign investments, particularly as these companies act as the government's vehicle for investing abroad part of its surplus funds. Thus, direct investments abroad, long-term securities and loans account for over 76 per cent of the foreign assets held by these companies. In addition, they play an important role in channelling local funds into the Euro-bond market. In 1976 they participated in bond issues denominated in KD and other currencies totalling KD2412 million, of which KD127 million were marketed in Kuwait, compared with KD1153 million and KD179 million respectively in 1975.

However, in spite of their increased importance in the Euro-bond market, their role in local bond issues and syndicated loans has been modest. This is mainly due to the greater prominence that was given from the start to foreign investment and the scarcity of good long-term investment opportunities locally. Their local assets, so far, consist mainly of deposits with local banks and real estate investments, particularly following the marked rise in land values and rents in recent years.

Although these companies have made serious efforts to develop a KD bond market, there are still major problems in this direction. Apart from the general obstacles mentioned earlier in this chapter which include shortage of qualified personnel, a narrow customer base, an inadequate knowledge of the Kuwaiti dinar abroad and the occasional resistance to Kuwaiti participation in underwriting bond issues, there are two serious problems that specifically relate to the development of the KD bond market:

1. Lack of risk sensitivity: It has been indicated that despite considerable risk disparities, almost all of the KD issues sold so far have carried coupons of between 8¼ and 9 per cent. 'Attracting a prime credit by offering a lower coupon would require a considerable educative effort of investors by the underwriters....'[23] Thus, it is the responsibility of the investment companies to make the necessary effort to achieve a greater measure of maturity in the market and upgrade the quality of the bonds offered.

2. Inadequacy of the secondary market: This problem has a significant effect on the degree of liquidity of bonds issued in Kuwait and the future development of the market. The cause of the problem is partly related to the lack of risk sensitivity referred to above which limits the investors' interest in changing positions. It was also caused by the absence of suitable institutions. This, however, should be gradually eliminated with the recent formation of the Arab Corporation for Trading Securities which is designed to make a market in bonds floated locally. It is expected to contribute significantly to the growth and maturity of the local bond market and to help develop Kuwait's financial sector.

INTEREST RATES

Kuwait's interest rate structure had, during the years 1961–77, a maximum legal ceiling of 7 per cent per annum. Interest rates were allowed to fluctuate below that level; however, due to inter-bank agreements, the degree of fluctuation has been relatively small since 1969. Interest paid on private time and savings deposits generally ranged between 3·5 per cent and 5·5 per cent per annum and varied according to the deposit's amount and duration. Rates paid on advances and discounts were close to the maximum and occasionally the effective rate (including commissions and other charges) went over the 7 per cent ceiling rate. On the other hand, medium and long-term loans had been rare and until 1975 were only extended by the Credit and Saving Bank. However commercial banks would normally renew their credit facilities to established clients on a regular basis.

As explained earlier, the legal constraint on interest rates restricted the role of the Central Bank in conducting monetary policy. Moreover, with the rise in interest rates in the major financial centres, the financial position of the commercial banks was sometimes adversely affected as private savings found their way abroad and the spread between deposit and lending rates was considerably reduced. In view of these considerations and after persistent pressure by the Central Bank, the law was amended in early 1977 vesting the power to fix maximum lending rates with the Central Bank. Surprisingly enough, however, the ceiling was kept the same, but the interest rate structure became generally lower as the maximum rate was designed to be inclusive of all commissions and bank fees. In these circumstances, it was difficult for Kuwaiti banks to compete with banks elsewhere, particularly those offshore in Bahrain, which could pay 6–6½ per cent for KD deposits, and there was a danger that a KD market would develop outside Kuwait.[24] Thus, the Central Bank announced on 14 February 1977, new regulations according to which the ceiling on the effective rate chargeable on KD secured loans not exceeding twelve months was set at 7 per cent, for unsecured loans for the same period 8½ per cent and for other KD loans 10 per cent. Loans denominated in foreign currencies are not subject to these limits. The rate for savings accounts was set at 4½ per cent. These rates are subject to periodic review by the monetary authorities. Although the situation is more flexible now that the Central Bank has the power to regulate interest rates according to prevailing local and international market conditions, it is still early to judge the effectiveness of monetary policy under the new circumstances. Nevertheless, the Central Bank is likely to play a more active role in influencing the country's economic conditions from now on.

THE KUWAITI DINAR

Since the establishment of the Kuwaiti dinar in 1961, its value was pegged to sterling until 1967. However, at the time of the British devaluation in 1967 it was effectively pegged to the US dollar and, even though it was revalued in terms of the latter in 1971 and 1973, it continued to be pegged to that currency until 18 March 1975, with the Central Bank observing the IMF's 2·25 per cent margin on either side of parity. As of that date, Kuwait broke the dinar's link with the dollar and adopted a new exchange rate policy under which the rate is determined according to the performance of a basket of major currencies through which Kuwait's major transactions are carried out. While the composition of the basket has never been disclosed, it seems certain that the dollar has the most important weighting. This has had significant repercussions with the recent fall of the dollar. Due to this heavy weighting, the Kuwaiti dinar has not appreciated against the dollar as much as some other major currencies. This seems to reflect in part the policy of the Central Bank in avoiding major revaluations in the KD in order to safeguard the financial position of the banking system which has sizeable dollar holdings. An added point to note is that greater knowledge of Kuwait's foreign exchange policy would facilitate and encourage bond issues denominated in KD as the lack of such knowledge is considered a major constraint on this activity as mentioned earlier.

As part of the government's efforts to promote regional cooperation, an Arab Monetary Fund has recently been created which represents only a beginning in the direction of monetary integration. However, more serious discussions are now underway for the establishment of a monetary union of the Arabian Gulf states. There are clearly a number of benefits which would be obtained from such a union including a more efficient division of labour and capital by means of eliminating distorting exchange rates, the provision of greater potential for lending and borrowing and a reduction in exchange transaction costs. While these are important, the union's most significant benefit would lie in its contribution towards Gulf economic integration which would have substantial advantages in view of the limited size of the individual states. This, however, is a matter for political decision and requires much further consideration to assess its true prospects and potential.

PRICES

Although average prices in Kuwait had been 20 to 30 per cent higher than in such neighbouring countries as Iraq, Iran and the Eastern Mediterranean countries, they were relatively stable during most of Kuwait's growth experience in the sixties. The differences in food prices, rents and other living costs were adequately compensated by generally higher wages and salaries in comparison with the levels prevailing in other countries in the region. However, as import prices began to move up at an accelerated rate in the late sixties and early seventies, prices in Kuwait took a sharp turn upward and inflation became one of the country's most serious problems. In spite of the fact that available price indices are not reliable enough, their general trend and magnitude indeed confirm the overall dimension of the problem. The country's GNP deflator almost doubled between 1969 and 1975.[25] By the same token, the wholesale price index and the cost of living index increased from a base of 100 in 1972 to respectively 156 and 139 in 1976.[26] These indices, however, do not obviously tell the full story, for in the case of some items the rate of inflation was truly phenomenal, e.g. rent has gone up by more than four times since 1974.[27]

With Kuwait's heavy dependence on imports, the main cause of inflation should be obvious. However, the rise in import prices was certainly not the only cause of recent inflation in Kuwait. Inflationary pressures were greatly aggravated by the rapid increase in domestic demand, the quasi-monopolistic situation in certain sectors of the economy and the relatively inelastic supply of imported products caused by port congestion, delays in delivery, etc. This combination of factors were largely responsible for the rise in domestic prices to the extent of 20 per cent more than in import prices.

The government has since 1975 taken numerous measures designed to alleviate the effects of inflation in Kuwait. These include price support policies to minimise the impact on the low income groups. In two years (1975 and 1976) the government spent over KD20 million on supporting such essential products as meat, rice, milk, sugar and vegetable oil. The subsidies, which represented for some products up to 50 per cent of the market price, averaged a total of KD10 ($35) per person annually. These subsidies were undoubtedly of major benefit to the poorer members of the community as they were mainly paid on the staple products. Other measures included a ban on re-export of food-stuffs and building materials, reorganisation and expansion of the port facilities and the increase of domestic production of some products. In addition, the previously mentioned appreciation of the KD relative to the US dollar absorbed part of the foreign inflationary pressures. With these measures and the relative slow down in world inflation, there are clear indications that the situation improved significantly during 1977 and early 1978. However, the cost of living has already outpaced the levels of wages and salaries and is now considered to be higher than in many industrialised countries.

THE KUWAIT STOCK MARKET

A total of forty-two public shareholding companies have been established in Kuwait since 1952, of which about a half have been established since 1970. Twenty-two are exclusively privately owned, eighteen are owned jointly with the government, and two are now fully owned by the public sector, as well as Kuwait Airways and the Kuwait Oil Company. A classification of the private and joint companies according to economic activity is given in Table 10.4 below.

At the end of 1977, the number of issued shares was estimated at seventeen million with a total par value in the order of KD110 million and a current market value of approximately KD2·1 billion. With government owning approximately 25 per cent of all shares, and about 30 per cent banned from trading until balance sheets covering a full year's operation of the companies concerned have been issued, the number of shares placed on the market was estimated at the end of 1977 at no more than 32 million. The relatively small number of available shares, combined with a scarcity of domestic investment opportunities, a high measure of monetary liquidity and speculation, have resulted in a high

TABLE 10.4   Classification of public shareholding companies

Economic activity	Number of companies
Banks	7
Insurance	4
Investment	4
Industrial	12
Real estate	3
Shipping	2
Transport	2
Trade and services	6
Total	40

volume of trading and a rapid increase in share prices during the years 1970–6.[28] The ratio of the monthly trading average to the number of shares on the market reached 6 per cent at times of active trading during the period from 1972 to 1976 and averaged more than 4 per cent.[29] The rise in share prices was also phenomenal; in the period from the end of 1970 to the end of 1973, average share prices increased three-fold, followed by more than a 125 per cent rise during the years 1974–6.[30] However the share boom came to an end at the beginning of 1977 primarily as a result of the excessive speculatory attitude that was followed by a relatively mild decrease in liquidity. Many share prices were down as much as by 25 to 40 per cent from their 1976 peak levels and trading shrank considerably. The government was prompted in December 1977 to declare its readiness to buy shares at minimum purchase prices in order to support the market and enable those who were compelled to sell to do so without pulling down share prices still further.[31] This measure is in clear conformity with the government's paternalistic attitude which was discussed earlier in the book. However, the implications of this precedent are very serious, particularly regarding the utilisation of public funds, its inequitable application, its psychological effects on future speculation and its result of increasing government control. This measure helped to increase the level of trading activity in early 1978 as well as to precipitate a modest rise in share prices and the government now has the opportunity to use the purchased shares for the purpose of preventing a recurrence of a speculative spell in the market. The recent increase in the volume of trading and in share prices was further assisted by a split of up to 10 to 1 in some company shares during the second quarter of 1978. This action raised the number of shares on the market to over 200 million and escalated the volume of trading.

The remarkable growth in the volume of trading and the share boom, referred to above, occurred despite the non-existence of a formal stock exchange until 1977. Trading before that date was carried out in brokers' offices with inadequate information on the companies' financial conditions and movement of share prices. The situation has improved since mid-1977 with the completion of a temporary building for the stock exchange and the introduction of measures designed to upgrade the monitoring of market trading, as well as the preparation of a share index and the dissemination of data on trading transactions. Nevertheless, there is still room for improvement, particularly with regard to regulating and organising margin purchases and forward sales and streamlining the flow of information about the financial results of the shareholding companies. In addition, it is important to increase the volume of trading activity in all shares so that market prices can be established on a daily basis. This has been partly achieved recently through the mentioned splitting of existing shares in order to reduce the unit price. Other measures in this direction should include reducing the limit on the size of individual transactions. Finally, the role of the brokerage institutions should be reviewed and licensing of dealers should be done in accordance with criteria of specialisation, proficiency and financial capability.

Unless it is properly organised and regulated with a view to protecting the public interest without undue intervention by the government, it would be difficult for the stock market to develop into a viable and effective institution that would help in mobilising savings and channelling funds to productive activities in the country. Since Kuwait's stock market is still in its infancy, special care and attention should be devoted to safeguarding its growth and development.

Annex to Chapter 10

The identical results obtained with the two approaches that determine the change in the money supply may be verified mathematically with the aid of the balance of payments identity. This may be demonstrated as follows:

The balance of payments identity for the 'local economy' is stated below (this should not be confused with the overall balance of payments condition mentioned in Chapter 7).

1. $X - R - M + (Gn + \Delta GD) = \Delta A + \Delta F$

where X = Non-oil exports and re-exports
M = Expenditure on imported goods and services
R = Remittances and net private capital transfer minus income from assets held abroad
ΔA = The change in foreign assets held by the banks
Gn = Net government domestic expenditure
ΔGD = The change in government deposits with the Central Bank and the commercial banks
and ΔF = The change in foreign assets held by the Central Bank

And according to the 'traditional approach', the change in the money supply is determined as follows:

2. $\Delta Mo = \Delta L - \Delta GD^{32} - \Delta K + \Delta A + \Delta F$

where ΔMo = The change in the supply of money and quasi money
ΔL = The change in the banking system's claims on the private sector
ΔK = Net change in the banking system's equity position

Equation (2) may be rewritten as follows:

3. $\Delta A = \Delta Mo - \Delta L + \Delta GD + \Delta K - \Delta F$

Substituting equation (3) for ΔA in equation (1) gives:

4. $X - R - M + (Gn + \Delta GD) = \Delta Mo - \Delta L + \Delta GD + \Delta K - \Delta F + \Delta F$

After re-arranging the terms and omitting ΔF and ΔGD, equation (4) becomes:

5. $\Delta Mo = Gn + \Delta L + (X - R - M) - \Delta K$

Equation (5) gives the 'alternative approach' for determining the change in the money supply.

11 Kuwait's Role in International Finance

It need hardly be remarked that the recent changes in the world order have seen many emergent countries gain control of their resources and the changes in the price of oil have transferred much of its value to the producer countries which hitherto had passed to the extractive companies and their home countries. This has placed a remarkable degree of power in the hands of a new group of operators on the world's industrial and financial markets. The changes in oil prices and in the relationships between emergent nations and the former colonial or imperial powers are essentially interdependendent, in that the ability to influence prices undoubtedly depended at least in part on the ability of producer countries to exercise their sovereignty. It is essential to recognise, however, that these are two separate but equally important elements in the development of the new structure of financial arrangements which are arising in the world. Their separateness is stressed because the transfer of ownership of financial assets should not in itself be cause for concern. International markets exist for precisely that purpose. When a substantial group of operators entering any market, however, are motivated by a different set of principles and objectives from those under which existing operators work, it is often then that concern is expressed as to the effect of the operations of the newcomers on the existing patterns of relationships and the balance of power between existing groups. It must be emphasised that the change taking place is in the power over real resources, but this basic fact is neglected by those people whose nations see their relationships with others via patterns of monetary flows, currency exchange rates and deficits and surpluses on balances of payments.

One of the special features in the transfer of power has been that those to whom it has been transferred have almost exclusively been in the 'less developed' category. Consequently, their power over resources has not been an addition to an existing economic power base, but rather a complete transformation of it. The accepted rules of development require the effective allocation of capital which is in short supply to activities which maximise the productivity of other factors of production which are present in comparative abundance. Where capital is suddenly the factor available in abundance, however, then it is often necessary to keep it 'in store' until it can be used. Thus, when there is a newly acquired control over a comparative abundance of capital outside a country's borders, this is acknowledged by financial instruments which are nothing more than acknowledgments of debts, and these are deployed on the world's money markets until the money or physical assets which they represent are needed by their owners. The rate at which they will be absorbed depends upon the total quantity available and the 'absorptive capacity' of the owning country. However it may be also be that the monetary and physical assets abroad may be more valuable to their new owners, as revenue earners, than an equivalent investment in their own country. Under these circumstances they may not be liquidated for reinvestment at home, but used to create an income flow from abroad. This choice, however, is the prerogative of their owners and it is increasingly evident that this is precisely the choice that they are making. It is increasingly evident too that the inability of the rest of the world to understand their motives and to adjust conventional attitudes to allow for them is a fundamental element in the economic and financial crises which have bedevilled the seventies.

A conceptual optimisation model was outlined in Chapter 9 for oil-based economies faced with choices of extraction versus conservation, and home development versus foreign investment, as a means of maximising their share of the world's productive resources in the future and thereby securing future income flows, especially against the time when oil resources are exhausted. This theme was continued and the development of Kuwait's oil industry, manufacturing activities and infrastructural development in terms of maximising the value added which accrued to the country and increasing the country's absorptive capacity for home investment was discussed. Investment abroad creates income which can be spent on consumption or investment goods for domestic use or it can be reinvested abroad to augment future income flows. Investment at home, however, may be in infrastructure or in new technology to increase the productivity of existing factors of production or it may increase production directly by adding to the existing quantity of productive capital and thereby extend the existing capital base.

The deployment of capital abroad by a capital surplus economy, therefore, should be seen as an integral part of a strategy, and the form and structure of a country's portfolio of foreign assets should be regarded as one aspect only of a wider deployment of a total quantity of assets. This basic fact is persistently ignored by many of the pundits who comment on the 'oil surpluses' and how they should be deployed. Using the existing markets and their structure as a frame of reference, they derive criteria for their judgement from accepted principles of those markets' operations. The surpluses are judged according to their effect upon the markets without reference to the aspirations of their owners. Thus, so many commentators see favourable and unfavourable balances of payments caused by oil price rises as temporary phenomena which should be corrected by the normal workings of the existing system. Exchange rates should alter, demand should be managed by fiscal and monetary means. Taking one year with another, countries will ideally waver either side of a neutral balance. The world's financial markets are supposed, under ideal conditions, to bring about this adjustment. However, this requires that all countries party to the operations 'play the game' according to the rules drawn up in agreements made for their mutual benefit. One of these is that the import demands upon each other should alter as the measures outlined take effect: oil exporters should buy more imports; oil importers should buy less oil. Yet this is precisely what most operators are seeking to avoid — the oil producers, because of absorptive capacity problems and the need to reserve income for the future, the industrial states because of their need for oil.

While current events create balance of payments difficulties, therefore, the problem is not a balance of payments problem and the conventional approach is not applicable. With limited absorptive capacity, the oil states cannot immediately increase their imports to match their exports, unless of course they are willing to squander their capital (i.e. oil transformed into money) entirely on consumption goods. Reduction in demand in the deficit countries has little effect, as the problem is created by outflow of a single resource from producer countries and the reduction in demand in industrial countries is largely translated into reduction in demand on each other, reductions which cannot be taken up by the oil-producing countries for the reasons mentioned. Also, instead of falling currency values creating extra demand, they merely imply that assets held in monetary form abroad are worth less to the oil producers. Thus, with the failure of these existing balancing mechanisms, there will be a net outflow from the oil-producing groups for many years, at least until the annual gross outflow is exceeded by the purchase of goods for use at home. Without the adaptation of the money market mechanisms to permit the aspirations of the oil-producing countries in surplus to be realised, and with the failure of the industrial countries in deficit to realise the true nature of those aspirations and thereby to permit these surpluses to be invested in real tangible assets in their countries, the financial authorities in the industrial world will go on attacking 'wrong problems with wrong weapons'.

There was a glimmering of recognition of the events which were to come in the outline of reform drawn up by the 'Committee of Twenty' of the IMF[1] in 1974, yet the proposals formulated still saw the surpluses of the oil countries as abberations in the existing system, not as symptoms of fundamental change. There was recognition of the need to harmonise the work of the IMF with the World Bank and GATT, but the general proposals for reform were based upon the need to improve the existing situation by 'tightening up the rules' and ensuring that means were available for early balancing adjustments. Thus, the outline for reform contained the statement:

> . . . There shall be a better working of the adjustment process in which adequate methods to assume timely and effective balance of payments adjustments by both surplus and deficit countries will be assisted. . . .[2]

Even though there was an evident recognition of the oil surplus problem later in the outline,

> It is agreed that in the revised adjustment procedures, as also in relation to convertibility, separate arrangements will need to be made for a limited number of countries with large reserves deriving from depletable resources and with small populations, e.g. certain oil-producing countries.[3]

However there appears to have been little attempt so far to make those arrangements in a manner which will accommodate the aspirations of such countries, and those which have been made appear to have been designed to protect the existing system.

The size of the surpluses by themselves is extremely large, although as a proportion of world liquidity they are not nearly as conspicuous. Preliminary data on an accrued basis published by the IMF in March 1975[4] showed these surpluses as $70 billion in total in 1974. The estimated surpluses for the years 1974 to mid-1977 are as shown in Table 11.1 and their deployment is worthy of deeper attention. The sudden price and other changes of 1974 saw a phenomenal increase in surpluses for that year and the deployment was

TABLE 11.1   Estimated deployment of oil exporters' surpluses
(Billion $US)

Year	1974	1975	1976	1977	1977[c]
U.K.					
British government stocks	0·9	0·4	0·2	−0·2	—
Treasury bills	2·7	−0·9	−1·2	−0·1	−0·2
Sterling deposits	1·7	0·2	−1·4	0·5	0·3
Other sterling investments[a]	0·7	0·3	0·5	0·2	0·4
Foreign currency deposits	13·8	4·1	5·6	3·4	0·2
British government foreign currency bonds	—	—	—	0·2	3·4
Other foreign currency borrowing	1·2	0·2	0·8	—	—
Total	21·0	4·3	4·5	4·0	4·1
US					
Treasury bonds and notes	0·2	2·0	4·2	2·0	4·3
Treasury bills	5·3	0·5	−1·0	0·5	−0·8
Bank deposits	4·0	0·6	1·6	—	0·4
Other[a]	2·1	6·9	7·2	3·9	5·0
Total	11·6	10·0	12·0	6·4	8·9
Other countries					
Bank deposits	9·0	5·0	7·0	4·0	8·5
Special bilateral[a][b]	11·9	12·4	10·3	6·1	11·2
Total	20·9	17·4	17·3	10·1	19·7
International organisations	3·9	4·0	2·0	0·2	0·3
Total	57·0	35·7	35·8	20·7	33·0

SOURCE: Bank of England, *Quarterly Bulletin*, Volume 16 No. 3, 1976,
        Volume 17 No. 3, 1977, Volume 18 No. 1 1978
[a] Includes holdings of equities and property, etc.
[b] Includes loans to developing countries
[c] Provisional

almost a 'holding' operation with investments largely in current or fixed deposits with UK or American banks. 1975 and 1976 saw the complete eclipse of the importance of Britain in this market and the pattern of distribution settled down. As may be seen, by no means all of these surpluses are floating around in the world's currency market as so many critics imply. Around 30 per cent has been finding its way into special bilateral arrangements including help to developing countries, between 5 per cent and 10 per cent to international organisations and around 20 per cent in 'other investments' which includes purchase of assets in companies and real estate, notably in the United States and Britain.

As these categories are all rather loose, it would be difficult to express precise proportions for any particular sub-groups, but it is evident that a good 50 per cent can be accounted for by the three groups mentioned. As to the other groups, it is not possible to estimate how much of the investments would have been bought by other surplus countries. Had the oil prices not risen, and oil resources not been nationalised, then the surplus countries would undoubtedly have been confined to the industrialised world, while the debtors would have been other industrial countries and most of the developing world. Had the United States been the surplus country, then most of the balancing transactions would have taken place in US dollars, and the US would have continued as the world's creditor. The markets would not have found it unusual, and the United States would have been able to absorb their debtors' obligations. Now, however, with the US as a debtor, there is an inflation in the Euro-dollar market due to the increasing claims on the United States which can only be met eventually in dollars, thereby increasing foreign claims on the United States.

The problems which have arisen, therefore, cannot have been because of the size of the surpluses, nor can the size of them as claims be regarded as a threat when compared with the assets held abroad by some of the major countries. The US assets held abroad were $4500 billion in 1971 and these had accumulated at a rate which saw a doubling every ten years. The total financial assets held abroad by the oil producers is unlikely to exceed 3 per cent of those held by the United States, 40 per cent of the world's productive capacity is now under American control, 65 per cent of the world's equity and 55 per cent of total fixed interest securities and negotiable instruments. In no way can the oil states' accumulations ever be a threat to such power. However the transfer of the control of the oil revenues from the traditional centres of monetary manipulation, where they were used as a balancing factor in 'traditional' countries' calculations, at the precise time that they so greatly increased in value undoubtedly had an initial traumatic affect which triggered a 'traditional' response completely unsuited to the actual situation which was being created.

KUWAIT'S EMERGENCE INTO THE INTERNATIONAL MARKET: THE EARLY YEARS

Under the original oil agreements, Kuwait's income from oil was very small when compared with the present day. In the immediate post-war years there was only one oil company, the Kuwait Oil Company, which controlled the extraction and export of the whole of the country's crude oil. Gulf and BP, the two foreign partners in the company, each paid their contributions to the government of Kuwait through an account in London. BP paid directly in sterling, Gulf in dollars which were converted into sterling. The rates were fixed in sterling and paid into the British Bank of the Middle East in London. These payments were made quarterly and, apart from the few local taxes raised, were the revenue to the state budget. These funds were transferred to the account of the government at the local branch of the British Bank of the Middle East as required. There was also a small addition to revenue from the Neutral Zone concession to Aminoil after this was granted which was paid in dollars, but amounted only to about 6 per cent of total government oil revenue. The state normally kept its expenditure within the budgeted receipts and usually budgeted for a small surplus which was transferred annually to a reserve account also held in London.

It must be remembered that at this time sterling was still a reserve currency and the maintenance of the value of that currency was one of the cardinal aims of successive British governments. Kuwait's relationships in trade were strongly orientated toward Britain and, with most of its revenue being held for a short time only in a London account, the problem of protection of its value against possible devaluation was not of paramount importance. Also, under an agreement with Britain during the 1940s, Kuwaiti government investments in Britain were, and still are, exempt from British taxation. The maintenance of reserves and the handling of accounts in London, therefore, made good sense especially as politically Kuwait maintained strong links with Britain under the Protectorate Agreement.

The reserve account was divided between investments in the money market, bonds and first class equities. The Kuwait Investment Board[5] was established in London in 1952 to handle government investments and some further diversification occurred. Investments were also made in Europe (up to about 10 per cent of total) and as the output of the Neutral Zone increased, so did the interest of those responsible for Kuwaiti investments increase in American investment possibilities. Kuwait was fast moving towards complete independence from Britain and toward the establishment of her place in the world's councils of nations and her view of her reserves and their deployment, small though they still were, was rapidly changing toward their use in a development strategy. The attitudes nurtured during this period, prior to the ending of the agreement with Britain in 1961, laid the foundations of future developments in her financial affairs and the way she responded to later changes.

THE CHANGING ATTITUDE FOLLOWING 1961

It was from the reserve account after independence in 1961 that Kuwait actively began the encouragement of indigenous activities in the home country. This she undertook especially in the joint sector. Faced with a narrow economic base and the urgent need for development, she entered many activities, either as banker to encourage others to join or as a collaborator when the entrepreneurship of a part of the private sector appeared to need support in what was considered a worthwhile enterprise from the national point of view. Often, too, the government collaborated in joint investment ventures in order to take advantage of specialised expertise and so that investment could be handled on its behalf by others. Thus, as well as entering such ventures as the Kuwait National Petroleum Company, the Kuwait Flour Mills Company, the Kuwait Transport Company and the Kuwait National Industries Company, as it did in 1962, it also promoted or joined a series of investment and financial companies between 1961 and 1965, some of whom were quickly to become international names in the financial world. The Kuwait Investment Company was set up in 1962, and the Kuwait Foreign Trading, Contracting and Investment Company in 1964. The Kuwait Hotels Company in 1962 was a venture for both home and overseas investment, and has become a very important operator in this specialised industry throughout the world.

With the marrying of government money with private, the private enterprise collaborators provide more drive than might come from a civil servant bound by different management considerations. Also the combination of a Kuwaiti company with foreign expertise was to enable investment abroad (e.g. in hotels and other developments) to be used for creating a specialised expertise among Kuwaitis.

As far as Kuwait's foreign portfolio was concerned, it was quickly spread among fixed interest investments in the British, European and American markets. At the same time, Kuwait also began lending to other Arab countries both through loans to governments and also via agencies in respect of specific activities or projects. Central Banks in many Arab countries received deposits from Kuwait at this time. Thus, the Kuwait financial sector was to a great extent anticipating the country's future role and was already deploying its foreign and home assets in a manner which was in accord with the policies that were to be formally stated in later years. With the prime motive of protecting the country's assets, the financial authorities also sought to ensure that, where possible, those assets would be deployed to the enhancement of both the home and other Arab economies. Unfortunately, of course, the absorptive capacity at home coupled with the administrative and political restrictions in some fellow Arab states made investment difficult. Consequently most of the reserves were deployed abroad via London, as the greater proportion of income was still being received in sterling.

In 1967 there was a major devaluation of sterling by 16 per cent and with it the devaluation of a major portion of Kuwait's foreign assets. This immediately provoked Kuwait into reconsidering its relationships with London, and she began an urgent reappraisal of her foreign portfolio and investment policy. Even at this time it was obvious that sterling would not remain a major reserve currency for much longer and negotiations were carried out with Britain to ensure that compensation would be paid on investments if the value of sterling fell below $2·40 to the pound. At that time Kuwait's foreign reserves were of the order of $0·7 billion. This was small by present day standards, but of course quite large compared with the size of the Kuwaiti economy at the time, with a GNP of around $2 billion.

1973 ONWARD, THE FOUNDATIONS OF THE PRESENT SITUATION

1973, or more exactly the period 1971–4, saw a complete change in the relationship of Kuwait with the international financial markets. In 1971 the world monetary system went through a period of such difficulty that from the point of view of states such as Kuwait it had effectively collapsed. Kuwait could no longer rely on the safeguarding of its assets by the efforts of others in managing their exchange rates and, with the growing importance of her reserves relative to her current account balances, the problem of portfolio management now became of vital importance, including the need for diversification. By 1974, however, the need for portfolio diversification was given a new dimension, for the price hikes saw such an increase in the revenues of Kuwait, like those of all other oil-producing states, that her portfolio needed not only to be protected from the point of view of uncertainty, but also to be diversified over time as the need for the protection of reserves over a much longer period immediately became apparent. By the time of the price increases, her reserves were in the order of $1·8 billion, and this base had been accumulated over twenty years. Its diversification began by shifting the emphasis from London to New York. The current account cover was kept in dollar bonds and Euro-dollars since it is difficult to diversify on a current account basis without speculation.

The reserves became so large, and the annual additions of such a magnitude, that some investments would not need to be liquidated for some thirty to forty years. Indeed, with the estimates of oil reserves, the reserves were likely to be accumulating beyond the foreseeable future. The managers of the reserves were thus faced with the problem of finding sound investments which would maintain their value in the face of inflation and at the same time show a reasonable yield. The net balance of current account transactions on the balance of payments for the years 1971–7 were:

(Million KD)

1971	1972	1973	1974	1975	1976	1977
420·8	448·8	979·8	2137·4	1939·0	2104·0	1794·0

In the same years oil receipts and government investment income were:

(Million KD)

	1971	1972	1973	1974	1975	1976	1977
Oil receipts	527·9	548·5	1084·6	2369·3	2289·0	2615·0	2587·0
Investment income*	108·7	125·5	141·4	202·6	334·0	441·0	492·9

* Government, Commercial banks and investment companies only.
N.B. To 1976, data are for financial years 1st April to 31st March.

The current account surplus figures contain both public and private balances. While the receipts were growing each year, there were three upward leaps in 1973, 1974 and 1976 due to the price changes. From 1974 onward, the emphasis was on the deployment of resources for the long-term future. The reserves of oil were such that with the introduction of conservation policies, Kuwait would be able to regard it as a store of wealth for over eighty years and, given current price levels, even at the rate of internal development expected, annual receipts could reasonably be anticipated to cover annual needs until well into the foreseeable future. To support this view, the balance of payments accounts in Table 5.4 for 1975 and 1976 show some most interesting pointers. As shown above, the balance of current transactions were KD1939 million and KD2104 million for the two years respectively.

Even though the current balances included results of transactions in the private sector, the overwhelming proportion of these balances were created by oil receipts. The net additions to the government funds abroad required new placements each year which were out of all proportion to those available only a few years previously. Bearing in mind the time lag between investment and receipt of interest, the figures for the last two years' investment income were only beginning to show the upturn from the previous years' increases in investment. The actual receipt of investment income itself, therefore, is bound to become more and more significant even if receipts from oil remain static.

In 1974 Kuwait's policy on long-term investment took a different direction and evolved along new lines. The allocation of general reserves was roughly 60 per cent in equities, industry and real estate, and 40 per cent in bonds and first class medium and long-term securities of over seven years' life. The investment in equities was as a hedge against inflation, while the bonds and securities were to provide a turnover of liquid capital. The Kuwait Investment Office continued its work in London, but the investments in the United States were handled by agents. Kuwait formulated the general investment strategy, while its representatives translated it into local detail. Given the 'comfortable' situation of Kuwait's anticipated future, however, this policy was based upon three main tenets—safety, income and capital appreciation. There was a general need for secrecy in these matters and investments were spread among 'the seventy-five companies', i.e. the seventy-five companies deemed most reliable on the New York Stock Exchange.

Very soon, however, with the increase in revenues, it was obvious that Kuwait could well be on the way to being a large holder in all seventy-five if her policy continued. In economic terms, she was no longer a marginal operator. If restricted to the same group, each year's purchases would have a significant effect upon ownership and also upon the market prices of shares in the companies involved. Another strategy needed to be evolved since the Kuwaiti authorities wished to remain 'low key' in their dealings. Any sudden reaction against foreign ownership within major companies would adversely affect not only the safety of investments but also the ability to invest elsewhere. Portfolios were created, or existing ones developed, in other countries and equity portfolios outside America and Britain were handled by banks in Germany, Switzerland, France, Belgium, Holland and Japan. The same rules of safety, income and capital appreciation were to apply with the same division of responsibility for general policy and detailed application. The main area of operations continued to be in the United States, however, for, even though international diversification may seem to be sensible, the size of the US market is so great that its relative safety at least is assured.

As well as the further diversification into other countries, Kuwaiti investments went outside the 'seventy-five' and into more speculative enterprises. This was a matter of necessity rather than choice and helped to maintain as much secrecy as possible in those markets where significant purchases require disclosure. At the same time Kuwait adopted a further policy of choosing certain companies which she felt would be advantageous to her policy and to concentrate some investment in them. This may seem counter to a policy of diversification, but in many ways the concentrations were 'diversified' in various sectors of economic activity.

In 1974 Kuwait entered, through the Kuwait Investment Company, the real estate market in strength. This included the purchase of Kiawah Island, off the East Coast of America, as the site of a major holiday resort. In the same year Kuwait bought out St Martin's Properties in London, a property group with wide interests, but at that time in urgent need of liquidity. This proved to be an astute purchase for after settlement of the firm's obligations by its new owners, the value of the company increased substantially. This purchase also gave Kuwait an entrée into the UK property market at a time when that market was depressed. The development of this interest has been such that she may now be one of the market's biggest, if not the biggest, operator.

The purchase of St Martin's, and also real estate activities in America, brought adverse publicity to Kuwait's financial activities. Many countries require disclosure, either through the Stock Exchange or directly via the government, of purchase of a given level of interest in a major company. In many cases the adverse publicity was based upon leaks rather than official disclosures and Kuwait now has an arrangement in London that, in conforming to the rules of disclosure, the information is made known to the government but remains undisclosed to the general public.

THE CURRENT INVESTMENT CLIMATE

It must be remembered that markets thoughout the world are not open to any investor to buy or sell at will. Each has its own rules and each is operated within the law of the country in which it is situated. If Kuwait wished to operate on a 'low key', it would be useless to operate in a market where complete disclosure is required. Furthermore, it may be better to operate through companies controlled by Kuwait than to operate directly. The purchase into property and insurance companies is an example of how this may be done. This is a convenient way of

preserving anonymity and shunning publicity, especially when safety
and not control is the object of the exercise. Kuwait may be confined to
certain markets by other policies of foreign governments. For example,
if Kuwait and other oil states wish to maintain at least some of their
current account balances in short-term funds, or even some of their
longer-term investments in government securities, there must be
sufficient securities available for their entry into the market not to
create speculation. Alternatively, if the value of a country's currency
fell, or interest rates altered so that security values changed drastically,
a move out of the market by a major operator might prove disastrous.
The original concepts of the reserve currencies were based upon the
strong economies of their countries (US and Britain). Now, however,
the strongest economies are West Germany and Japan, but with the
world situation as it is, those countries have no wish to see their
currencies develop into reserve currencies, a development which might
hinder their industrial sectors' progress. With a buoyant economy,
there is no need for a government to borrow from the market in the
same way as it would under conditions of depression. Thus, the supply of
'government paper' is restricted in precisely those countries which,
given its aim of investing for safety and security, Kuwait would find
attractive. If Kuwait were able to spread its short-term investments into
more currency areas, then the purpose of diversification would be
better served and the risks to world currencies in general would be
lessened as the need to take defensive action in the face of changes in
currency values would not have such a traumatic effect. At the present
time, the amounts available for new investment annually are such that
with the narrow markets open to the investors acting on behalf of the oil
producers, the placements are almost invariably large enough to be
significant and can often have a marked effect.

As for Kuwait's long-term investments, these are spread widely and,
where concentration in certain firms in an industry has taken place, this
has been undertaken for specific reasons connected with other policies.
The importance of long-term investments has also been given added
poignancy by the creation of the Reserve Fund for Future Generations
in August 1976. This fund was given an initial transfer of 50 per cent of
the General Reserve Fund, i.e. KD632·7 million, and was to receive 10
per cent of the state revenue annually plus all profits earned on General
Reserve Fund holdings. It commenced with a fund of KD850 million. It
will be handled in the same way as the GRF, but its capital and proceeds
are designated for the future and are declared inviolate.

While the concept of a reserve for future generations may seem laudable, it is difficult to envisage its practical significance. As maintained earlier, the whole of the capital of states such as Kuwait needs to be deployed in a manner which will sustain national growth into and during the non-oil period. It is not a question of setting some of the present income aside for the future, but rather of ensuring that the future and the present are integrated in a way that national growth throughout the whole period is maximised.

So far, only direct government activity has been discussed, and that purely in foreign investment. The activities in investment have not been confined to areas outside Kuwait, however, and neither has all Kuwait investment been undertaken by the government. The state has also sought to instigate investment by the private sector and has stimulated joint sector financial institutions for this purpose. These financial institutions have been developed, therefore, not as means of profiting by financial manipulation but more as instruments for the channelling of finance into desired developments. They were to be part of the development of a financial infrastructure which is as essential as a physical infrastructure to economic diversification. The two majors in the joint sector which have already been mentioned are the Kuwait Investment Company (KIC) and the Kuwait Foreign Trading Contracting and Investment Company (KFTCIC). Established respectively in 1962 and 1964, they have recently come into their own as vehicles of government and private investment, both at home and overseas. The former is 50 per cent government-owned, the latter 80 per cent; together with the Kuwait International Investment Company, a privately owned venture, they form the major Kuwait powers on the foreign investment scene.

It may be too early to judge the performance of the Kuwait institutions in fulfilling the twin objectives of managing investments and promoting internal development, since the large waves of available finance have only recently hit them. It may be that, even though they may be already part of Kuwait's financial infrastructure, the economy may as yet not be sufficiently developed to provide enough avenues for local investment. In the international sphere, however, they have become more important and there is no doubt that their development in international markets will stand them in good stead at home and also assist in the fulfilment of the state's other objectives. Kuwait joined in the creation of a number of joint banking ventures in Europe and elsewhere, the most notable being Banque Arabe et Internationale d'Investissement, Union de Banque Arabe et Francaise and the United

Bank of Kuwait, with further subsidiaries being established elsewhere throughout the world. Through these, Kuwait plays an ever-increasing role in the world's money markets.

As mentioned earlier, there are other wider policies to be considered by state or semi-state institutions, notably national security, and also policies of integrated Arab development and contributions toward the advancement of less developed nations generally. The last, will be dealt with in the next two chapters, but activities of some of the financial institutions not concerned with aid can still have an 'aid dimension'.

FOREIGN OPERATIONS OF FINANCIAL INSTITUTIONS

During 1974, the KIC, KFTCIC and the KIIC, together with the Al Ahli Bank and the Commerical Bank of Kuwait, handled over fifty bond issues and syndicated loans on foreign markets. Often these activities were carried out with other organisations abroad; for example, with others, the KIC arranged a loan of KD5 million to the Asian Development Bank in April 1974. In March of that year KFTCIC arranged an issue of bearer bonds for Sudan and, in June, KIIC managed a note issue for the Philippines, acting together with a number of foreign banks and financial institutions. In September KFTCIC were reported to be arranging a KD100 million loan to Yugoslavia; in December the KIC was reported as the sole backer for two large bond issues, one of $15 million maturing in 1984 at $10\frac{1}{4}$ per cent for the European Investment Bank. This marked the first time that a single Middle East investment organisation had acted as sole organiser of a loan to a major Western financial institution.

During 1974, however, a number of other institutions were established with overseas financial interests. The Kuwait Financial Centre, a joint business venture between the International Bank of Washington and a group of Kuwaiti businessmen was formed to provide finance for brokerage and import/export credits. The Kuwait Commercial and Industrial Investments Company was formed to invest in securities and other projects and to carry out research into avenues of investment at home and abroad. The Tourism Enterprise Company was formed with the government as the biggest shareholder, other shareholders being Kuwait Hotels Co, Kuwait Airways and the Kuwait Real Estate Company. This is an example of an 'interlocking' company bringing together various interests for mutual benefit by coordination.

By 1975, the KIC, KIIC and the KFTCIC (the 'three Ks') were among the leading issue-managing institutions and Arab investors accounted for 20 per cent of the world's credit securities for the last quarter of 1974. Although, as mentioned earlier, much activity in 1974 was in the nature of a holding operation with the large funds being devoted temporarily to short-term securities, facts such as these were viewed with awe and consternation by the world's press. During 1975, the pattern of company formation in Kuwait was totally different from 1974; contracting and manufacturing companies were now in the majority of the new formations, many with foreign participation. However, activity abroad in 1975 was still very active, and the 'three Ks' managed or co-managed forty-eight bond issues totalling $1·16 billion. Other smaller companies were engaged in ventures of a similar nature totalling almost $100 million more.

The pattern of overseas investments had also changed from 1974 onward, with far more foreign 'joint venture' activities being undertaken, and the floating of issues for specific industrial developments. These included petrochemical and pipeline developments, joint engineering ventures, real estate and joint investment companies, as well as projects for specific development in the Arab world. The variety of the form of the investments was only matched by the variety of their locations; Kuwaiti interests spread to every continent at this time. An examination of these investments, and those which followed from 1974 onward, indicate an emerging pattern. The aim to invest where possible in the Arab world was obvious; this was entirely in accord with the declarations of the Arab summit conferences and was an adherence to established policy. Furthermore, the upstream and downstream investments in oil became more evident. Investment in petrochemicals and refining abroad was to secure an outlet for Kuwaiti crude and Kuwait also invested heavily in pipeline construction to supplement her investment in tankers. As for non-oil diversification, investment took place in food processing, engineering and other industries. This was a means of gaining expertise in those industries which would be of use as a non-oil development strategy for Kuwait. These patterns continued to develop into 1976 and 1977. The movement 'upstream' into industries linked to current developments is useful in securing procurement and also assists in improving procurement terms. Investment in shipyards and ship repairs enables Kuwait to take full advantage of the concessions available in the Western shipbuilding countries for such purposes as employment creation and regional development and to give her own shipping interests priority if ever the need arose.

Thus, in spite of many restrictions on her activities in foreign investment imposed by countries in which the markets are centred, Kuwait has achieved a remarkable degree of success, in the four short years since the price increases, in evolving and following a complicated policy. Consistent with the overall policy of the government to serve the national well-being when oil is no longer available, to diversify the economy and to aim toward an overall development of the Arab world, Kuwaiti investments have followed a pattern of:

(1) safety, both through the avoidance where possible of risky enterprises and also by wide diversification,

(2). investments abroad which will assist home development via better procurement, securing of markets or the sharing of expertise, and

(3) many joint ventures in the Arab world.

Undoubtedly the third has been the most difficult from the banking point of view. For example, up to KD500 million has been invested in loans to British local authorities when interest rates on these reached 14 per cent per annum. These are good risks, yet Arab local authorities have a far greater need for finance but at a greater risk. Active steps are being taken to improve guarantee arrangements in the Arab world, therefore, so that this imbalance may be rectified. The Inter-Arab Investment Guarantee Corporation is an example, and it is almost certain that there will be more investments in both the Arab and other developing countries as their conditions improve and the risk of loss is reduced. Already some 50 per cent, an increasing proportion of total investments, are moving in this direction. In addition, the Kuwait Real Estate and Investment Consortium, a joint sector investment company, has been particularly active in carrying out investment projects throughout the Arab world. A dozen or so projects have to date been initiated in such important sectors as housing, tourism, and office accommodation.

This examination of Kuwait's investment policies and activities overseas must inevitably be cursory. There is no doubt that the external strategy is an integral part of an overall strategy for the use of the assets available to Kuwait (oil, real capital and monetary assets) and that this is not confined to the disposition of government funds but also relates to investments through the joint sector institutions. The concept of 'oil surpluses' is, in fact, already outdated and, if it ever existed at all, it was confined to 1974 and perhaps early 1975. With the evolution of an overall strategy, receipts from oil are now being deployed in ways quite similar to any portfolio management under a set of preconceived constraints and objectives, except that these constraints and objectives are derived from political as well as economic considerations. With the government and the joint sector institutions so prominent in the market, the direction of the general pattern of Kuwait's investment is determined. The private sector investments are able to exploit other avenues at will; many of these are obviously in areas where initial opportunities have been created by the government and joint sector institutions.

KUWAIT AS A FINANCIAL CENTRE

The magnitude of the 'financial surpluses' has led many to suggest that Kuwait might develop as a financial centre. The growth of the financial sector already mentioned and the natural expertise which the Kuwaitis have displayed lends support to these suggestions. This is particularly so in view of the need to diversify the sources of income and the potential need to employ a specialised and educated labour force. Evidence from other financial centres indicates that they make a substantial contribution to value added and employment in this proposed way.

However, in spite of the presence of many attributes such as the rapid increase in the number and variety of financial institutions as well as much of the necessary infrastructure such as telecommunications and air transport, such a development requires the expansion of both the demand and supply of financial facilities. Although domestic demand has been increasing in recent years, it is still small relative to the supply of funds as is evident from the shortage of financial instruments, the substantial KD deposits of the commercial banks with the Central Bank and the size of the foreign exchange assets held by the banking system. This situation has mainly resulted from the narrow production base referred to earlier and the insufficient domestic investment opportunities available. However, if these problems were to be overcome, this would only support the emergence of a domestic capital market of a more mature nature. The main attributes for the establishment of an international centre are already present. The world in general has free access to Kuwaiti capital via the existing institutions. What is not present is that whole pattern of banking activities which is normally concerned with dealing in debts and currency exchange. Kuwait is well able to do this on the world markets anyway, and it is probable that the presence of a large number of foreign institutions on Kuwaiti soil, creating an international centre in the accepted physical sense, would in reality imply the borrowing of Kuwaiti money by others in which to perform business in the market–business which Kuwait can adequately do for itself and which it is actually doing on a relatively limited scale at present.

In this regard, Kuwait is fundamentally different from Bahrain in that the latter is merely an offshore centre in which dealings are almost entirely undertaken in foreign currencies, since it does not have the substantial surpluses that are available to Kuwait. The problem facing Kuwait is, therefore, clearly of a different nature because it is more concerned with the investment of its KD surpluses. Although there is scope for following Bahrain's example, this would only provide marginal benefits compared with the main activity of handling its own KD investments. Furthermore, if these marginal activities, for example in Euro-currencies, were to have a detrimental effect on that main activity because of speculative operations affecting the KD, the drawbacks could outweigh the benefits to Kuwait of adopting the Bahrain pattern. While the government's reservations in this matter are thus recognised, efforts should be made to promote the main activity already mentioned by introducing measures aimed at broadening the demand base to encompass not only an enlarged domestic market but also increased regional and international participation. These measures should include not only the increase of the financial facilities available but also a clear and explicit policy concerning the Kuwaiti dinar. At the moment, there is an eagerness by lenders and a corresponding reluctance by borrowers to deal in this currency. This may be alleviated with the gradual emergence of a futures market in KDs, which would increase short-term stability, provided the explicit policy mentioned above is forthcoming.

While this examination so far has dealt with the deployment of Kuwait's foreign financial resources on a commercial basis, much of its foreign activity is also directed towards its growing relationships with the rest of the developing world. This is also to be seen as part of its overall strategy, although the actual commercial return is not commensurate with other forms of investment. The next two chapters are devoted to this important aspect of its resource deployment.

12 Transfer of Resources: a Case of 'Collective Self-Reliance'

BACKGROUND

Kuwait foreign aid, initiated even before the country's independence in 1961, has indeed been exemplary and for a long time unique among developing countries. Although until Independence it was confined to the construction of a few schools, health clinics and mosques, Kuwait foreign assistance soon evolved into a manifestation of the concept of 'collective self-reliance'.[1] Kuwait, which, in spite of its high per capita income, is still regarded as a developing country, has had one of the most impressive foreign aid records known to date. Taking into account Kuwait's concessional and non-concessional transfer of resources to developing countries, a staggering picture of the total capital flow emerges, irrespective of whether it is viewed in relative or absolute terms. But, before examining the country's record, describing the organisational set up and assessing the performance of Kuwait's efforts in the field of transfer of resources, we should attempt to explain the country's motives and objectives regarding such a transfer, particularly as far as aid-giving is concerned.

MOTIVES AND OBJECTIVES

Many interesting motives of granting aid have been suggested. Some are political in nature, some economic and some humanitarian.[2] A number of these motives have been criticised on the grounds that aid is normally administered in a way which often leads to results that contradict the donor's original motives[3] or that the motives of aid-giving may be in conflict with the real or long-term interests of the recipients. While some of the traditional motives of aid-giving are applicable to Kuwait,

209

many are completely irrelevant. As indicated in this connection in a recent article on OPEC aid, most OPEC members are small developing countries. None of them is a Super-Power with world-wide strategic interests, or an ex-colonial power with political and economic commitments to former dependencies. This raises the issue of motives, which differ from those of other donors in that they involve, in the case of OPEC, the relationships of Third World countries with each other and the mutality of their interests.[4]

Regarding the traditional motives of aid in the case of Kuwait, it has been indicated that there is a host of political, sociological and historical motives.[5] Although the exact motives might have changed with time, it is safe to say that in regard to the provision of aid to the Arab countries they consist mainly of the following: (1) a feeling of affinity towards the Gulf states and other Arab countries originating from tribal, nationalistic and religious links, (2) a desire to develop stronger ties with neighbouring countries to safeguard the country's independence and security, (3) a moral obligation to assist needy countries for purely humanitarian considerations, (4) a recognition of the importance of attaining greater regional political stability through improved economic conditions in the area, and finally (5) a means of acquiring greater international recognition and influence. Further occasional motives occur in the light of circumstances – for example, the financial support Kuwait pledged to Egypt and Jordan at the 1967 Khartoum Summit Conference, and additionally to Syria following the 1973 Arab-Israeli War. These were undoubtedly acts intended to consolidate the Arab world in the face of a threat to its collective identity. Hence, aid in this situation would be regarded as an act of solidarity. It would be difficult and perhaps pointless to evaluate the relative importance of these factors in determining Kuwait's motivation mainly because basic motives may change according to changes in the national, regional and international circumstances.

Following, however, the major rise in the oil prices at the end of 1973 and the expansion of the scope of Kuwaiti aid to cover developing countries other than the Arab states, the underlying motives became slightly different. Apart from the consequences of the 'oil revolution', Kuwait by that time had also acquired a significantly more influential position in the international community. While some of the country's earlier concerns about national security and Arab solidarity remained of paramount importance, Kuwait has become increasingly more concerned with safeguarding its economic interests by maintaining the real value of its oil-export earnings. Hence, as in the case of many OPEC members, aid has come to be regarded as a means of developing mutual benefits of the donor and recipient countries and thereby generating increased interest by the latter in sustaining the prosperity of the OPEC countries.[6] This factor was greatly enhanced by the efforts of many OPEC governments to strengthen the hand of other developing countries aspiring to reach more favourable terms in their relationships with the developed world. In addition, the success of OPEC in raising the price of oil has put the petroleum-exporting countries in the vanguard of the developing nations and they have thus assumed a leading role in the call for the establishment of the New International Economic Order. At the same time the oil-exporting countries seem to be aware that higher oil prices represent a financial burden on oil-importing countries of the Third World. However, 'The OPEC position is that oil price increases do not create a case for compensation through aid . . . but there is a case for alleviating burdens in the context of Third World solidarity to the extent that such a role could be played without appreciable harm to the donors.'[7]

On the other hand, the economic motives obviously assume greater significance in the case of non-concessional flows to developing countries. These motives differ in substance from those of the developed countries. With the substantial rise in the financial surpluses of Kuwait and other members of OPEC, particularly since 1973, there has been an increased search for new outlets for these resources, whereas the developed countries were in search of markets for goods and services and outlets for foreign private investments. However, in spite of the fact that in some cases developing countries provided more profitable and secure outlets for its surplus funds than the developed countries, there were also important non-economic factors that figured in Kuwait's motivation in this connection. These factors include, in particular: (1) the country's aim to develop stronger political ties with other developing countries, (2) its desire to acquire greater international recognition, and (3) a clear realisation that such non-concessional flows that would supplement its financial assistance to the developing countries would also contribute in a very positive way to the solidarity of the Third World.

While some may argue that it is premature to pass judgement on the motives underlying Kuwait's concessional and non-concessional flows, it is difficult to dispute the legitimacy of these motives. Even in instances where 'mutuality of interest' is established, the motives are still considered legitimate so long as there are no exploitative designs. There are clearly no indications to the contrary as regards Kuwait's financial flows to its fellow developing countries. Moreover, in spite of the importance of ascertaining the underlying motives, these flows should not be judged on the basis of the country's motivation alone. More importantly, they should be judged by the policies which have been followed by Kuwait and the results that have been realised to date. These are the aspects which will be evaluated in this and the following chapter. However, it is important to describe first the organisational set-up of Kuwait's foreign aid and to indicate the magnitude of the country's concessional and non-concessional flows to the Third World. As for the institutions concerned with the provision of non-concessional flows, they have already been described in the two preceding chapters.

THE ORGANISATION OF KUWAITI AID

The bulk of Kuwaiti aid has been extended on a bilateral basis through the following government channels: the Ministry of Finance, the Kuwait Fund for Arab Economic Development (KFAED) and the General Authority for the Arabian Gulf and South Arabian States. The Kuwait Fund, established in 1961 as a public corporation endowed with a legal personality, now has a declared capital of KD 1 billion (equivalent to approximately $3·5 billion). The Fund, which operates on a revolving fund basis, is the only organisation in Kuwait that provides concessional financing to economic development projects in the Arab states and other developing countries. In view of the importance of the Kuwait Fund not only in the context of Kuwaiti aid but also as a pace-setting and model organisation in the field of financial assistance, a full discussion of its policies and operations will be pursued at length in the next chapter.

The General Authority for the Arabian Gulf and South Arabian States, established in 1962 under the name of the Gulf Permanent Assistance Committee (GUPAC), was originally intended to provide grants to the Gulf Trucial Emirates mainly to finance social projects in such fields as health, education and housing.[8] Its scope of activity was gradually expanded to cover Bahrain, the Yemen Arab Republic (North Yemen), the People's Democratic Republic of Yemen (South Yemen), Oman, and more recently, the southern provinces of the Sudan.

The Authority's board is composed of the under secretaries of the ministries concerned (Health, Education, Housing, Public Works, Islamic Affairs and Information) and the Director-General of the

Kuwait Fund, and is chaired by the Minister of Foreign Affairs. The board is responsible for formulating the general policies of the Authority and approving its programme of operations. The Authority's resources which have been steadily increasing are provided by the Kuwait Government in the form of annual appropriations included in an exclusive supplementary budget which amounted in 1977 to KD12 million (equivalent to $42 million). This budget consists of three parts: the first two cover such current expenses as salaries, materials, rents and other general expenses pertaining to the Authority, its offices in the recipient countries and the running costs of the projects administered by the Authority, e.g. schools, hospitals, health clinics and mosques. The third part consists of the capital appropriation required for the construction works and supply of equipment for new projects.

The Authority's operations include a total of approximately 120 schools of all levels, several teachers' institutes, 10 hospitals, about 20 health clinics and the University of Sana'a. They also include the provision of teachers and medical staff, the construction of residential facilities for students, teachers and medical staff, and a settlement programme in the southern provinces of the Sudan. The Authority is responsible for the staffing and operation of all these facilities except those in the six Emirates (Dubai, Ajman, Ras Al-Khaima, Sharjah, Um Al-Quoun and Fujaira).[9] This summary of the Authority's operations indicate the importance of its role in promoting education and improved medical services in the Gulf states, North Yemen and South Yemen. These operations will have a positive effect on the future social and economic development of these countries.

The third channel of bilateral aid is the Ministry of Finance which draws on the state reserves to provide extraordinary financial assistance to the developing countries. Decisions to provide this type of aid, including the amount and terms, are usually made at the highest political level in the country. However, this type of bilateral aid normally consists of grants or highly concessionary medium and long-term loans, central bank deposits and guarantees of commercial loans to developing countries. The major form of this aid is the financial support provided by Kuwait to Egypt, Jordan and Syria to compensate them for lost income resulting from the Israeli occupation of their lands and to support their economies in the face of their disruption following the 1967 and 1973 wars. Also included in this type of aid is the provision of balance of payments support which is not covered under the Charter of the Kuwait Fund. This outlet also provides a suitable source of aid in emergency situations. Because of its nature and the decision-making process involved in aid provided directly by the government, political considerations are normally more prominent in this case than in other forms of bilateral aid. Such political motives as national security, good-will and regional stability are particularly relevant in this connection. It should be noted, however, that except for two minor instances this form of aid has been provided without ties to any source of procurement or otherwise.[10]

Kuwaiti aid through multilateral institutions has assumed greater importance in recent years and has covered a wider range of organisa-tions. In addition to such widely known multilateral institutions as the UN agencies, the World Bank and the IMF, Kuwait's multilateral assistance now covers a variety of regional institutions many of which have recently been created by the Arab countries and OPEC. Kuwait has taken a leading role in the establishment of the Arab Fund for Economic and Social Development (AFESD), the Arab Bank for Economic Development in Africa (ABEDA), the Special Arab Aid Fund for Africa (SAAFA), the Islamic Solidarity Fund, the Islamic Development Bank, the OPEC Special Fund, the newly created Gulf Organisation for Development of Egypt (GODE) and the Arab Monetary Fund (AMF).[11] In addition to its financial support of these organisations, Kuwait has taken a keen interest in their management and has helped in enhancing their operations. Kuwait has also supported such regional institutions as the Asian Development Bank (ADB) and the African Development Fund (ADF) and has played a leading role in the support of multilateral institutions involving other developing and developed countries including the new International Fund for Agricultural Development (IFAD), the proposed Solidarity Fund of Non-Aligned Countries and the projected Common Fund for Commodities.

Kuwait has also acquired an esteemed position through its active role in support of the World Bank, its participation in the replenishment of the IDA resources and its initiative to establish the Third Window to enable the World Bank to extend concessionary loans to developing countries ineligible for IDA assistance. It has also joined in the IMF Oil Facility which was created in 1974 to assist countries experiencing balance of payments difficulties attributed to the rise in oil prices.[12] In addition, Kuwait has contributed generously to virtually all UN agencies and programmes including, in particular, the United Nations Relief and Works Agency (UNRWA), the United Nations Children's Fund (UNICEF), the United Nations Development Programme

TABLE 12.1   Development finance organisations (basic information)

Organisation	Year established	Membership[1]	Authorised capital (in US $ million)	Kuwait's share (%)	Eligible countries	Scope of activity[2]
AFESD	1971	A	1400	18·75	ARAB	L,T
ABEDA	1974	A	742	14·70	AFRICAN[3]	L,T
SAAFA	1974	A	200	15·00	AFRICAN[4]	O
IS. BANK	1975	I	2300	5·00	ISLAMIC	L,T,E
OPEC	1976	O	1600	9·00	DEVELOPING	L,B
GODE	1977	A[5]	2000	35·00	EGYPT	B
IFAD	1977	J	1000	3·70	DEVELOPING	G,L,T
ADF	1972	J	407	3·92	AFRICAN	L,T
AMF	1975	A	910	10·00	ARAB	B

[1] A,O,I,J, are respectively: Arab, OPEC, Islamic and joint membership of developed and developing countries
[2] G,L,T,E,B are respectively: Grants, loans, technical assistance, equity and balance of payments support.
[3] Only non-Arab African countries
[4] Only non-Arab African countries. Correspondingly, a trust account was created by the Arab oil exporting countries (OAPEC) to assist Arab countries affected by the rise in oil prices which was administered by AFESD.
[5] Only Saudi Arabia, Kuwait, UAE and Qatar contribute to this organisation.

(UNDP), the United Nations Industrial Development Organisation (UNIDO), the World Health Organisation (WHO) and the UN Capital Development Fund.

Table 12.1 below gives some basic information about some of the new development finance organisations to which Kuwait subscribes. A complete summary of its bilateral and multilateral financial flows broken down into their concessional and non-concessional components will be provided later in this chapter.

MULTILATERAL VERSUS BILATERAL AID

As a major donor, Kuwait is increasingly faced with the question of whether to give greater prominence to multilateral or bilateral channels. As will be shown in the following section, bilateral aid has represented to date a far larger proportion of Kuwait's total financial assistance to the Third World. But multilateral aid has not been neglected, as evidenced by the rising number of regional organisations that Kuwait has helped set-up in recent years, and its long-standing support of the international organisations referred to earlier. However, in evaluating Kuwait's current policy of giving substantially more aid on a bilateral basis, it is necessary to examine the known shortcomings of bilateral aid in the context of Kuwait's economic and political circumstances.

Major criticisms have been voiced of bilateral aid, emphasising mainly that it is often a means of exerting political pressure and that it represents neo-colonialism and the continuation by other means of previous domination of developing countries.[13] However, it has been argued, perhaps more convincingly, that bilateral aid is generally less effective and less efficient than multilateral aid because: (1) it is often based on irrelevant criteria which favour political ends rather than national economic considerations, (2) it has the tendency to give excessive emphasis to large technical projects and grandoise schemes that show the extent of the donor's generosity, (3) it is normally tied to the purchase of goods and services produced in the donor country, hence restricting international competition, and (4) it results in the proliferation of aid administrations that tends to dissipate the limited supply of personnel with sufficient knowledge and experience in development finance. As regards the political arguments against bilateral aid which, according to Mikesell, are perhaps of greater relevance to the debate,[14] it should be noted that except in as far as it has an interest in developing stronger ties with other LDCs and in safeguarding its national security, Kuwait, as explained earlier, has no designs to exert political pressure, or assume a dominating position over the recipient countries. Moreover, the feeling among the latter of 'ambivalence to the erstwhile colonial administrations' in many traditional donor countries is completely irrelevant in the case of Kuwait.[15] Itself a developing country, Kuwait has given particular attention to this point and the main source of its bilateral aid, the Kuwait Fund, has had an established attitude of empathy towards the recipient countries which has succeeded in inspiring more confidence in its motivations and objectives.[16]

Although many of the other criticisms apply in varying degrees to bilateral and multilateral aid alike, most do not seem at all relevant in the case of Kuwait. For example, except in the two instances referred to earlier, Kuwait's bilateral aid has been completely untied. As regards the aid criteria and the distribution of aid among recipient countries, it will later be shown that the Kuwait Fund, which administers a principal part of Kuwait bilateral aid, applies conventional criteria of ascertaining technical soundness and economic viability of projects and gives due regard to such considerations of aid distribution as need, performance and absorptive capacity. With the proliferation of bilateral and multilateral aid organisations, coordination is recognised as an important requisite to increase the effectiveness of aid. In this connection the Fund has been very active in coordinating its operations with those of other bilateral aid agencies and with those of major international lending organisations. Thus, the problems of overlapping and duplication of efforts have been greatly minimised.

Finally, UNCTAD has argued that the major advantage of multilateral aid centres on the ability of multilateral institutions to be 'particularly effective in supporting sound development programmes because they are in a position to take an objective view of such programmes and to base their decisions exclusively on development'.[17] However, given a sufficient degree of freedom of action and administrative independence, national development institutions could very well acquire this objectivity without being influenced by the conflicting interests and objectives of member countries which are often inherent in the policies and procedures of multilateral institutions. As will be illustrated in Chapter 13, Kuwait's bilateral aid has realised this important advantage by means of the Kuwait Fund. Notwithstanding this point, Kuwait has also recognised the advantages of collective and concerted efforts and hence has assumed, as mentioned above, an active

TABLE 12.2   Comparison of administrative expenses

	Ratio of administrative expenses to annual lending operations (%)
ABEDA (1976)	5·0
Arab Fund (1977)	2·0
Asian Development Bank (1976)	2·5
Kuwait Fund (1976/77)	1·1
Abu Dhabi Fund (1976)	1·8

role in many international and regional organisations and a leading role in the setting-up of a number of specialised aid institutions.

Nevertheless, it should be noted that there seems to be evidence that the administration of some multilateral regional aid institutions is significantly more costly than that of bilateral aid institutions. Although it is difficult to make a meaningful comparison without taking into account differences in circumstances and in the range of activities, this observation appears to be borne out by the ratio of administrative expenses to the size of annual lending operations of a number of bilateral and multilateral regional institutions as shown in Table 12.2.[18]

FINANCIAL FLOWS

The record of Kuwait's financial flows to other developing countries covers a period of almost a quarter of a century. Its two bilateral aid institutions, the Kuwait Fund for Arab Economic Development and the General Authority for the Arabian Gulf and South Arabian States, already have a history behind them of more than fifteen years. Given the scanty data available for the years prior to 1973, it would be difficult to determine the volume of Kuwait's financial flows during the first twenty years. However official development assistance (ODA) extended on a bilateral and multilateral basis prior to 1973 is estimated in the order of $1·65 billion consisting of $280 million in loan commitments from the Kuwait Fund, $190 million in grants from the General Authority and over $1·15 billion[19] in grants and concessionary loans from the state reserves. This estimate of ODA for the first twenty years represents about 55 per cent of its counterpart for the years 1973–6. This comparison, however, should not detract from Kuwait's efforts prior to 1973 because the country's total oil receipts during the years

1946–72 was almost equivalent to the total receipts in the years 1973 and 1974. Furthermore, when related to the country's GNP, the average ratio of annual ODA commitments to GNP is estimated at well over 5 per cent.[20] It should also be noted that this impressive aid effort occurred during the country's earlier stages of development, i.e. when it was in the process of building up its infrastructure and hence its resource and foreign exchange requirements were, in relative terms, much greater than in recent years. As for Kuwait's non-concessional flows to developing countries, which were mainly extended by the Ministry of Finance and the joint sector investment companies (the Kuwait Investment Company and the Kuwait Foreign Trading, Contracting and Investment Company),[21] and other financial institutions, they included purchases of KD bonds issued by the World Bank and the Asian Development Bank amounting to approximately $350 million, in addition to loans, deposits and government investments in developing countries in the order of $150 million. Not counting private foreign investment, Kuwait's total financial flows to the developing countries during the period prior to 1973, are thus estimated at a staggering sum of $2·1 billion.

On the other hand, the record of Kuwait's financial flows to the Third World since 1973 has not only been substantial in relation to GNP, but has also been very impressive in terms of absolute magnitudes as well. In the four years from 1973 to 1976, Kuwait's net financial flows calculated on a net disbursement basis totalled approximately $5·4 billion.[22] As shown in Table 12.3, these flows represent on average well over one-fifth of total OPEC net flows and more than 4 per cent of the total net flow of all the DAC countries combined. To put Kuwait's net flows in the right perspective, they should be related to the foreign exchange needs of the developing countries. In this connection it is important to note that the 1974 net flows represented approximately 6 per cent of the combined trade deficits of the developing countries during the same year.[23] The record is significantly more impressive when related to Kuwait's GNP. Its total net financial flows averaged almost 11 per cent of GNP during the years 1973–6 compared with an average of 0·9 per cent for all the DAC countries and 0·81 per cent for the United States in the same period. The ratio of Kuwait's net flows to GNP is in fact greater than the figure stated here mainly because a large part of the country's oil revenues is a mere transformation of a depleting resource and thus should not all be regarded as value added.[24] In view of this, the World Bank proposed for the purposes of this comparison reducing the GNP of the major oil-exporting countries by a 'depletion factor' of 30

TABLE 12.3   Kuwait's financial flows to the third world (Million $US)

	1973	1974	1975	1976	TOTAL
Total net flows	550·0	1250·1	1711·2	1874·8	5386·1
Total net flows/GNP (%)	9·17	11·46	11·44	11·50	10·89*
Total net flows/OPEC net flows (%)	31·6	21·0	20·9	23·5	22·62
Total net flows/net flows of DAC countries (%)	2·2	4·4	4·2	4·6	4·03
A. Concessional Flows					
1 Commitments					
Bilateral	366·3	726·1	1096·3	544·7	2733·4
Multilateral	12·5	112·8	93·7	210·8	429·8
Total	378·8	838·9	1190·0	755·5	3163·2
2 Net disbursements					
Bilateral	311·8	556·3	910·3	376·3	2154·7
Multilateral	33·5	65·2	65·0	150·6	314·3
Total	345·3	621·5	975·3	526·9	2469·0
Net disbursements/ GNP (%)	5·76	5·70	6·52	3·23	5·3*
B. Non-Concessional Flows					
1 Commitments					
Bilateral	264·7	574·4	1683·7	1347·1	3869·9
Multilateral	171·8	61·5	85·0	876·4	1194·7
Total	436·5	635·9	1768·7	2223·5	5064·6
2 Net disbursements					
Bilateral	37·9	607·4	743·9	1076·9	2466·1
Multilateral	166·8	21·2	−8·0	271·0	451·0
Total	204·7	628·6	735·9	1347·9	2917·1

SOURCE: OECD, *Development Cooperation − Efforts and Policies of the Members of the Development Assistance Committee 1977 Review*, November 1977.
* Arithmetic mean for the period.

per cent.[25] Such an adjustment in Kuwait's national accounts would raise the ratio of net financial flows to GNP to almost 16 per cent.

Regarding the record summarised in Table 12.3 the following major observations may be made reflecting clearly the significant effort Kuwait has made in the field of transfer of resources:

1. The sum of net financial flows consistently increased during the years 1973–6.

2. Total commitments for the years 1973–6 totalled $8·23 billion, of which almost 40 per cent was provided on a concessional basis. This

component includes contributions to IDA IV and the Third Window of the World Bank amounting to, respectively $27 million and $20 million. Moreover, in 1977 Kuwait committed to IDA V a sum of $200 million representing almost seven and a half times its contribution to IDA IV.

3. The ratio of non-concessional commitments to total commitments increased from an average of 49 per cent during 1973–4 to 75 per cent in 1976. Although it is too early to deduce a trend from this data, this development seems to reflect Kuwait's increasing awareness of the need to cultivate new avenues of financial cooperation of mutual benefit by investing in Third World countries.

4. Total net disbursements of ODA flows accounted during the period under consideration for over 46 per cent of Kuwait's total net flows.

5. Net disbursements of bilateral concessional and non-concessional flows represented approximately 86 per cent of total net financial flows.

6. Net disbursements of ODA flows averaged during the years 1973–6 5·3 per cent of GNP whereas the target for the Second Development Decade set by the UN was 0·7 per cent. Partly due to lower oil revenues and the previously mentioned increase in non-concessional flows, this percentage decreased in 1976 to almost half its level of the year before. Nevertheless, as shown in Table 12.4, Kuwait's performance is still far superior to those of the leading DAC countries.

7. Non-concessional flows consisted of equity participation, bond purchases, central bank deposits and loans with a grant element of less than 25 per cent. These flows had a remarkable growth record in the period from 1973 to 1976 with multilateral institutions accounting for 23.6 per cent of new non-concessional commitments compared with only 13 per cent in the case of concessional flows. This development is due mainly to increased borrowing by the World Bank and other international organisations from the oil-exporting countries.

8. Apart from the exclusion of Kuwait's contribution to the IMF Oil Facility totalling $795·9 million during the years 1974–6, it should be indicated that there is no precise estimate of the amount of the total official and private non-concessional flows to developing countries. This is mainly due to incomplete information regarding direct investments undertaken by various public and private companies.

9. Data on concessional flows in 1977 show bilateral and multilateral commitments of $215 million and $1134 million respectively, totalling $1349 million, and bilateral and multilateral disbursements are shown as $792·2 million and $211·0 million, totalling $1003·2 million. While there are no complete statistics on other financial flows

TABLE 12.4   Ratio of net ODA disbursements to GNP (per cent)

YEAR	KUWAIT	OPEC	DAC	FRANCE	JAPAN	SWEDEN	UK	US
1973	5·76	1.41	0.28	0.55	0.22	0.55	0.29	0.21
1974	5·70	2.01	0.31	0.56	0.23	0.72	0.32	0.22
1975	6·52	2.70	0.33	0.58	0.21	0.82	0.34	0.24
1976	3·23	2.14	0.31	0.58	0.18	0.81	0.35	0.23

SOURCE: OECD, *Development Cooperation, 1977 Review*, November 1977, p. 168 and OECD *Statistical Tables*, 4 November 1977, pp. 8–11.

since 1976, preliminary figures indicate that the rising trend has continued into 1977 and 1978 despite the decrease in the current value of Kuwait's oil receipts and surplus funds. However, while its support for the multilateral institutions is contunuing, a greater proportion of the concessional and non-concessional flows are being provided on a bilateral basis through Kuwait's growing financial institutions.

In addition to the volume and breakdown of net financial flows into concessional and non-concessional components, the 'quality' of ODA flows is of great importance in judging the performance of different donors. Usually, this is expressed primarily in terms of the percentage of grants to total concessional flows and the extent of the grant element incorporated in the ODA loans.[26] As Table 12.5 shows, while the quality of Kuwait's foreign aid compares favourably with those of other members of OPEC, it is often less concessionary than that of many DAC donors, whose aid is generally tied. Moreover, there has been a drop in the overall grant element of Kuwait's ODA flows since 1974. However, as indicated earlier, this has been partly offset by the rise in total financial commitments, particularly those of a non-concessional nature. Another important factor that reflects the quality of ODA flows is the geographic distribution of the donor's bilateral concessional assistance. Kuwait's record on this count shows considerable improvement in recent years with the number of recipient countries increasing from five in 1973 to nineteen in 1974 and twenty-six in 1975. In addition, the percentage of ODA extended on a bilateral basis to the

TABLE 12.5   Quality of ODA flows (per cent)

	Grants as a share of ODA commitments		Grant element in ODA loan commitments		Grant element of total ODA commitments	
	1975	1976	1975	1976	1975	1976
KUWAIT	74·2	57·9	50·5	46·7	87·3	77·6
OPEC	48·2	62·9	46·4	45·4	72·3	79·3
DAC	69·3	69·6	62·7	62·3	88·6	88·5
FRANCE	83·1	83·4	45·0	43·7	90·7	90·6
JAPAN	35·4	48·2	53·9	51·5	70·2	74·9
SWEDEN	95·4	98·4	82·6	93·3	99·2	99·9
U.K.	91·1	94·8	65·2	55·0	96·9	97·6
U.S.	58·1	58·8	65·3	65·0	85·4	85·6

SOURCE: OECD, *Development Cooperation, 1977 Review*, p. 189.

Arab countries decreased from 98 per cent in 1973 to 84 per cent in 1976.

As for the sources of ODA flows, it is important to note that the Kuwait Fund has become considerably more important as a source of bilateral concessional flows in recent years. Unlike the period prior to 1973, the Fund accounted in 1975 and 1976 for more than 60 per cent of Kuwait's ODA disbursements on a bilateral basis. The bulk of the remainder was extended directly by the government and deducted from its financial reserves. On the other hand, the major proportion of concessional flows to multilateral organisations was provided to regional institutions. In 1974, a large part went to the Special Arab Aid Fund for Africa (SAAFA) designed to assist African countries to overcome balance of payments problems resulting from higher oil prices, whereas in 1975 and 1976 the bulk of the concessional flows went to such new development organisations as ABEDA, GODE, the Islamic Development Bank and the OPEC Special Fund.

EVALUATION OF THE AID RECORD

In this chapter an attempt has been made to explain how Kuwait has deployed a substantial proportion of its natural resources to assist other developing countries. It appears that this deployment has taken place in accordance with accepted aims which form part of the country's overall strategy of resource allocation. It must be evident that, having regard to the high ratio of concessional and non-concessional flows to GNP, Kuwait's efforts in this field have indeed been noteworthy. In addition, political considerations in allocations appear to be of far less significance than in most donor countries. Since such considerations are almost entirely applicable to bilateral aid only, their lack of significance in Kuwait's aid policies will be verified in the next chapter which is devoted to a discussion of the policies and operations of the major bilateral aid organisation of Kuwait.

13 The Kuwait Fund: Sixteen Years in Development Assistance

During the first twelve years of its history, the operations of the Kuwait Fund were confined to the Arab countries. In this first phase of its existence it concluded a total of forty-seven loan agreements amounting to KD134 million or to approximately $402 million. A second phase started in July 1974 when the Fund's Law and Charter were amended shortly after the 'oil revolution' increasing its declared capital from KD200 to KD1000 million (equivalent to more than $3·5 billion) and extending its scope of activity to cover not only the Arab countries but other developing countries as well. During the last four years, the Fund provided eighty-four new loans totalling KD390 million (equivalent to about $1·4 billion), raising the total number of loans to over 130 and the sum of commitments to KD524 million (approximately $1·8 billion). Mainly because of its relatively limited resources the Fund's operations in the first phase were rather modest compared with its present level of activity. However, it was during this phase that the Fund evolved its policies, work guidlines and its informal *modus operandi*, and acquired a measure of international reputation and prestige of impressive proportions.

The motives underlying Kuwait's assistance to developing countries have already been discussed, but it is important at this juncture to examine the justification for establishing an organisation such as the Fund as its instrument for providing this assistance. In this respect, Robert Stephens states

> The Kuwait Fund originally was established in December 1961, on the last day of Kuwait's first year of national independence. The Fund thus had its origins in a time when Kuwait was looking for recognition of its new status and for international support ...[1]

He then proceeds to explain that, in its effort to secure support for its application for membership of the United Nations, Kuwait was trying

225

to promote an image of itself different from that of an extravagant newly-rich Bedouin sheikhdom. Thus, it was resolved to set up, 'an international aid fund to show the world and the Arab countries in particular that Kuwait was a responsible member of the international community and ready to use its new wealth to help those in need.'[2]

Another important reason for deciding to channel a major part of its bilateral aid through the Fund emanates from a deep conviction on the part of the Kuwait Government that this would be the most effective way of developing the productive capacities of the recipient countries, an objective that also coincided with its underlyi..g foreign aid motives referred to earlier. It was fully realised that an organisation such as the Fund would be able to allocate its resources efficiently and in a manner that would best safeguard the interests of the beneficiary countries. These are basically the reasons the Kuwait Government has continued to place such a great emphasis on the expansion of the Kuwait Fund and the chanelling of an increasing proportion of its bilateral aid through this organisation.

While it might appear that a substantial part of this work is being allocated to this one organisation, this is because the Fund is an essential instrument in Kuwait's allocative policy and serves as a model in its structure, method of operation and pattern of growth for many newer institutions in Kuwait and abroad. Even though the allocations are not being made on a commercial basis, Kuwait has taken a lead in world affairs by recognising the need for the development of the Third World. This is regarded as a prerequisite for future world prosperity and security in which Kuwait obviously has a vital interest. Furthermore, it was for so long a unique institution and its history is a worthy case for study in its own right.

In order to appreciate fully the experience of the Fund in the field of development finance, it is important to examine its organisational aspects, policies, procedures and operations. Hence this chapter is designed to highlight the major issues pertaining to the Fund's experience and to discuss its current problems, future prospects and role in international development assistance.

ORGANISATION AND MANAGEMENT

According to Article 1 of its Charter, the Kuwait Fund, 'is a Kuwaiti Public Corporation with an independent legal personality as well as financial and administrative autonomy under the supervision of the

Prime Minister who shall be the Chairman of its Board of Directors.' This article sets the grounds for the Fund's administrative autonomy which has been a major factor in its success.[3] The Kuwait Fund is, therefore, governed by a Board of Directors which consists of eight Kuwaitis 'of recognised competence' appointed by the Prime Minister who himself is *ex officio* Chairman of the Board. The Prime Minister can delegate the Minister of Finance to act as Chairman in his place. The Fund's Charter provides for the appointment by the Chairman, on the recommendation of the Board, of the Director-General who is in charge of administrative, financial and technical matters and is responsible for the day to day operations of the Fund.

Article 5 of the Fund's Charter further provides that the Board of Directors is the supreme authority of the Fund and that it determines general policy and gives final approval to loans and to the Fund's own accounts. It has been indicated, however, that in practice, 'the Director-General plays a very influential, indeed decisive, part, in both the formulation and the execution of policy.'[4] Moreover, the fact that the Charter left many major areas uncovered has enhanced the role of those responsible for the Fund's management, and has stimulated them to greater endeavour and imagination.

The remainder of the Fund's organisational structure is very simple; it consists of: the Operations Department, the Finance Department, the Research Department, the Administration Department and the Office of Legal Advisers. There has been no justification for a formal geographic division in the organisation of the Fund, particularly because of its relatively small professional staff which consists of about forty members of several different Arab nationalities. The work in the Fund is mainly based on the 'task force' approach with close and informal collaboration among the various departments.

THE FUND'S RESOURCES

Besides setting the Fund's declared capital at KD1000 million, Article 3 of the Law provides for payment of KD400 million out of government reserves by transfers made from time to time according to the needs of the Fund.[5] This Article also provides for payment of the remainder of the Fund's capital out of the public revenues of the state by the appropriation of a percentage of the said revenues annually. Accordingly, a total of KD508 million had been paid up by the government by the end of the financial year 1977/8. Although this article implies that the

Fund's ability to lend is partly influenced by government decision which determines the amount of paid-in capital, it was interestingly argued that, by linking the Fund's additional capital to revenues, which, for all practical purposes means oil revenues, the mutuality of interest in Kuwait's sustained prosperity between donor and recipients has been consolidated.[6] Nevertheless, it should be recognised that the main constraint on the capital of the Fund had been the relatively limited size of government resources before the oil 'revolution'.

The Fund's Law also provides the Fund with the power to borrow and issue bonds within the limit of twice the amount of its capital plus its reserves. There has been no occasion yet to exercise this power as it appears that the Fund management is awaiting full payment of the declared capital, especially since borrowing is apt to increase the interest rate structure applied by the Fund.

Finally, it should be noted that the Fund's Charter requires that net profits be credited to a reserve account until accumulated reserves represent 20 per cent of the Fund's capital. 'Thereafter, net profits shall be added to the capital of the Fund, provided, however, that the reserves shall always remain equal to twenty per cent of the capital.'[7] Apart from helping to strengthen the Fund's financial position, this requirement has been effective in augmenting its resources by a sum of about KD135 million by the end of 1977/8 and hence has considerably enhanced the Fund's lending capacity.

THE FUND'S POLICIES

Other than the codified policy limitations provided in the Charter, there are very few written policy directives in connection with the operations of the Fund. Thus, the Fund's operations are characterised by a great measure of flexibility in handling the different financing problems it encounters. In addition, the provisions of the Charter are broadly worded and general enough not to restrict the management of the Fund in its handling of new situations. These points will be clarified below in the discussion of the Fund's statutory limitations.

Eligible Recipients
As indicated in Article 2 of the Charter, 'The purpose of the Fund is to assist Arab and other developing states in developing their economies ...'. Due to shortage of staff, the Fund's operations have been confined so far to Africa, Asia and two European countries, Malta and Cyprus,

and the management expects to commence operations in Latin America in the financial year 1979 / 80. Such known considerations as need, performance, access to foreign capital and absorptive capacity are very important in allocating aid among the various countries. As to whether or not the Fund's assistance should be limited to governments, the Fund's interpretation of the Charter has been that eligible recipients 'comprise governments, public or semi-public entities, as well as private or mixed enterprises undertaking development projects. Regional or sub-regional entities can also benefit from the Fund's activities.'[8] In cases where the borrower is other than the government of the country concerned, a guarantee agreement must be concluded with that government. The purpose of restricting the Fund to development projects is to avoid getting involved in purely profit-motivated activities. However, the distinction between the two is often very difficult to determine. On the other hand, the requirement of a guarantee agreement is designed for the protection of the Fund's resources and to ensure the recipient government's knowledge of the new obligation and its participation in safeguarding the country's interest in regard to the assistance provided by the Fund.

Forms of Aid
The Fund's Charter defines in general terms the type of assistance that may be provided. Accordingly it has been interpreted to include the following forms of assistance: (1) direct loans, (2) grants-in-aid to finance sectoral studies, pre-investment studies, identification of investment opportunities, feasibility studies, project preparation, training and other types of technical assistance, (3) advisory services relating to the financial, technical, economic and legal aspects of development projects, policies or institution-building and (4) provision of guarantees for the obligations of governments and corporate entities. Of these four principal forms of assistance, only the first three have so far been provided; guarantees, however, become an important form of assistance especially when shortage of funds is a constraint on its operations notwithstanding the fact that such guarantees constitute contingent liabilities on the Fund.[9] This form of assistance may also be very useful in situations where the Fund's guarantee can secure easier terms of finance for the recipient country. As in most other lending institutions, this type of operation has not yet received the kind of attention it warrants. Apart from above, the Fund's policy has excluded financial assistance for budgetary or balance of payments purposes, as well as equity participation.

On the other hand, while the Fund's Charter provides for extending assistance for financing projects as well as programmes, the policy of the Fund has given far greater prominence to the former. There are, however, assistance operations in the Fund's experience which fall in the area of the latter, including financing programmes in the power sector which encompass generation, transmission and distribution of electricity, as well as loans provided on a 'line of credit' basis to a number of industrial banks. There are other cases where there is sufficient justification for giving greater emphasis to programme financing, particularly where projects are highly interrelated or have similar physical requirements, or where the proper execution of the entire investment programme determines the efficacy of the individual investment projects.[10]

Limits of Financing

According to its Charter (Articles 14 and 15), the Fund is precluded from: (1) financing more than 50 per cent of the total cost of any project or programme, and (2) financing the local cost component of any project or programme. The Charter, however, provides that the Board of Directors may, by a majority of two-thirds of the members present, approve the relaxation of these two limits in exceptional cases. Such cases include, with regard to the first, situations where 'the necessary financing for a vital project or programme cannot otherwise be obtained on reasonable terms',[11] and with regard to the second limitation, situations where the country is unable to mobilise sufficient local resources to finance the project under consideration.

The rationale for the 50 per cent limit is not based purely on economic considerations. The Fund's view is that the proper implementation of any project requires the full support of the government of the recipient country which can be more readily secured when it is committed to take part in its financing. In addition, the Fund regards itself not only as a source of finance, but also as a catalyst that helps the recipient country to mobilise additional foreign exchange financing for the project,[12] thereby releasing some of its own funds for other projects in the same country or elsewhere.[13]

On the other hand, the rationale for the second limitation is largely economic. It embodies the distinction between the saving and foreign exchange constraints which has been widely accepted in the literature. The Fund's position in regard to this matter is that in most developed countries additional investment is constrained solely by shortage of foreign exchange and thus its financing should be confined to the foreign cost component of the project.[14] However, it is also recognised that, in some developing countries, income levels are so low that sufficient domestic resources cannot be mobilised to meet the country's investment requirements.[15] In these circumstances the Fund normally relaxes its second limitation which precludes financing of local costs. The Fund has encountered many such situations, the most striking of which was a loan of KD15 million to finance a power project in India where the full amount of the loan was utilised almost exclusively to finance locally produced goods and services.[16] It was considered that the level of consumption could not be reduced further to make available the investment goods required. However, the Fund ensured by special covenants in the loan agreement that the foreign exchange proceeds of the loan would be utilised to supplement the country's food import requirements and other essential consumption and capital goods.

Sectoral Distribution
The Fund's Charter is very general in regard to the sectors in which assistance can be provided; all projects that promote development are eligible for Fund assistance. However, the policy of the Fund in this connection has been rather restrictive. Assistance has been mainly confined to agriculture, transport, power, industry, storage and technical assistance. Projects in education, housing, family planning, water supply and sewerage have been almost totally excluded.[17] While the Fund recognises their importance, it was felt that another Kuwaiti institution, the Gulf Authority, was more responsible for such social projects and that the Fund needed to specialise in those basic sectors which would more directly affect the structure of the Arab economies, e.g. infrastructure. Moreover, it is believed that such projects as education and training should be incorporated in a broader development project in industry, agriculture or transport to avoid providing the wrong type of education or graduating a large number of students who would not have suitable employment opportunities. Therefore, Fund assistance to education and training has been provided only as part of its support of such major development schemes as the Rahad irrigation and Sennar sugar projects in the Sudan, the Tihama agricultural project in Yemen and to industrial development banks where resources were allocated for training and higher education of their staff. Finance for housing has also been provided on a limited scale as part of major development projects.

Currency of Aid

The Fund's Charter stipulates that the Kuwaiti dinar shall be the monetary unit of account in all its assistance operations, and also, until July 1978, that the Kuwaiti dinar should be based on the gold parity specified in the special agreement with the International Monetary Fund at the time of signature of an agreement for a loan or other type of financial assistance.[18] The justification for the first part of this stipulation is obvious in the case of a bilateral aid organisation such as the Kuwait Fund. The second part, however, was intended to safeguard the interests of the Fund and the recipient against either a possible devaluation or revaluation in the value of the Kuwaiti dinar as defined in the Central Bank's agreement with the IMF.[19] In the circumstances of a capital-surplus country dependent on a wasting resource such as oil, it is normally fair to incorporate this type of stipulation in long-term loan agreements. Although this was a maintenance of value clause, it should not be misconstrued as requiring the Fund and the recipient to adjust the unwithdrawn balance and the outstanding amount of the loan in accordance with any possible change in the value of gold in terms of which the par value of the Kuwaiti dinar was expressed. The Fund's interpretation was that 'gold' in this stipulation served as a yardstick to define the Kuwaiti dinar at the time of signing the loan agreement.[20]

Financial Terms and Conditions

The only financial condition specified in the Fund's Charter is concerned with the imposition of 'a service charge of one-half of one per cent annually on the amounts withdrawn from the loan and outstanding, to cover administrative expenses and other costs incurred in the execution of the loan agreement.'[21] The Charter, however, also indicates that the Board of Directors shall have the power to determine the form and terms for the participation of the Fund on the recommendation of the Director-General.[22] There is, therefore, a large measure of flexibility in deciding the financial terms and conditions of the Fund's assistance. As explained in the Fund's documents, however, this is normally done in the context of the grant element to be embodied in its assistance operations. The Fund's view is that the level of the grant element should be determined according to the economic conditions of the recipient country and the specific circumstances of each project. In practice, however, the Fund tries to be as consistent as possible in determining the interest rate which represents a major variable in the grant element leaving the grace and repayment periods to vary more freely. Hence, apart from certain exceptional cases, the Fund normally charges, exclusive of the service charge, an interest rate of 2·5 per cent for agricultural projects and 3·5 per cent for industrial, transport and power projects.[23] Therefore, the grant element in the Fund's lending operations ranges from a low of 25 per cent to a high of 86 per cent with a weighted average for agricultural projects of 57 per cent, power projects 44 per cent, transportation projects 46 per cent and industrial projects 37 per cent, giving an overall weighted average of about 50 per cent. If grants-in-aid are taken into consideration, the grant element in the Fund's assistance operations would average approximately 60 per cent.[24]

It should be indicated in this regard that in view of the increased debt-service burden of many developing countries, it would be helpful if aid institutions follow a more flexible approach in determining their terms of lending. It has been proposed that aid institutions may decide the grant element as a percentage of the proposed loan and alllow the recipient to select among the various combinations of interest rate (provided that it does not fall below the institution's actual cost of borrowing plus the fixed service charge), grace period and maturity of loan in accordance with the country's projected debt-service position. If given the option, developing countries might find it better from the standpoint of their projected debt-service situation to pay a higher interest rate with an extended grace period and loan maturity than otherwise.

Other Conditions

Apart from the financial terms and conditions, the loan and guarantee agreements incorporate standard conditions designed mainly to ensure the completion of the financing plan, the borrower's preparedness to make additional funds available for the project as and when required, the proper implementation of the project and that international competitive procedures would be followed in the procurement of all goods and services whose costs exceed a specified minimum limit. In addition, the loan and guarantee agreements include special covenants that vary according to the circumstances of the project and the recipient that are designed, among other things, to safeguard the financial position of the organisation or agency responsible for carrying out the project and to secure a competent management and trained staff for its operation. Also, the agreements often include covenants that aim at spreading the benefits of the project to as broad a base of the country's nationals as possible and to ensure that other requirements (physical or otherwise) needed to maximise the benefits of the project will be provided.

Co-financing

The Kuwait Fund policy favours participation in joint or parallel financing with other bilateral or multilateral aid agencies. This form of assistance has been considerably expanded in recent years and has emanated from two main considerations: (1) the Fund's lack of familiarity with some African and Asian countries in which operations were initiated after July 1974, and (2) to overcome the constraints on its operations stemming from the shortage of staff. Consequently the number of assistance operations co-financed with the World Bank, Arab Fund for Economic and Social Development, African Development Bank, Asian Development Bank and other aid institutions have totalled approximately twenty since 1974, or about 30 per cent of the Fund's operations during the last four years. While this development has helped in expanding its volume of lending, there are indications that because of occasionally conflicting disbursement procedures, the pace of disbursement has been relatively slow. In view of this, there is a growing tendency in the Fund to favour co-financing on a parallel rather than a joint basis.

In addition, there has been an increasing appreciation of the importance of coordinating the Fund's activities with the growing number of bilateral and multilateral aid institutions. Progress in this direction has been made but in fact there is still some degree of unwarranted overlapping and duplication of effort. It is therefore essential that many of these institutions should cooperate more effectively to streamline their activities with the aim of minimising the degree of duplication in project appraisal, follow-up and matters of disbursement. Apart from reducing their administrative expenses, such coordination would also help the recipient countries in planning their operations and would enhance the impact of the combined financial assistance provided by the donor institutions.

Joint Projects

The Fund's Charter provides for the possibility of participating in the financing of projects or programmes undertaken by two or more countries on a joint venture basis. The most notable operation of this type has been a loan of KD21·5 million ($75 million) that the Fund recently promised to the Organisation for the Development of the Senegal River Basin which comprises Mali, Mauritania and Senegal.[25] This is a major multi-purpose development scheme that consists of several sub-projects located in the river basin surrounded by the three countries. The Organisation is empowered to borrow from external sources with the joint guarantee of the member states and will repay its financial obligations from the revenues it collects from the sale of electricity, water rights and similar dues. There are also major indirect benefits that will accrue to the member states which range from increased agricultural productivity, as in the case of Senegal and Mauritania, to obtaining an outlet to the sea as in the case of Mali.[26]

However, notwithstanding this important project, the Fund's role in financing joint projects has been very modest indeed. The explanation normally given in defence of the Fund's policies in this area of operation is that political conflicts among many neighbouring developing countries render joint projects very difficult to organise and there is no guarantee that they would operate smoothly once implemented. This is borne out to a large extent by the record of the Arab Fund which was set up six years ago with the primary aim of promoting Arab economic integration by identifying and financing joint projects.[27] Nevertheless, it would seem that more can be done in the identification and support of joint projects, particularly since there are many small projects involving no more than two countries, e.g. in the field of transport, power generation and water supply, that would greatly improve the allocation and utilisation of resources on the regional level.

There are, on the other hand, numerous national projects with significant regional and international benefits which the Fund has supported. Such projects include the Suez Canal reopening and expansion projects,[28] the modernisation of the railways in the Congo and the Kenana Sugar project in the Sudan. Projects of this type promote regional economic cooperation and should therefore be given greater support by development finance institutions.

Allocation of Aid Among Recipients

The Fund's policy in regard to allocation of aid is very flexible. The Fund emphasises, however, its political and ideological neutrality in cooperating with recipient countries to the extent that it can be characterised as being apolitical. Assistance has been provided to countries with such different political systems as North Yemen and South Yemen, Morocco and Algeria, and Jordan and Syria. The Fund's philosophy is that even though social and political factors have an important impact on development, it should not be involved in suggesting social or political changes.[29] Political conflicts between neighbouring countries have also not affected the Fund's operations as evidenced by the assistance provided to India, Pakistan and Bangladesh as well as to Thailand and Vietnam.

The Fund is considerably more selective on the basis of economic criteria such as need (per capita income), population, performance, absorptive capacity and access to foreign capital. However, there are no definite and rigorous bases for its allocation. Per capita income seems to weigh heavily as a criterion but, as often indicated, countries with good performance in development and in their utilisation of previous loans from the Fund should not be penalised for having a relatively higher per capita income than others. This explains the Fund's greater support to Tunisia compared with North Yemen. The Fund also recognises the importance of absorptive capacity in allocating aid, although it does not always appear to be a constraint, as in many developing countries there is a sufficient number of projects eligible for financing. Finally, availability of foreign capital is also an important consideration for the Fund and it is evidently related to the country's overall growth performance mentioned above.

Lending Programme

In spite of the developing countries' persistent calls on aid institutions to supply them with medium or long-term lending programmes, many donors are not prepared to do so. This is particularly true of many bilateral aid institutions. The Kuwait Fund's policy in this regard is consistent with that of most bilateral organisations, as it makes known its financing on a project by project basis. The explanation of this behaviour seems to rest mainly on the Fund's concern to maintain maximum flexibility in dealing with the recipient countries. However, increased knowledge by the developing countries of the amounts of assistance forthcoming from various sources is apt to improve their allocation of foreign funds and to facilitate the formulation of long-term development programmes by these countries. The Fund has recently started to move in this direction by making its future operations known to the recipient countries up to two years in advance.

Project Evaluation

Due to its nature, project evaluation is referred to in the Fund's Charter in general terms only. It is indicated that consideration of loan applications should be guided by such recognised principles of development finance as: (1) the degree of importance of the project or programme and its priority rating, (2) the completeness and accuracy of the cost estimates and (3) the adequacy of the economic and technical evaluation of the project.[30] Other than this, there seems to be no written policy guidelines concerning the approach and criteria applied in project evaluation. Nevertheless, a review of a sample of the Fund's appraisal reports of projects financed during the last fifteen years clearly reveals that the Fund has evolved a special pattern of project evaluation. Although the specific approach and criteria used differ slightly according to the circumstances of each project, the general pattern may be outlined as follows:

(a) The Fund largely operates on the principle of respecting the priorities of the recipient country. As explained by the Fund's management, this principle emanates from a belief that the recipient countries are generally in a better position to determine their own priorities. However, apart from ensuring that the project meets certain minimum standards of technical soundness and economic viability, the Fund also takes an active role in ascertaining that the country's priorities are based on rational and legitimate considerations.

(b) In establishing the technical soundness of a project, the Fund ensures that all the relevant components of the project have been properly incorporated. This is usually followed by an investigation of the salient features of the project's description and technical properties. There are clear indications that major technical changes were made at the request of the Fund in numerous projects.

(c) Having established the project's technical soundness, the next step is to ascertain its economic viability. This is normally done following a thorough investigation of the market prospects and projection of input and product prices. The project's economic viability is generally analysed using shadow prices of foreign exchange, skilled and unskilled labour and excluding all forms of taxes and duties. After making the necessary adjustments in a project's costs (capital and recurrent) and revenues, the economic rate of return is deduced and/or the benefit-cost ratio is estimated on the basis of an assumed opportunity cost of capital (usually 10 per cent). The decision on whether or not to proceed in financing the project normally takes into account the outcome of this analysis.[31] However, as the Fund's project appraisal reports indicate, the Fund has no formal cut-off point as regards either the economic rate of return or the benefit-cost ratio.[32] The project's economic viability is then subjected to a sensitivity analysis to determine the most probable economic rate of return for the project in the light of assumed changes in capital cost, operating cost, rate of production, product prices and date of completion.

(d) Although the Fund attaches particular significance to indicators that are designed to ensure the efficient utilisation of capital, it does not base its decisions purely on such criteria. It also takes into account the social implications of the project and its impact on employment, income distribution, rural and urban development and the attainment of balanced regional development. These implications however are not incorporated in the analysis through quantifiable factors that enter into the estimation of the project's rate of return or the benefit-cost ratio as often suggested in recent manuals on project appraisal.[33] They are normally treated in an explicit manner, particularly when it is believed that such social implications figure in a significant way in the objectives of the project under consideration.[34] It is important to note that, apart from the greater emphasis sometimes placed on the social implications, the Fund's approach in treating such aspects in a qualitative rather than a quantitative manner resembles those of many other development aid institutions including the World Bank.

(e) The Fund's appraisal reports also indicate that adequate consideration is given to the project's financial viability and to the safe-guarding of the financial position of the organisation responsible for carrying out the project. The purpose of this is mainly two-fold: (1) to ensure that the project and the organisation concerned will not become a burden on the recipient's financial resources and (2) to secure part of the funds required for the future expansion of operations in the sector to which the project belongs. This is particularly relevant in the case of projects in power and industry. However, there also seems to be a recognition that tariff rates for electricity are often considered a fiscal policy instrument and hence could not be set independently of the government's other fiscal tools.

(f) Finally, the Fund's appraisal reports indicate that attention is usually paid to the managerial requirements and assessment is made of the capabilities of the organisation responsible for carrying out and operating the project. The Fund often requires the formation of a project implementation unit to ensure that the project will be properly executed. Financing is sometimes provided by the Fund to staff such a unit with the required expatriate personnel and to cover the cost of the project's training component. However, in the Fund's experience, the development of a methodology for considering management matters, based on techniques of evaluation using conventional criteria, is an urgent necessity.

Disbursement Procedures

As explained in a special Fund document, the disbursement procedures are basically designed to ensure that the financial assistance provided by the Fund is spent for the project or programme for which the finance was originally extended.[35] These procedures also enable the Fund to monitor the procurement of all required goods and services, facilitate project follow-up and to make sure that international competitive bidding referred to earlier is always adhered to.[36]

THE KUWAIT FUND'S OPERATIONS

Development of Loan Operations
The Fund's loan operations as shown in Table 13.1 have increased at a very rapid pace since 1972/3 reaching by the end of the financial year 1977/8 a total of KD524 million in commitments of which KD390 million were provided during the last four years. However, prior to 1974, loan commitments and disbursements displayed major annual fluctuations which in the case of the former were due to variations in the availability of funds as mentioned earlier. On the other hand, fluctuations in disbursements could in part be attributed to fluctuations in the size of new commitments, but their main cause seems to lie in the occasional delays in project execution. The slow rate of disbursement is a major problem encountered by aid institutions and relates normally to a host of factors as will later be explained. As for the ratio of disbursements to total commitments, it peaked at 72·6 per cent in 1972/3, but has declined since because of the sharp increase in new commitments.

Sectoral Distribution of Loan Operations
The four main sectors in which the Fund has been active are: electricity, transport (including communications and storage), agriculture and industry. Of these, the first two have received a total of 54·8 per cent (27·4 per cent each) of the Fund's total commitments. They are followed by industry (including loans to industrial development banks) and agriculture. However, as shown in Table 13.2, the relative shares of these sectors differ from one group of countries to another. In the case of Arab countries, transport, communications and storage have had the largest share indicating a greater emphasis on infrastructure, with industry occupying second place followed by agriculture and electricity. Although the Fund's record in the non-Arab countries is too short to reflect any definite pattern, there are however two interesting observations: (1) infrastructure and agricultural projects have received about 93 per cent of the loans provided to the African countries, and (2)

TABLE 13.2   Sectoral and geographical distribution of Fund loans 1962/3–1977/8

Country group	Agriculture	Transport[1]	Electricity	Industry[2]	Total	Group share (%)
Arab countries						
Amount (KD thousands)	74,790	130,930	64,890	79,480	350,090	66·77
Sector share (%)	21·36	37·40	18·54	22·70	100·0	—
African countries						
Amount (KD thousands)	13,310	24,500	16,370	4,500	58,680	11·20
Sector share (%)	22·68	41·75	27·90	7·67	100·0	—
Asian countries						
Amount (KD thousands)	12,200	9,800	74,850	16,345	113,195	21·58
Sector share (%)	10·78	8·66	66·13	14·43	100·0	—
European countries						
Amount (KD thousands)	—	1,130	—	1,200	2,330	0·44
Sector share (%)	—	48·5	—	51·5	100·0	—
Total						
Amount (KD thousands)	100,300	116,360	156,110	101,525	524,295	100·0
Sector share (%)	19·13	31·73	29·78	19·36	100·0	—

SOURCE: *Kuwait Fund Annual Reports*
[1] Including communications and transport
[2] Including industrial development banks

TABLE 13.1   Kuwait Fund loan operations 1962/3 –1977/8 (Million KD)

Year	Commitments		Disbursements		Repayments		Outstanding loans		Ratio of 3 to 1(%)
	Cumulative (1)	Annual (2)	Cumulative (3)	Annual (4)	Cumulative (5)	Annual (6)	Cumulative (7)	Annual (8)	
1962/3	14·5	14·5	0·8	0·8	—	—	0·8	0·8	5·6
1963/4	20·5	6·0	5·3	4·5	—	—	5·3	4·5	24·4
1964/5	37·8	17·3	15·8	10·5	—	—	15·8	10·5	41·8
1965/6	46·6	8·8	24·2	8·4	0·2	0·2	24·0	8·2	51·9
1966/7	56·5	9·9	30·8	6·6	0·7	0·5	30·1	6·1	54·4
1967/8	67·4	10·8	37·1	6·3	1·8	1·1	35·3	5·2	55·0
1968/9	68·6	1·2	45·0	7·9	4·1	2·3	40·9	5·6	65·6
1969/70	71·6	3·0	51·8	6·8	6·2	2·1	45·6	4·7	72·4
1970/1	80·8	9·2	57·2	5·4	9·8	3·6	47·4	1·8	70·8
1971/2	94·0	13·2	66·5	9·3	14·3	4·5	52·2	4·8	70·7
1972/3	103·0	9·0	74·8	8·3	18·7	4·4	56·1	3·9	72·6
1973/4	134·0	31·0	83·4	8·6	24·0	5·3	59·4	3·3	62·2
1974/5	161·0	27·0	91·3	7·9	29·3	5·3	62·0	2·6	56·7
1975/6[1]	320·4	159·4	135·9	44·6	36·7	7·4	99·2	37·2	42·4
1976/7	435·0	114·6	188·0	52·1	44·0	7·3	144·0	44·8	43·2
1977/8	524·3	89·3[2]	244·0	56·0	52·5	8·5	191·5	47·5	46·6

SOURCE: *Kuwait Fund Annual Reports*
[1] This financial year comprises fifteen months (1 April 1975 to 30 June 1976) because of the change in the financial year from 1 April–31 March to 1 July–30 June.
[2] This amount includes loans approved by the Fund of KD 35·8 million, but for which agreements had not been signed before the end of the financial year.

power projects account for over 66 per cent of the loans extended to the Asian countries. The first observation partly reflects Africa's need to develop its infrastructure as well as its agricultural potential and is generally in line with the efforts to increase world food production; the second is an indication of present efforts to increase the supply of electric energy as a prerequisite of industrial development in many Asian countries.

Geographic Distribution of Loan Operations

As indicated in Table 13.2 the Arab countries have received almost 67 per cent of the Kuwait Fund loan commitments since 1962. The remaining 33 per cent has been shared mainly by the Asian and African countries with about 22 per cent and 11 per cent respectively. However, this imbalance in favour of the Arab countries is due to the fact that the Fund's operations were confined to this group until about four years ago. Therefore, it is more relevant to compare the respective shares of the loans provided since 1975. As shown in Table 13.3, these shares display a greater degree of balance in the allocation of loans.

Classification of Loan Operations according to Per Capita GNP

As explained above need is an important criterion in the allocation of aid. Loans committed since 1975 are thus classified in Table 13.4 according to the various categories of per capita GNP. The table shows that countries with per capita GNP of less than $265 received more than 46 per cent of the loans committed during the period from 1 April 1975 to 30 June 1978, whereas countries in the upper income category (over $1075) received less than 5 per cent. It appears, therefore, that the Fund's performance in relation to this indicator is generally satis-factory, especially as there are other important criteria that were mentioned earlier which also have a bearing on allocation.

TABLE 13.3   Geographical distribution of Fund loans
1 April 1975—30 June 1978

Countries	Number of countries	Number of projects	Amount (Thousand KD)	Share of total (%)
Arab	13	38	189,080	52·0
Non-Arab African	16	19	58,680	16·2
Non-Arab Asian	12	18	113,195	31·2
European	2	2	2,330	0·6
Total	43	77	363,285	100·0

TABLE 13.4   Allocation of loan commitments according to per capita GNP, 1 April 1975–30 June 1978

GNP Per capita	Number of countries	Amount (Thousand KD)	Share of total (%)
Less than $265	23	168,905	46·5
$265–$520	14	137,000	37·7
$520–$1075	3	41,400	11·4
More than $1075	3	15,980	4·4
Total	43	363,285	100·0

Technical Assistance

The Fund's technical assistance activities have considerably increased in importance since 1972. A total of forty technical assistance projects have so far been approved for a sum of approximately KD6·0 million (equivalent to about $21 million). Several of these operations are considered to be provisional grants because, in the event of the Fund agreeing to extend a loan to finance a project based on a technical assistance study, the amount spent thereon would become part of the loan. However, most of these operations are outright grants covering a wide spectrum of activities that include project identification studies, techno-economic feasibility studies, detailed engineering works, sectoral surveys, training and resident technical assistance missions. The main purpose of these operations is to identify, analyse and prepare projects in countries that do not have the capabilities or the means to undertake such studies. Other than the provision of formal technical assistance, the Fund appraisal reports indicate that it also performs an important advisory role and assumes an active part in assisting many recipients to negotiate with consultants, contractors, suppliers, other lending institutions and occasionally foreign shareholders.

Other Activities

The Kuwait Fund undertakes numerous activities which are designed to contribute to the development of Third World countries through means other than the provision of loans or technical assistance. These activities include helping in the establishment of national, regional and international development organisations and representing the Government of Kuwait on the management of such organisations to which Kuwait subscribes. In this context it should be noted that the Fund took an active role in drafting the Agreement and Charter of the Inter-Arab

Investment Guarantee Corporation, the internal regulations of the Arab Fund, and legal documents for such multilateral and national institutions as the OPEC Special Fund, the Solidarity Fund of the Non-Aligned Countries, ABEDA, GODE, the National Bank for Development of Industry and Tourism in Lebanon and the Industrial Bank in North Yemen. It also represents Kuwait in many multilateral organisations including the IBRD, the Development Committee of the World Bank and IMF, ADF, the Arab Fund, ABEDA, the Inter-Arab Investment Guarantee Corporation, the OPEC Special Fund and the UN Programme for the Control of Onchocerciasis.[37] Moreover, the Fund has recently completed a joint assignment with the Arab Fund and the Kuwait Institute for Scientific Research for the preparation of the preliminary studies for the establishment of a new Arab Fund for Scientific and Technological Development.

MAJOR PROBLEMS OF THE FUND

The Fund faces such common problems as inadequate information concerning the economies of many recipient countries, insufficient knowledge in some developing countries of the procedures followed by development aid organisations and the lack of sufficient commitment on the part of administrators in many recipient countries. In addition, it is confronted with a number of others which are felt to be of particular importance, namely:

1. Cost over-runs. Given the rapid increase in prices in the last few years, it has become very difficult to estimate accurately project costs even with the incorporation of a price escalation contingency representing at times up to 60 per cent of basic cost. These circumstances have resulted in many cases in cost over-runs of more than 100 per cent of the original cost estimates and have caused major problems during project implementation. Unlike the World Bank, which normally does not finance cost over-runs, the Fund follows a flexible approach. In countries where reliable cost estimates are difficult to prepare, either because no similar major projects were implemented in those countries before or because extraordinary transport and political problems are likely to result in over-priced tenders, the Fund normally permits the project executing agency to proceed with tendering procedures and delays the preparation of final cost estimates and the decision on the amount of the loan until the bids have been received.

However, in some other cases, cost over-runs are due to many development institutions basing their amount of financing on cost estimates developed at the feasibility stage. These estimates are referred to as 'factored estimates' and are usually prepared by assessing historical unit prices and adjusting them according to experience of similar projects and conditions. As explained recently, however, by the International Federation of Consulting Engineers, 'Factored estimates only give an order of magnitude of the costs involved and no better estimate can be prepared since detail plans and specifications are not available, general and specific conditions inherent to the project are not known.'[38] Therefore, it is useful for lending institutions to put off a final decision regarding the amount to be made available until complete cost estimates, based on detailed plans and specifications, more definite unit prices and an estimate of contractors' indirect costs, have been prepared.

2. Low rate of withdrawals. As noted above, this is a major problem encountered by many development aid organisations. Apart from its obvious implications for project implementation and the realisation of anticipated benefits, this problem affects the net flow of resources, i.e. disbursements minus debt service, to the recipient country, and raises the effective cost of borrowing due to the commitment charge imposed by some institutions. In order for this problem to be analysed properly a comparison should be made between the projected schedule of withdrawals with the actual amounts withdrawn over the period of project execution. The annual shortfalls should then be related to the amount of outstanding commitments.[39] The main causes of the problem are presumed to be as follows:[40]

(a) Delay in declaring the effectiveness of the loan agreement due to lengthy ratification procedures in the recipient country, the requirement of cross-effectiveness with other loan agreements and the imposition of such additional conditions as the formation of a project implementation unit, appointment of a project manager or selection of supervision consultants.

(b) Delays in project preparation and last minute changes in project description and components.

(c) Unavailability of local contractors to carry out the work and the need to allow longer time for foreign contractors to mobilise and become familiar with work conditions in the project area.

(d) Lengthy and complex disbursement procedures applied by many development aid organisations and the lack of knowledge and experience with these procedures in the recipient countries.

It is difficult for an aid organisation to overcome all these problems.

However, there is a tendency now to introduce increased flexibility in matters relating to effectiveness of loan agreement and disbursement procedures. In fact, the Kuwait Fund imposes now the cross-effectiveness condition in exceptional cases only and is gradually simplifying its disbursement procedures.

3. Decline in the real value of the Fund's resources. This is a serious problem for any development organisation with fixed resources, i.e. one that operates on a revolving fund basis, because of its major consequences on its future lending capacity. Given the high rate of world inflation, especially in prices of manufactured goods and construction materials, project costs are steadily increasing. For example, the average cost of installing a 25mW thermal power station escalated from $6,250,000 in 1965 to about $13,000,000 in 1975. By the same token, the average cost of constructing one kilometer of paved road increased from $100,000 in 1968 to $260,000 in 1976. In the absence of periodic replenishments of the Fund's capital, the real value of its financial resources will inevitably decrease unless the average yield is equal to or greater than the average rate of inflation. It should be noted, however, that the average yield earned on the Fund's resources during the last ten years was in the order of 6 per cent per annum compared with an average annual rate of inflation of at least 8 per cent during the same period, and more than 12 per cent during the most recent five years.[41] Hence, it is estimated that the real value of the Fund's resources as of 1968 has decreased at a compounded rate of about 2 per cent annually.

Moreover, the World Bank projects a rate of inflation of 8 per cent per annum over the next four years followed by an average of 7 per cent. Assuming an average annual yield of 5–6 per cent on the Fund's total resources as of 1978, their real value would decrease on the basis of a 2 per cent differential by approximately 25 per cent after ten years. This clearly implies that, barring a replenishment of its capital, the Fund's lending capacity will be 25 per cent less than its level in 1978.[42] On the other hand, augmenting the Fund's financial resources through borrowing would maintain, or even increase, its lending capacity in the future and, as indicated before, the Fund is authorised to borrow up to twice the sum of its capital and reserves. However, unless the rate of interest on loans to recipient countries is increased to cover at least the cost of borrowing, the expansion of the Fund's lending capacity along these lines would speed up the dimunution of the real value of the Fund's capital and reserves.

Correspondingly, the problem of inflation and the resulting decline in the real value of the Fund's resources will be inevitably reflected in the amount and terms of assistance made available to the recipient countries. However, in the event of maintaining the amount of gross lending by the Fund at a fixed annual level,[43] the above problem would be further aggravated by the decrease in the current value of the net flow of resources – after allowing for debt service – to the recipient countries. The magnitude of the decrease in the net flow of resources will, of course, depend on the financial terms of the loans extended by the Fund. It is, however, estimated that, assuming an average interest rate of 3 per cent per annum and a maturity period of twenty-five years including five years grace, the net flow of resources would decrease after ten years by about 40 per cent in current terms.[44] The combined effect of the decline in the net flow of resources and the decrease in its real value will significantly curtail the real value of additional resources made available to the developing countries. This may be illustrated by assuming that the amount of lending is maintained at a fixed annual level of KD100 million, the average terms of lending are the same as indicated above and that the rate of inflation is 7 per cent per annum. The Fund's net flow of resources to recipient countries would decrease under these assumptions to approximately KD60 million per year in current terms after ten years and to about KD30 million in real terms. This means that the net flow of resources would represent in real terms only 30 per cent of the present level of gross lending.

The joint effect of the decline in the net flow of resources and the decrease in its real value makes it imperative for the Fund to augment continually the annual volume of its lending operations in order to maintain its developmental role. Given the analysis discussed above, this requires a replenishment of the Fund's resources not only through borrowing but also through increasing its capital. This problem will arise after the full payment of the Fund's declared capital which is likely to occur in about five years from now. It is an essential matter for the future role of the Fund to which the Kuwaiti authorities and the management of the Fund should give very careful thought. In view of the need to maintain its developmental impact, the Fund might also consider adopting a more selective approach to the allocation of aid which would concentrate its activities on those developing countries with the most critical problems and in sectors where development finance is less forthcoming.

ASSESSMENT OF THE KUWAIT FUND ROLE

Evaluating the contribution to development of financial and technical assistance requires ideally not only an analysis of the impact of such assistance on the growth records of the recipient countries, but more importantly a thorough examination of the circumstances pertaining to the assistance operations and their role in overcoming strategic shortages in specific human and material resources. This would be a very difficult task to undertake in evaluating any development aid institution and it obviously goes much beyond the scope of this study. In addition, in view of the Fund's limited resources relative to the enormous capital requirements of the developing countries, it is believed inappropriate to assess the role of the Fund and perhaps those of most other institutions in terms of the criteria mentioned above. Nevertheless, it is evident from the aid record reviewed earlier that the Fund's assistance operations have noticeably augmented the resources available to the developing countries and have played an important role in helping to mobilise domestic and foreign funds to be deployed for development purposes. In fact, there are many instances, particularly in relatively small countries, where the financial assistance provided by the Fund could be regarded as a major aggregate supplement to domestic resources which was markedly effective in increasing the level of investment and augmenting the growth rate of the recipient countries. Such instances include loan operations in many small African and Asian countries where the amount of financial assistance provided by the Fund represented up to 60 per cent of their national income and several fold the rate of investment. Even in large developing countries, the Fund's financial assistance represented an important addition to their resources enabling them to carry out essential components of their development programmes. Furthermore, there are indications that the Fund's catalytic role and activities in such fields as technical assistance, training and the promotion of appropriate development policies in the beneficiary countries have been of substantial value, especially in the least developed countries where the need for these forms of assistance is particularly urgent.

The Fund's role can also be assessed by inference from various observations and indicators. In this, emphasis will be placed on such broad aspects as the magnitude of the Fund's financial assistance, its role in assisting recipient countries to mobilise additional resources, its record of project completion and of disbursement and its performance in the allocation of aid. As mentioned earlier, the magnitude of annual commitments displayed wide fluctuations during the first ten years which were due in large part to variations in the amount of funds available. This problem however has been minimised following the five-fold increase in the Fund's declared capital in 1974 which also resulted in a substantial rise in the average size of annual commitments – from KD11 million ($33 million) during the years between 1962/3 and 1973/4 to KD97·3 million ($340 million) during the years from 1974/5 to 1977/8.[45] Although part of this increase was offset by the sharp escalation of prices, there has undoubtedly been a marked rise in the real value of the Fund's annual commitments.

As for the Fund's role in mobilising resources it should be indicated that the total cost of projects financed during the years 1975/6–1977/8 is estimated at KD1·94 billion (equivalent to approximately $6·8 billion) of which the Fund provided a total of KD363 million, representing about 20 per cent of the total cost of the projects. The ratio of Fund financing to the total cost of individual projects has ranged from a low of 6 per cent in the case of countries with easy access to foreign capital such as Morocco, Cyprus and Malaysia to 100 per cent in such least developed countries as Somalia, Mauritania and the Comoros Islands, with an average ratio of 35 per cent. These figures indicate not only the extent of domestic resources the recipient countries were encouraged to mobilise, but also the significant catalytic role of the Fund in mobilising additional funds from external sources. Although it is difficult in cases of joint financing to determine the party that assumes the catalytic role, the Fund's appraisal reports indicate that it was very active in promoting many important projects with other development assistance organisations and thereby obtaining the additional financing required.

Regarding project completion, the evidence indicates that of the 130 projects financed until 30 June 1978 a total of 40 projects had been completed. Of these, it is estimated that about 23 were completed according to schedule and 17 had delays averaging around eighteen months. The remaining 90 projects are in various stages of execution, including 77 projects (86 per cent) that were financed during the period 1975/6–1977/8, many of which have not yet commenced construction. This clearly indicates the need to expand the Fund's activities in project follow-up and supervision in order to avoid problems of delay and loan administration resulting from the substantial rise in new commitments in recent years. Nevertheless, the Fund's disbursement record has been generally satisfactory and, while the ratio of disbursements to commitments has varied with annual commitments, the Fund's disbursement record compares favourably with those of other development aid organisations.

Finally, the Fund's performance in aid allocation is believed to be superior to many other bilateral donors. As indicated earlier, 84 per cent of the loans committed during the years 1975/6–1977/8 were

TABLE 13.5   Comparison of Kuwait Fund and DAC allocations

Per capita GNP of recipient countries	Less than $265	$265–$520	$520–$1075	More than $1075
Kuwait Fund (% of 1975/6–77/8 commitments)	46·5	37·7	11·4	4·4
DAC bilateral ODA (% of 1975/6 disbursements)*	41·2	19·0	13·1	17·6

*Unallocated 9·1%

provided to countries with a GNP per capita of less than $520 whereas
the average for bilateral ODA provided by the DAC members was
about 60 per cent and only 53 per cent in the case of the United States
during the same period. Table 13.5 compares the Fund's overall
allocation with that of the DAC countries.

In concluding this chapter, it should be recalled that the basic motive
for channelling a substantial proportion of Kuwait's bilateral aid
through the Kuwait Fund is that the assistance provided through this
instrument would be an effective way for developing the productive
capacities of the recipient countries. There is now considerable evidence
that this has been achieved. As explained earlier, the Fund's operations
have contributed in a very positive and tangible way to building up the
infrastructure of many developing countries and augmenting their
production possibilities. Moreover, the Fund has succeeded in
maintaining a strong financial position that will provide a base for the
continued expansion of its activities. The manner in which the Fund has
gone about deploying its resources and developing its methods of
operations is therefore of particular significance to other institutions
and countries with circumstances similar to those of Kuwait.

14 Problems and Prospects

This concluding chapter is not intended to be a summary of the main body of the rest of the book, but is designed instead to highlight some of the salient problem areas in the Kuwait economy whose importance became evident in the light of this study. These problem areas are not only to be found within the boundaries of the country but also extend to include Kuwait's relationships with the rest of the world. While focusing on these separately, it must be emphasised that in most cases they are basically interrelated and often may not be of a purely economic nature. In addition to defining major problem areas, this chapter is also designed to examine the likely future pattern of the development of Kuwait as it is seen to be emanating and the possible changes in international and other circumstances which may affect it.

SOME MAJOR PROBLEMS

1. It has been emphasised throughout the whole of this study that the economy of Kuwait is heavily dependent upon its relationships with the rest of the world, via trade, investments and flows of labour. In fact, it is almost meaningless to discuss its development without discussing its foreign relationships as an integral part of the whole. While this is inevitable for a small developing country dependent upon a single natural resource, it has clearly left Kuwait highly vulnerable to many possible changes over which it sometimes has had limited influence.

In trade, world conditions in the oil industry for a long time restricted its revenues and, while developments since 1973 have changed the balance of power within the industry, the industry itself is still dependent upon world market conditions which may be greatly influenced by technological changes and alternative sources of energy. There are significant monetary complications both for Kuwait and the international monetary system flowing from this which will be touched upon later, but dependence upon a single exhaustible resource is in itself a source of extreme vulnerability that cannot be over-emphasised and which will inevitably be present for a long time to come. This may, of

251

course, be countered somewhat by industrial diversification, and this is the expressed policy of the government, but most diversification seems to be occurring within the oil industry, notably into downstream activities, so that given the interdependence of these and their total dependence on initial oil output, the economy's overall vulnerability has been little affected. Diversification into non-oil based activities would be more effective and these should be widened and further developed.

Trade being a two-way process, Kuwait's dependence on imports is another important cause of vulnerability and this is bound to continue given the country's limited production base. While this may be offset somewhat by greater regional cooperation, the country's dependence on imports will remain a fundamental part of its economic structure.

It has been emphasised throughout this work that oil exploitation in countries like Kuwait is essentially a transformation of one form of wealth into another. As explained earlier, much of this transformation has been into assets held abroad, resulting in Kuwait's accumulation of several billion Kuwaiti dinars worth of foreign investments. While this provides an alternative source of income and reduces dependence on oil alone, it carries with it a number of other uncertainties.

The third form of external dependence arises from the high proportion of expatriates in the labour force. This is becoming of increasing consequence to Kuwait's future development, not only in terms of its effect on the work force structure, but, perhaps more importantly, because of its effect on labour supply in other countries in the region and the resultant availability of labour to Kuwait in the future. There are of course much wider implications of a sustained influx of foreign labour and economic policies should be formulated in the light of these. Notably the plans for industrialisation cannot be formulated on economic criteria alone, but require an explicit population policy that aims to satisfy both economic and other long-term objectives, and at the same time contribute to the solution of the general labour problem.

2. Estimates indicate that at the current rate of extraction, Kuwait's known oil reserves will last upwards of eighty years. In view of this, and the indication that oil will remain a main source of energy and an important source of raw materials, oil production is expected to continue to play a predominant role in the Kuwait economy for the foreseeable future. Oil export earnings of Kuwait, and those of other members of OPEC, are becoming increasingly affected by developments in the international monetary system. In spite of the control

gained over pricing and production by these countries, the real price of oil is determined by factors over which they have little control. This real price is governed by inflation and the value of the US dollar in which payment is made. Due to the chronic trade deficits of the United States, resulting in large part from the oil import bill projected at $45 billion for 1978 compared with $27 billion for 1975, the value of the US dollar has been declining relative to major world currencies including many of those of the OPEC countries. Any attempt to counteract this by raising the monetary value of oil will result in further weakening of the US dollar on account of the increase in the US trade deficit, particularly as US imports constitute approximately 30 per cent of total OPEC exports. Many European countries have succeeded in adjusting to this problem, but the US has so far seemed unable to do so.

Suggestions that oil prices be linked to currencies other than the US dollar, e.g. to DMs or SDRs or a basket of currencies reflecting the pattern of imports of the OPEC countries, would merely amount to the indexation of the price. It should be recognised that this would help to safeguard the export earnings of OPEC. Nevertheless, it would still increase pressure on the US dollar in which actual payment will almost invariably be made. Furthermore, as the bulk of these export earnings will be converted into dollar assets, it will adversely affect their future value so long as the US trade deficit is maintained at the current level. This poses a dilemma for the oil-exporting countries in terms of the setting of oil prices and the safe-guarding of the value of their dollar assets into which a substantial part of their physical assets are transformed. While this problem could be ameliorated by capital transfers, the normal mechanism, enshrined in the Bretton Woods Agreement, dictates that it should be attacked through currency value changes or alternatively through domestic deflationary measures in deficit countries. The inapplicability of the first has been discussed. The second, on the other hand, is of limited usefulness in this case since, due to the lack of substitutes for oil, this mechanism would entail deflating the US economy to levels which cannot be regarded as feasible.

3. Apart from the problem of maintaining the value of foreign assets held by Kuwait in the face of declining exchange rates of the US dollar, which is the world's major reserve currency, such assets are steadily falling in value due to world inflation. While this may be partly offset by effective portfolio management, there appears to be substantial resistance in some industrial countries to diversification of investments into real assets by the oil-exporting countries in order to hedge against this. It would seem that there is a very definite preference on the part of

those responsible for foreign investment for allocating a greater proportion of their portfolios to such long-term investments, which normally would offset many of the problems in connection with the trade deficits of the United States, and possibly others. However, failing this, a major part of these foreign assets are diverted to the money markets in the form of short-term securities and deposits which could contribute to the instability of the international monetary system through changes in portfolio preferences.

4. A further problem concerning the foreign assets being accumulated by Kuwait and other OPEC countries relates to the inevitable long-term uncertainties in the countries in which they invest. As well as the normal problems inherent in any foreign investment activity, the very magnitude of the oil-exporting countries' investments adds a further source of risk. Future return flows to meet these countries' requirements may constitute such a large sum relative to the exports of the host countries that some forms of restriction might be imposed and their owners' legitimate aspirations frustrated. This is an increasingly significant element in the motivation of greater regional cooperation and investment in developing countries, where their interests may be safeguarded to better effect in the long run.

5. Of the other forms of financial cooperation, foreign aid has its own special problems, notably that the fall in the real value of the Kuwait Fund's resources constitutes a problem of far-reaching consequences. This fall in the real value, combined with the rise in debt service of the developing world, is rapidly diminishing the real net flow of resources from the Fund to the recipient countries, thus decreasing its role as one of the world's major aid institutions. To counteract this trend, the resources of the Fund will need to be augmented sufficiently to expand its flow of resources to the developing countries in order to sustain its role. At best, however, this can only be regarded as a temporary expedient. Thus other forms of financial cooperation, such as have been indicated, will inevitably be sought by countries such as Kuwait to establish a more balanced pattern of international cooperation.

6. The employment structure which has evolved from policies designed to provide security of income to Kuwaitis resulted in the concentration of Kuwaiti employees in the public sector. The combination of job security and increased general prosperity has instigated a general apathy in public employment, while the increasing opportunities in the private sector, notably higher incomes and better personal prospects, attracts the more able and enterprising. This is creating a widening gap between the efficiency of public and private

administration, which has particularly serious implications in view of the fact that far greater responsibilities fall upon the government due to the rise in the oil revenues and its expanding role both in the local economy and on the international scene. This apathy has been aggravated by a number of factors, including the social stratification and reliance on other segments of the population; the spread of wealth, which has resulted in additional sources of income; the uninterrupted progress of the economy which fosters expectations of its continuance and finally the creation of aspirations, especially among the highly educated youth, which cannot always be satisfied.

7. The rapid expansion of Kuwait has necessitated a substantial influx of labour and resulted in raising the proportion of non-Kuwaitis to well over 50 per cent. It must be remembered also that the oil period has witnessed a considerable amount of naturalisation, so that, as well as the dichotomy between the Kuwaitis and the non-Kuwaiti population, there is also an increasing degree of dilution of the original Kuwaiti society. The problems likely to arise from this are related to the lack of harmony among the various groups, particularly as they enjoy different privileges and economic benefits. This problem will become more significant as soon as the rate of economic progress begins to slacken and the individual groups become yet more protective. Further implications concern the resultant transitory attitude of a large section of the population with the consequent lack of a sense of belonging and a sufficient degree of responsibility.

These problems have been heightened by current policies which preclude the non-Kuwaiti population from enjoying equal welfare benefits and economic opportunities. Personal relationships have inevitably reflected these differences and are tending to reinforce them. While attitudes and policies such as these are understandable, they do not appear justified or equitable. In addition, their consequences must not be overlooked, particularly in view of Kuwait's increasing dependence on imported labour and the rise in competition from other similar countries in the region whose policies may be more liberal.

8. The private sector has also developed a set of attitudes which, although different from those in the public sector, are equally a source of concern. Following inflation, sudden large increases in wealth and serious shortages and bottlenecks in various sectors, the prospect of quick and large profits quickly generated a climate of speculation. Apart from serious distortions in the price structure, this has increasingly turned the private sector's attention to short-term gains instead of long-term investment precisely at the time when the latter is

needed. This climate can only be sustained by continued inflation and ever-increasing government expenditure, failing which there must inevitably be an interruption in this process and some serious repercussions on the development of the domestic economy (non-oil) in which the private sector is paramount. When there are occasions of difficulty, as indeed there have been, government is called upon to intervene in cases where such intervention was not fully justified; this has tended to accentuate the dependence on the government and to augment the general paternalistic attitude. This in turn further encourages speculative tendencies.

9. A number of problems are inherent in the welfare system and the manner in which it is financed. The feeling of apathy has already been touched upon and the growing attitude of rights to welfare without a corresponding contribution undermines the sense of national responsibility. Further problems will be created in regard to the financing of the welfare system if non-tax government revenues become insufficient for this purpose. A complicating factor in that event would be that non-Kuwaitis, who do not share fully in all the benefits, would presumably be expected to share in their financing.

10. The rate of population growth and projected economic expansion as more of the oil revenues find their way into the domestic economy may contain a built-in dynamism the consequences of which are not yet fully realised. As these developments crucially depend upon power and water supply based upon gas, the government's conservation policy may well come into conflict with these forces since the rate of gas production depends on the rate of oil extraction. Although, in the long run, other sources of energy, such as nuclear reactors, may be developed, this could well pose a problem in the intervening period.

11. The crucial dependence of public utilities on gas poses a further problem that will extend to the country's current efforts to industrialise. As long as the demand for gas is lower than the supply created by the oil production then its price can legitimately remain low. However, as soon as alternative uses become available, such as LNG exports or industrialisation, to absorb the excess capacity, a cheap pricing policy will have serious distortive effects on the general price structure. The implications of this should not escape policy-makers and officials concerned with the planning of future industrialisation projects. Furthermore, this problem may, in the long-run, have consequences for conservation policy and it calls for a periodic review of the country's cheap energy policy in the light of possible increases in demand and changes in technology.

12. This study has highlighted the difficulties facing a government with insufficient instruments of economic control. The lack of taxation on either income or expenditure, except for minimal custom duties, the absence of a national debt, a fairly stable interest policy and the genuine shortage of financial instruments have all constrained government efforts to control liquidity and inflation. Although this is essentially a short-run problem concerned with achieving a smooth and orderly performance of the economy, it also has long-run repercussions because of the resultant changes in attitudes and expectations.

PROSPECTS

Having reviewed some of the problems facing the Kuwait economy, it remains obvious, in view of the oil reserves and the financial resources available, that the country's prospects are indeed favourable. This is particularly so if many of those problems can be overcome in order to maintain and foster social harmony and to sustain smooth and uninterrupted growth. The changes since 1973 have placed vast financial resources in the hands of the government and a substantial quantity of these has yet to be used in the domestic economy. It is therefore expected that, as the productive capacity of the country increases and more of these funds find their way into local use, the coming phase of development will prove more significant and of greater consequence than the boom period of the mid-fifties to the early sixties.

As previously mentioned, the known oil reserves of Kuwait are estimated at 71·2 billion barrels in addition to 35,550 billion cubic feet of natural gas, which represent respectively about 11 per cent and 2 per cent of the world's total known reserves. In spite of technological developments in the field of energy production and consumption, oil is anticipated to remain a substantial source of the world's energy requirements. More importantly, it should be noted that, given the low costs of production of oil in Kuwait in comparison to other major producers, Kuwait oil will remain exceedingly profitable even if other fields become uneconomic. From 1969 to 1973 Kuwait's costs of production per barrel were 7 US cents. At full production over many years to come, they should not vary far from that figure at constant prices. Yet forecasts for 1985 by OECD, *(Energy Prospects 1985, OECD, Paris, 1974)* show estimated costs in that year as between $0·15 and $0·20 for the Arabian Gulf as a whole, $1·5–$2·0 for the North Sea, $3·30 to $6·70 for United States medium cost wells, and $6·50 $7·50 for synthetic crude from coal, all at 1972 prices. In addition, it is important to to indicate that OPEC has become increasingly more effective in determining prices and also, to some extent, production. In spite of occasional differences among members, recent experience indicates that it will continue to play a crucial role in safeguaring their interests, particularly if arrangements can be made to overcome the impediments to the maintenance of the real value of oil revenues and other problems related to the international monetary system to which reference has been made. There is also no doubt that, under pressure, OPEC, like similar organisations, would become more rather than less cohesive.

Moreover, this analysis has clearly shown that oil revenues in the case of Kuwait have in large measure provided merely a source of foreign income to cover foreign exchange requirements for imports and remittances. This source from a purely economic point of view, and regarding it in this context, will be gradually supplemented, and could conceivably be replaced, by income from investments abroad. Such supplementation is already occurring, for as mentioned income from foreign investments now covers upwards of 40 per cent of the country's import bill. Although carried to its ultimate conclusion this would imply Kuwait's becoming a *rentier* economy, with obvious implications regarding uncertainty and the limits to its control over the sources of this income, from the strictly economic point of view this proposition is not entirely implausible. This is particularly so in view of the difficulty of ensuring the real value of income from oil itself and may be viewed as a form of diversification of sources of income. However, with the emerging importance of this source relative to oil, there will be a need for Kuwait to devote increasing attention to the management of its foreign assets and their augmentation, within a context of overall optimisation of its national resources, as has been stressed throughout this study.

As the income from both oil and foreign investments are subject to differing sets of uncertainties, efforts are being made to diversify into other economic activities in order to reduce the degree of vulnerability of the overall economic system. These efforts are directed to diversification within the oil industry as well as into non-oil related activities, such as services and small-scale industries. While the uncertainties affecting both oil receipts and income from investments abroad are the subject of forces, some of which are beyond Kuwait's control, in some the ability to diversify in the local economy is more dependent upon Kuwait's development of its own infrastructure and policies concerning the size and composition of population and regional cooperation.

According to this analysis, especially that in Chapter 7 the ability to diversify, which relates directly to the country's absorptive capacity, is determined by the development of its infrastructure measured in terms of government developmental expenditure. Obviously, limits are imposed upon the degree of feasible diversification by the pattern of natural resource endowment, the size of the market, Kuwait's geographical location and other factors. However it appears from observation of recent experience that a certain degree of diversification into industry, trade and services is possible given the provision of appropriate infrastructure. In this connection, attention to the improvement of existing infrastructure, especially by the removal of bottlenecks, seems to offer a better prospect for diversification than its overall extension. Current government plans in this field, aimed at improving the country's absorptive capacity, should make conspicuous further diversification a real prospect. This however is, as mentioned, dependent upon the government's policy on the size and structure of the future population, and the problems created by the lack of clear direction in this matter have already been stressed. Without knowledge of the probable future labour force or of the size of the market, investment in new activities must inevitably be inhibited. Action in this direction is particularly needed in view of current labour shortages.

There are obvious prospects for further diversification into oil-related industries, and into other downstream activities, as well as into high energy based industries, provided suitable petrochemical developments are instigated to supply the feedstocks. Although these prospects still remain subject to the overall uncertainty applicable to the oil industry, they should not be overlooked, especially if equitable arrangements can be made with international corporations prevalent in these industries to obtain the necessary patents, expertise and market outlets. There is no doubt that ways and means are available to make such developments attractive, e.g. by subsidised power or oil-based feedstock, provided that in the long-run the value added and other benefits accruing to Kuwait would justify such concessions. There is therefore a need for much more rigorous project evaluation, not only for the vetting of proposals received, but more importantly for the identification of large-scale activities that Kuwait should attempt to develop. This identification should also include investigation of the most appropriate form of project execution, e.g. through the public or the joint sector, and whether foreign participation would be advantageous.

It must be remembered that the entrepreneurial skills of the Kuwaiti

population are another indigenous resource and, with the greater availability of abundant capital, the possibility of developing other sources
of income should be increasingly pursued. As well as the scope for non-
oil related manufacturing industries, these resources point toward
further expansion in trade, shipping and financial services.
Historically, trade has occupied a major role in Kuwait and current
trade practices and policies were designed to foster this. Consequently
there are ample opportunities for the continued development of
Kuwait as a re-export centre. Shipping too, offers suitable opportunities in view of the country's maritime tradition, the availability of
capital and her increasing role in international trade. The country's
commitment to the promotion of indigenous development in the long-
run is evidenced by its emphasis on technological research. Apart from
a 5 per cent levy on corporate profits, which is earmarked entirely for
that purpose, the government devotes substantial funds to various
research institutions with the aim of developing a strong technological
base which would further enhance the country's future prospects.

Finally, although Kuwait has witnessed a rapid increase in both the
number and diversity of its financial institutions, there is clearly a broad
scope for further expansion. There have been suggestions that Kuwait
be developed as an international financial centre. Kuwait's money is
freely available to the world without the presence of foreign
institutions, however, and such a market would require supplies of
financial instruments not otherwise needed. But, it could emerge as a
financial centre for the region and for other countries seeking financial
services from this area. This could serve as a real and viable form of
diversification and, although past experience indicates that the
government has not been active in promoting this type of development,
recent signs, such as the increase in foreign institutions taking part in
the financial sector of Kuwait, lead to a belief that a change in attitudes
may be taking place.

It has been stressed that, given the limited production and market
base of the country, the scope of diversification will always be
constrained. Some of the constraints can, however, be overcome by a
greater measure of regional cooperation and this has long been
recognised by Kuwait. This was made explicit in the First Five Year
Plan, and has been evident in government policies and activities. Given
the overall size and future prospects of the regional market, many
industries could become viable. Attention hitherto has, however, been
devoted to the reduction of tariffs among some of the countries in the
region which has had limited effect on the expansion of regional trade

due to the lack of a sufficient degree of complementarity in production among countries concerned. Instead, greater emphasis should be placed on the development of joint projects in inter-related industries, and other economic activities designed to reinforce existing complementarities and promote trade. Kuwait investment in these types of projects within the region would not only contribute to the realisation of further economic integration, but would also provide additional outlets for utilising the country's financial assets. Not only would this be in keeping with the policy on Arab development, but would provide added security against risk.

As for the remainder of the developing world, aid in its present form cannot be regarded as a permanent form of cooperation in all cases. Therefore other forms of economic cooperation must be sought which would be more mutually beneficial. The development of joint venture investments should gradually overtake aid in its present form. An effective combination of aid and such investments in many developing countries would not only serve the legitimate interests of Kuwait, but could be a means of sustaining the rate of concessional flows to these countries. Greater attention should now be paid to these possibilities and there is much scope for a degree of originality in developing appropriate new methods. If these developments imply the forging of new links between Kuwait and developing countries and between those countries themselves, this will be to the advantage of both Kuwait and the world at large, where the existing economic order is proving to be inadequate.

Lastly, acceleration of development implies proliferation of problems which require wider participation in their solution. This inevitably entails the broadening of the basis of national leadership. In the case of Kuwait such problems are already arising and many have been articulated earlier. The realisation of many of the prospects identified in this study is conditional on the solution of these problems. This clearly indicates the need for reinforcing the existing leadership by expanding the spectrum of sources on which it is based. There is ample evidence of emerging availability of Kuwaitis of suitable calibre for this to be achieved. Some are already in a position to accept greater responsibility and others should in due course acquire the necessary skills and experience to take their place in that wider leadership which will be inevitable if Kuwait is to achieve the goals which the country has set for itself.

Notes

CHAPTER 2

1. See H. R. P. Dickson, *Kuwait and Her Neighbours* (London: Allen and Unwin, 1956); also many references in H. A. Al Ebraheem, *Kuwait: A Political Study* (Kuwait University, 1975) to which the early part of this chapter owes much.
2. These are quoted by Al Ebraheem from Abu Hakima *History of Eastern Arabia* (Beirut: Khayat, 1965).
3. See W. G. Palgrave, *A personal narrative of a year's journey through Central and Eastern Arabia, 1862–1863* vol. 2 (London: Macmillan, 1865) p. 386.
4. Al Ebraheem, op. cit. p. 40, quoting A. T. Wilson, below.
5. Arnold T. Wilson, *The Persian Gulf: an Historical Sketch from the Earliest Times to the Beginning of the 20th century* (Oxford: Clarendon Press, 1928) pp. 252–3.
6. See *inter alia* E. M. Earle, *Turkey the Great Powers and the Baghdad railway* (New York: Macmillan, 1923).
7. An interesting result of this trade is that the width of rooms in Kuwait were to a great extent dictated by the length of mangrove poles.
8. Statist, 20/11/1964.
9. For this and the subsequent proceedings up to 1934 see F. H. T. Chisholm, *The First Kuwait Oil Concession* (London: Frank Cass & Co. Ltd, 1975).
10. This statement is of course essentially relative and in present day terms both proposals appear derisory. While APOC offered an initial down-payment of £750, Holmes offered £2000 and, while APOC offered the Sheikh an annual minimum payment of £2300, Holmes offered £3000!
11. The Kuwait Neutral Zone is an area of land, south of Kuwait roughly 100 kilometres square. This is administered and 'owned' jointly by Kuwait and Saudi Arabia under an arrangement created at the Uquair Conference of 1922 convened to settle the borders in this area. While Iraq and Saudi Arabian delegations included their own nationals (Ibn Saud himself being a member of the latter delegation) Kuwait was represented by the British Political Agent only. During the conference it was obvious that the possibility of mutual agreement was remote. Thus a substantial tract of the Najd claimed by Ibn Saud was 'given' to Iraq and in turn much of the land formerly agreed as belonging to Kuwait by the Anglo-Turkish Convention of 1913 was again 'given' to Ibn Saud probably as a placatory gesture. Two neutral zones, one between Kuwait and Saudi Arabia, the other between Saudi Arabia and Iraq, were at the same time created to be jointly administered. These arrangements, in which Kuwait had no direct part but whose interests should have been safeguarded by the British Political Agent

under the 1899 Agreement, reduced the country from about 38,000 square miles to a third of that amount. In the early sixties a border was formerly delineated dividing the Kuwait–Saudi Arabia neutral zone between the two countries, but with an agreement on joint exploitation of the oil deposits on a 50-50 basis.

12. It should be pointed out that there was more than a suspicion at that time that the well-paid directorship insisted upon by the Sheikh was in fact being sought on behalf of Holmes who, although he was a negotiator for KOC, was in fact still maintaining independent contact with the Sheikh.

13. Op. cit., p. 82.

CHAPTER 3

1. Income and public revenue estimates are based on information from an article by Fakhri Shehab. 'Kuwait: A Super Affluent Society', *Foreign Affairs*, vol. 42, pp. 461–74 (April 1964).

2. This hypothesis was developed in M. W. Khouja, *Distinguishing Properties of the Kuwait Economy*, the Kuwait Economic Society, March 1973.

3. Apart from its present use in agriculture and gardening, a limited quantity of brackish water is normally added to the desalinated water to give a more natural taste and provide essential minerals.

4. Desalination plants use natural gas to fire their boilers which, in turn, produce steam to heat the sea water. The same boilers are also used to produce electricity by driving turbo-generators.

5. This is true in spite of the fact that until very recently there was neither a water distribution network nor a sewerage system; and even in 1977 these facilities have been installed in limited areas of the city only. In addition, visitors to Kuwait are astounded by the absence of paved sidewalks in many parts of the city, not to mention the congested airport which has long been obsolete and unbecoming of a country that has one of the highest levels of per capita income in the world. A new airport terminal however is in an advanced stage of construction.

6. According to one source, 'The concept of the Welfare State is part and parcel of the paternalist nature of Kuwait's Sheikhdom, though it owes a great deal in inspiration and form to Western models'. H. V. F. Winston and Zahra Freeth, *Kuwait Prospect and Reality* (London: George Allen and Unwin Ltd, 1972) p. 194.

7. The health situation also compared favourably to many of the most developed countries in the world. The following comparisons indicate the extent of the improvement in health services by 1957:

	Kuwait	Canada	UK	US
Number of inhabitants/physician	806	820	900	670
Number of hospital beds/ 1000 inhabitants	7·5	11·6	10·8	9·2

8. Evidence of this is found in the decline in the number of beds to about 4 per

1000 people in 1975 and the rise in the number of inhabitants per physician to almost 900.

9. Many suggestions have been put forth in this connection, e.g. an incentive system or a government subsidised health insurance scheme.

10. Estimate of the 1945 student population is obtained from Winstone and Freeth, op. cit. p. 196.

11. The adult education centres increased from 21 in 1965 / 6 to 123 in 1975 / 6.

12. Eligibility is based on such reasons as: poverty, disability, senility, sickness, orphanhood, etc.

13. The estimate of KD0·4/1000 gallons represents the difference between cost of production (KD1·1) with an imputed price for natural gas and the selling price to the public before transport (KD 0·7). The same applies for electricity. Both estimates should, however, be regarded as orders of magnitude only.

14. The main components of this estimate are education (KD60 million), health (KD28 million), family support (KD6·7 million), housing (KD4·3 million), water, electricity and food subsidies (about KD40 million in total, of which 50 per cent apply to the Kuwaiti population).

CHAPTER 4

1. This is also an indication that living conditions have sufficiently improved to induce more people to settle their families in the country and of the increased role of women in economic activity made possible through social and cultural transformation. In addition, the influx of more non-Kuwaitis into higher paid more regular employment encouraged family settlement.

2. Surprisingly, Yusif Sayigh applied a definition to Kuwait which included all people over the age of eleven, resulting in an estimate of 60·5 per cent of the total population as inactive in 1965. Hence, he states, '. . . the Kuwaiti labour force contains a category rarely encountered in labour statistics: that of people who are not in need of work-defined by the census report as those able to work but having no desire to work'. After offering some possible reasons for this phenomenon, he concludes that the main explanation is that the bulk of the category constitutes a *rentier* class. This conclusion would not be justifiable with a more meaningful definition of working age population, i.e. fifteen to sixty or even more preferably twenty to sixty. Based on a definition that if the labour force includes only people between the ages of fifteen and sixty, the inactive population would constitute about one-third in 1965; and it would have fallen to 6·7 per cent if he had considered the male population only. The corresponding figures for Kuwaitis and non-Kuwaitis would have been 19·8 per cent and 1·7 per cent respectively, which would constitute about 10,300 people in the case of the former and 2250 in the latter. (See Y. A. Sayigh, *The Economies of the Arab world. Development since 1945* (London: Croom Helm, 1978) p. 96.)

3. IBRD, *The Economic Development of Kuwait* (Baltimore, 1965) p. 4.

4. I. Najjar, *The Development of a One Resource Economy: A case study of Kuwait* (an unpublished dissertation, 1969) p. 67.

5. This policy has been criticised because of its adverse effects on the work incentives of non-Kuwaitis and its tendency to develop among Kuwaitis excessive job security and dependence on Government.

6. Although the sponsorship arrangement has been instituted in order to have a Kuwaiti assume the legal responsibility for the business and thus protect the interests of the community, it is sometimes regarded as the price of doing business in Kuwait. Therefore, a deposit, a tax or both would not only be more justified but would also be a more systematic way of regulating this activity.

7. See J. K. Al-Saadoun, 'Factors contributing to equality of income distribution in Kuwait', *Journal of the Gulf and Arabian Peninsula*, vol. 3, no. 12, p. 83 (October 1977).

8. This is confirmed by non-Kuwaitis who lived in Kuwait prior to 1946 who describe the friendly and hospitable atmosphere that prevailed when a limited number of foreigners worked and lived in the country.

CHAPTER 5

1. It has been argued, however, that such investments greatly contributed to the escalation of real estate prices in Egypt following 1973.

2. It is to be noted that the Inter-Arab Investment Guarantee Corporation was conceived in the late sixties as a means to encourage capital movement among Arab countries by providing insurance against non-commercial risks. However by the time it commenced operation in early 1975, risks of nationalisation and confiscation had been reduced and the corporation's capitalisation proved inadequate for major operations. Thus its role in promoting the flow of capital has been very limited.

CHAPTER 6

1. See Z. Mikdashi, *The Community of Oil Exporting Countries* (George Allen and Unwin, 1972).

2. See, for example, M. A. Adelman, *The World Petroleum Market* (Baltimore: The Johns Hopkins University Press, 1972).

3. C. Tugendhat and A. Hamilton, *Oil, the Biggest Business* (Eyre and Methuen, 1975) (Revised Edition).

4. An excellent discussion on terms of trade is to be found in Mikdashi, op. cit. pp. 157–95.

5. Mikdashi, op. cit. pp. 169–70.

6. Naiem A. Sherbiny, 'Arab oil production policies in the context of international conflicts' in *Arab Oil* edited by N. A. Sherbiny and M. A. Tessler, (New York: Praeger-Publishers, 1976).

7. Yusif A. Sayigh, 'Oil in Arab Development and Political Strategy: an Arab view', in *Arab Oil*, ibid., p. 262.

8. OPEC member countries approved a 'Proforma Regulation for the conservation of petroleum resources', in the Baghdad 17th Conference on 10 November 1968. The Proforma Regulation was presented to the Kuwait National Assembly in 1972 and was adopted under law No. 19/1973.

9. It is to be noted that Kuwait had extended extensive efforts during this conference to reach an agreement on a common price, but when it became apparent that consensus was unattainable, Kuwait decided to join the majority. See Central Bank, *Annual Report,* 1976, p. 26.

CHAPTER 7

1. This fall is also partly attributed to a reduction in the rate of production.
2. Due to lack of reliable estimates on depreciation, it was necessary to use data on a gross rather than net basis.
3. A price index for imported goods was available for part of the period only.
4. Part of this difference would be deposited in local currency in the banking system which would in turn utilise the bulk of this to acquire foreign assets. Consequently, this part would result in an increase in Kuwait's foreign assets.
5. For a full explanation and evaluation of the two methods see, Johnston, J, *Econometric Methods* (New York, McGraw-Hill, 1963).
6. Because, however, the small sample moments of the estimators are unknown, and may not even exist, the 2SLS estimates are not necessarily unbiased. Therefore, the best that can be said about simultaneous equation estimators is that they are consistent. See in this respect, C. F. Christ, *Econometric Models and Methods* (New York: John Wiley & Sons, Inc., 1966) pp. 480–1.
7. It should be indicated that the t ratios for 2SLS are asymptotic t-statistics because the small sample moments of the distribution of the estimates are unknown. The coefficients of determination (R^2) have been adjusted for the degrees of freedom in all equations estimated by the OLS method. On the other hand, the coefficients of determination for equations estimated by the 2SLS method have not been adjusted because adjusted R^2 are not obtainable by this method.
8. A downward shift had been expected *a priori*. However, because of the openness of the economy and the importance of the 'demonstration effect' among newcomers to Kuwait, this shift did not materialise.
9. For a comprehensive discussion of this concept, see O. Eckstein, 'Investment criteria for economic development and the theory of intertemporal welfare economics', *Quarterly Journal of Economics* February 1957, pp. 56–85, and J. H. Adler, *Absorptive Capacity: The Concept and its Determinants* (Washington: Brookings Institute, 1965).
10. Commercial banks have recently been required to maintain 25 per cent of their deposit obligations in liquid form and to keep at least 7·5 per cent of that in local currency. See Kuwait Central Bank, *Economic Report for 1976* (Kuwait, 1977) p. 50.
11. Unlike the method of deducing the reduced-form coefficients from the structural estimates, this method gives the statistical significance of the reduced-form estimates and makes it possible to focus on the pre-determined variables most relevant for explaining each of the endogenous variables. However, it should be noted that a severe multicolinearity problem normally exists in estimating reduced form coefficients by the OLS method. This presents a limitation on the multiplier analysis that follows,

but with the presence of non-linear equations in the model it would be difficult to deduce accurately the multipliers from the structural estimates.

12. The multiplier which incorporates the lagged effects should be larger, but in view of the weak response to the lagged variables in the structural equations, the difference would probably be relatively small.

13. Compared with 37 per cent in Iran, 26 per cent in Iraq, 55 per cent in Saudi Arabia and an average of 24 per cent for the industrialised countries in 1973. World Bank, *World Tables* (The Johns Hopkins University Press, 1976) p. 481.

14. This compares with 78 per cent for Saudi Arabia in 1973, 40 per cent for Iraq, 27·5 per cent for Iran and an average of 18·5 per cent for the developing countries.

15. The average for the countries of the Middle East was 26·3 per cent in 1973 with a high of 58·4 per cent for Jordan, 56·4 per cent for Lebanon, and 22 per cent for Saudi Arabia. Ibid., p. 409.

CHAPTER 8

1. Kuwait Planning Board, 1968.
2. See *Kuwait, Economic Growth, Problems and Policies* Riad El Sheikh (Kuwait University Publication 1972–3. Also Kuwait, *Economic Development and Regional Cooperation* Ragaei El Mallakh (University of Chicago Press, 1968).
3. We are using the term 'development' in its wider sense, rather than that implied by the more restricted economic interpretation which we would classify as economic growth only.
4. El Sheikh, op. cit.

CHAPTER 9

1. Chenery, Hollis B. 'Land, the Effect of Resources on Economic Growth' in *Economic Development*, edited by Kenneth Berrill (London: Macmillan, 1965).
2. The emphasis on this, and the growth of planning methods based upon allocation of capital, have been mentioned and criticised in the section on planning in Chapter 8.
3. But, one should perhaps note a remark by a prominent member of Kuwaiti society who had better remain nameless and who stated: 'Why the . . . should the Arab world invest its money in a non-optimal way to support the Western economies with their current levels of inflation and thereby assure that we pay more for the goods we buy from them than would otherwise be the case.'
4. This Ministry has now been divided into two, the Ministry of Finance and the Ministry of Oil.
5. This has the added benefit of avoiding major pollution problems for the city of Kuwait, where environmental problems are given high priority.
6. The address of Mr R. S. McNamara to the Board of Directors of the World Bank in 1974 drew attention to this dilemma, but the suggestion of an

automatic reduction of 30 per cent in GNP to allow for this highlights rather than solves the problem, and we would stress the need for a change in the accounting procedures so that valid comparisons can be made. At company level in the US and many other countries, the depletion of natural resources (e.g. in a mining company) is allowed against tax according to an agreed formula, but at the national level this is ignored, as historically new discoveries have kept pace with depletions. In the case of the US the assumption may no longer be tenable, and it certainly is not for Kuwait.

7. The Minister of Oil, quoted in *Financial Times* 25.2.1977.
8. This assumption is not a forecast of what it is believed will happen, but is merely a convenient choice for exposition. If the real return exceeds this rate, then reserves will build up more quickly and, if the rate falls short of this, then *vice versa*. If negative, then Kuwait will never be in a position to maintain its reserves at a sufficient level to cover its foreign requirements indefinitely.

CHAPTER 10

1. For a review of developments pertaining to this problem, see IBRD Mission's Report, *The Economy of Kuwait*, 1964. Part I.
2. The Kuwait Fund for Arab Economic Development which has been in existence since 1961 does not in effect constitute part of the financial system since its operations are mainly external.
3. IBRD, op. cit. pp. 37–8.
4. As indicated by the IBRD report, 'Instead of accumulating more cash to finance its growing transactions, the private sector relied on the banking system to provide for its financial needs, and invested abroad more of its liquid resources'. Ibid., p. 36.
5. *Financial Times*, London, 25 February 1976, p. 18.
6. Including four national companies and a number of Arab and foreign companies operating through local agencies.
7. A Kuwaiti company, the Bank of Kuwait and Middle East, was formed to take over the operations of the British Bank of the Middle East when its concession expired.
8. Kuwait's Company Law allows foreign participation in local companies provided that the capital share of the Kuwaiti ownership does not fall below 51 per cent.
9. Industrial Bank of Kuwait, *Charter*, Article 5.
10. Kuwait Real Estate and Investment Consortium, which includes government participation and invests in real estate projects throughout the Arab world.
11. *Financial Times*, London, 25 February 1977, p. 23.
12. This resistance was largely due to the reluctance of managers of international bond issues 'to get involved in the Arab boycott problems that might arise if a Kuwaiti house were in the management group'. Ibid., p. 23.
13. 'Money supply' used in this analysis refers to the sum of money in circulation, demand deposits and time deposits with the commercial and specialised banks.
14. It is assumed that other assets and liabilities of the banking system, e.g. government deposits and banks' equity, remain unchanged.

15. See, the Central Bank of Kuwait, *Economic Report for 1976*, Kuwait, 1976, p. 50.

16. The Central Bank of Kuwait, *Economic Report for 1975*, Kuwait, 1975, p. 58.

17. Other government foreign exchange funds (reserves) are administered by the Ministry of Finance and do not represent part of the monetary reserves of the Central Bank.

18. The IMF's Oil Facility is an arrangement created to provide short-term loans to member countries with balance of payments problems resulting from higher oil prices.

19. The ratio of the change in commercial banks' deposits to the increase in the money supply in 1976 is less than 8 per cent, and to the increase in the claims on the private sector is approximately 6 per cent.

20. Low elasticity of supply in the case of imported goods is due in large measure to domestic factors, e.g. port congestion, restricted competition, etc.

21. This point is further developed in S. Hoss 'Central Bank and monetary policy in Kuwait', a paper presented to the Kuwait Economic Society, 1972.

22. Interbank deposits consist mainly of short-term balances and would, therefore, enter as liquid assets for the purposes of the liquidity ratio required by the Central Bank. *Central Bank Report 1975*, p. 66.

23. Charles Welles, 'The rise and fall of the Arab underwriters', *Institutional Investor*, September 1976, p. 78.

24. See, *Financial Times*, London, Friday 25 February 1977, p. 23.

25. World Bank, *World Tables*, 1976, pp. 142–5.

26. The Central Bank of Kuwait, *Economic Report for 1976*, pp. 78–9.

27. There are clear indications that the rise in rent is not correctly reflected in the cost of living index.

28. For a discussion of the factors affecting share prices in Kuwait see, M. Khouja and W. Said, *The Kuwait Stock Market, Performance and Prospects*, The Kuwait Economic Society, June 1974, pp. 42–54.

29. In the New York Stock Exchange this ratio usually ranges between 2 per cent and 3 per cent.

30. Average share prices increased almost without interruption from KD15 in September 1970 to KD50 in December 1973 and to KD115 by the end of 1976. For the increase in share prices during the years 1970–3, see, Khouja and Said, op. cit., p. 40, and for the years 1973–6, see The Central Bank, *Economic Report for 1976*, p. 73.

31. Minimum share prices were set equal to the lowest prices reached during the period from 1 October to 17 December 1977. In the case of companies whose shares were not traded during that period, a committee was appointed to set the bases for determining their minimum prices.

32. A decrease in government deposits leads to an increase in money supply; hence the negative sign preceding it.

CHAPTER 11

1. IMF *Survey,* 8 October 1973 and 17 June 1974.

2. *First Outline of Reform* submitted to Board of Governors of IMF, Nairobi 24–28.9.74. Article 3.

3. Article 8, op. cit.
4. IMF *Survey*, 24 March 1975.
5. This consisted of five British bankers, chaired by the director of the Middle East department at the Bank of England. This Board was later replaced by the Kuwait Investment Office, still in London.

CHAPTER 12

1. This concept became prominent only recently following its use in connection with the UN General Assembly resolutions during its Sixth and Seventh Special Sessions calling for the establishment of the New International Economic Order.
2. See for example G. Ohlin, 'The Evolution of Aid Doctrine' *Foreign Aid Policies Reconsidered*, OECD, 1956, pp. 13–33; I. M. D. Little and J. M. Clifford. *International Aid*, Chicago, 1966; John White, *The Politics of Foreign Aid*, London, 1974; and the Pearson Commission Report, *Partners in Development*, New York, 1969.
3. As explained in P. T. Bauer, 'Foreign aid forever?'. *Encounter*, March 1974, pp. 23–5, in connection with such arguments for aid as the 'widening gap' and the 'moral obligation'.
4. I. F. I. Shihata and R. Mabro, 'The OPEC aid record', January 1978, a publication of the OPEC Special Fund, p. 1.
5. See Abdlatif Y. Al-Hamad, '*Address to a seminar on the Kuwait Fund*', a publication of the Kuwait Fund for Arab Economic Development, Kuwait, February 1971 (in Arabic) p. 4.
6. Shihata and Mabro, op. cit., p. 9.
7. Ibid., p. 9.
8. GUPAC was also involved for a short time in the financing of resource surveys, soil analyses and development of water resources. These operations, however, have been relinquished since they fall within the scope of the Kuwait Fund.
9. These functions were taken over by the Government of the United Arab Emirates after its establishment in 1972.
10. The only instances of tying aid to a particular source of procurement were when Kuwait provided fertilizer in kind as a grant and financed the sale of locally manufactured metal pipelines; both were extended to the Sudan.
11. The AMF is a regional monetary organisation designed to assist member countries to overcome temporary balance of payments problems through the provision of short-term credit facilities.
12. The IMF Oil Facility consists of non-concessional funds provided by a group of developed and oil-exporting countries.
13. For a discussion of the various criticisms of bilateral aid, see, T. Balogh, 'Multilateral versus Bilateral Aid', *Oxford Economic Papers*, new series, vol. 19, 1967, no. 3; reprinted in *Foreign Aid*, edited by J. B. Bhagwati and R. S. Eckaus (Penguin, 1970) pp. 203–22.
14. R. F. Mikesell, *The Economics of Foreign Aid* (Aldine Publishing Company, 1968) p. 254.
15. T. Balogh, op. cit. p. 207. In fact, it is argued that this attitude is also common among the staff of many leading international aid organisations.

16. See Abdlatif Y. Al-Hamad, 'Some aspects of the Kuwait Fund's approach to international development finance', a publication of the Kuwait Fund, December 1977, p. 8.
17. UNCTAD Secretariat, 'Growth and Aid', *Proceedings of the United Nations Conference on Trade and Development*, Second Session, New Delhi, vol. IV, 'Problems and Policies of Financing', New York. 1968, p. 4.
18. This comparison does not reflect the follow-up activities that need to be performed on account of previous lending operations. This aspect is of importance in the case of older institutions with a large number of projects in the implementation stage.
19. Approximately one-quarter of this amount was extended before 1967 to nine Arab countries (UAR $94·5 million, Iraq $84 million, Algeria $70 million, Lebanon and Morocco $28 million each, etc.); one-half to Egypt and Jordan under the Khartoum Agreement following the 1967 Arab–Israeli war to compensate the former for lost income resulting from the closure of the Suez Canal and to both for the disruption of their economies caused by the Israeli occupation of Arab land. The remainder was provided in grants and loans during the years 1967–72, a major part of which was extended through multilateral institutions.
20. In fact, Kuwait's net ODA disbursements in 1964 were estimated at 9·61 per cent of national income.
21. The role and activities of these institutions have already been discussed in Chapters 8 and 9.
22. The financial flows referred to in this section have been compiled by OECD (*Statistical Tables* dated 4 November 1977 and *Development Co-operation, 1977 Review*, November 1977). They are generally less than UNCTAD estimates. As explained by Shihata and Mabro, 'The major difference between the two sources seems to lie in estimates of non-concessional multilateral flows. OECD does not consider payments to the IMF Oil Facility as part of the relevant flows while UNCTAD does. The OECD argument is essentially that these payments did not constitute long term financial flows, but rather short to medium-term balance of payments assistance and did not diminish the donors' resources since they were able to draw on them whenever their own payments position so warranted.' Shihata and Mabro, op. cit. p. 7.
23. This figure is based on a World Bank Survey covering a sample of forty developing countries, which estimates the import requirements of the developing countries in 1974 at $96·3 billion and their total balance of trade deficits at about $22 billion.
24. See Z. A. Nasr, 'The Kuwait Fund scheme for the guarantee of inter-Arab investments', Kuwait Fund publication, May 1972, p. 30.
25. This suggestion, as indicated earlier, was made by the President of the World Bank, Robert McNamara in his September 1974 address to the World Bank Board of Governors.
26. For a discussion of the grant (or concessionary) element and its policy implications see J. A. Pincus, 'Costs and Benefits of Aid: An empirical analysis', in UNCTAD Second Session, volume IV. *Problems and Policies of Financing*, 1968.

CHAPTER 13

1. R. Stephens, *The Arab's New Frontier*, (London: Temple Smith, 1976) p. 53.
2. Ibid., p. 54.
3. The only matter that requires approval by the country's Legislative Authority is the Fund's administrative budget. (See, I. F. I. Shihata, *The Kuwait Fund for Arab Economic Development; A Legal Analysis*, a Kuwait Fund publication, 1973, p. 9, for the legal implications of this issue.)
4. R. Stephens, op. cit., p. 56.
5. Law No. 25 (1974) for the Reorganisation of the Kuwait Fund.
6. R. El-Mallakh, *Economic Development and Regional Cooperation: Kuwait* (Chicago: The University of Chicago Press, 1968) p. 184.
7. Article 28 of the Fund's Charter.
8. *Basic Information*, Kuwait Fund, November 1974, p. 5.
9. The activation of this type of operation by international aid institutions is currently under study by the Development Committee.
10. See H. W. Singer, 'External Aid: for Plans or Projects?' *Economic Journal*, vol. 75, 1965, pp. 539–45.
11. There have been many such occasions in the 'least developed countries', e.g. North Yemen, South Yemen, Mauritania, Bangladesh, Afghanistan, Rwanda and Somalia.
12. The Kuwait Fund has played a major catalytic role in arranging the financing of many projects, e.g. the Rahad Project in the Sudan (total cost KD95 million), the Pong Power Project in Ghana (KD70 million), the Selingue Dam in Mali (KD42 million) and the Guelbs Iron Ore Project in Mauritania (KD160 million).
13. See Interview with KFAED Director-General, *Middle East Journal*, January 1978, p. 82.
14. This, as indicated by V. Joshi, assumes that 'more saving can be extracted, but the possibilities of transforming consumption into investment domestically *and* through trade have fallen to zero'. V. Joshi, 'Saving and Foreign Exchange Constraints', in Paul Streeten (ed.), *Unfashionable Economics*, London, 1970. Also reprinted in G. M. Meir, *Leading Issues in Economic Development* (New York: Oxford University Press, 1976) p. 339.
15. It is important to note in this respect that, 'An increase in investment is constrained by "saving" if, at the margin, transformation possibilities (domestically and/or through foreign trade) still exist but cannot be utilised because domestic consumption has reached its minimum tolerable level.' Ibid., p. 339.
16. Kalinadi Hydro-electric Power Project, where the loan was justified on the grounds that while the goods and services required could be procured locally, it was difficult to do so because local resources could not be released for this purpose since consumption was already at its minimum level. See Loan Agreement dated 27 January 1976 concerned with this project.
17. The first water supply project was extended to Tunisia in late 1977.
18. As indicated in Article 16. However, the Fund's standard loan agreement

provides the option to the recipient whereby the Fund may act as its agent in effecting disbursements and accepting repayments in other fully convertible currencies on the basis of the current exchange rates.

19. It should be noted that no change in the par value of the KD has taken place since its introduction as the national currency of Kuwait in 1961.

20. In view of the recent international monetary reforms whereby gold has been effectively demonetised and the system of par values abandoned, the Fund followed the Central Bank's decision not to adopt a par value for the KD and decided in July 1978 to delete the gold clause from its charter and standard loan agreement.

21. Article 17.

22. Unlike other development lending institutions, the Fund charges no commitment fee on the unwithdrawn balance of the loan extended.

23. The exceptional cases include the least developed countries (e.g., North Yemen, South Yemen, Mauritania and Bangladesh) and the relatively more advanced developing countries (e.g., Malaysia, Cyprus, etc.), as well as industrial projects with foreign shareholding. The interest rate for the first group normally ranges between 0 per cent and 2 per cent, and between 5 per cent and 7 per cent for the other two groups.

24. These figures are estimated on the basis of the projected disbursement schedules of the various projects. However, because of normal delays in execution and a slower pace of disbursement than originally envisaged, the above estimates are believed to be overstated.

25. There is only agreement in principle; a loan agreement is yet to be concluded.

26. The immediate scheme consists of the Diama dam (designed to prevent the flow of sea water into the basin), the Manantali dam (designed to regulate the flow of the river so that it becomes navigable) and the construction of several ports along the river. The total cost of these components is currently estimated at $500 million.

27. As at the end of 1977, the Arab Fund participated in the financing of two joint Arab projects only: a telecommunications project involving Algeria and Morocco and a road between Aden in South Yemen and Taiz in North Yemen.

28. The economic rate of return of the expansion project calculated on the basis of global savings in transport cost is 30 per cent whereas the economic rate of return to Egypt based on the revenues of the Suez Canal Authority is estimated at only 15 per cent.

29. See R. Stephens, op. cit., p. 60.

30. Article 20.

31. In the case of power projects, the analysis is usually based on comparing the cost stream of the proposed project with that of the best possible alternative. The aim is to determine the least cost alternative for generating or supplying the power needed to satisfy the projected demand.

32. The economic rates of return on the Fund's projects have varied from a low of 3 per cent in the case of projects with important social considerations to a high of 45 per cent in the case of some industrial projects.

33. See for example UNIDO, *Guidelines for Project Evaluation*, New York, 1972, chapter 3.

34. The Fund's approach is summarised in Abdlatif Y. Al-Hamad, 'The employment and income distribution objectives in the Kuwait Fund development

assistance', in J. D. MacArthur and G. A. Amin (eds.), 'Cost-Benefit Analysis and Income Distribution in Developing Countries: A symposium', *World Development*, vol. 6, no. 2 (Oxford: Pergamon Press, February 1978) pp. 127–30.

35. *Disbursement Procedures*, Kuwait Fund (Kuwait, 1972).

36. Although the Fund as a rule requires procurement of goods and services on the basis of international competitive bidding to enhance competition and enable the recipient to obtain the most favourable prices, it normally provides a preference margin of up to 25 per cent to local bidders in order to offset the effects of tariffs and duties imposed on imported items that enter as intermediate inputs in goods procured locally.

37. It should be noted that the Fund pays, on behalf of the Kuwait Government, its contribution to such regional multilateral organisations as the Arab Fund, ABEDA, the Inter-Arab Investment Guarantee Corporation and the ADF. The total amount paid from Fund's resources to these institutions as of 30 June 1977 is KD50 million.

38. FIDIC, 'Estimating Costs of Construction', *NEWSGRAM* (The Hague, Netherlands, January, 1978) p. 1.

39. An elaborate analysis of this problem is given in a recent paper by M. S. Abu Ali, 'Delay in withdrawal of development loans', presented at the Arab Organisation for Administrative Sciences – Seminar on Investment Problems (Kuwait, December 1977). Forthcoming in *Journal of Oil and Arab Cooperation*.

40. Ibid., pp. 5–9.

41. This ratio of net income to total assets is attained in spite of the fact that the average interest rate on Fund's loans is less than 3 per cent. This is attributed to two main reasons: (1) Given the rapid increase in its capital and the slow pace of disbursement on new loans, over 60 per cent of the Fund's resources (capital and reserves) has been invested in high quality securities and bank deposits, and (2) A low ratio of administrative expenses to gross income – about 4 per cent, compared with 9 per cent for the World Bank (1977), 35 per cent for the Arab Fund (1977) and 41 per cent for the Asian Development Bank (1976).

42. Given the Fund's policy of restricting the level of total net commitments (gross commitments minus repayments) to the amount of available resources, the Fund's lending capacity in a given year would in fact be determined in the present circumstances (borrowing excluded) according to the following formula:

$$LC_t = PC_t + R_t + RP_t - GC_t + C_t - D_t$$

where LC_t = Lending capacity as at the end of year t.
PC_t = Total paid-in capital as at the end of year t.
R_t = Cumulative reserves as at the end of year t, are equal to last year's reserves plus net income in year t.
RP_t = Cumulative loan repayments as at the end of year t.
GC_t = Cumulative gross commitments as at the end of year t.
C_t = Cumulative loan cancellations as at the end of year t.
D_t = Equity participation in development institutions on behalf of the Kuwait Government.

43. For the purposes of this analysis it may be assumed that the Fund makes arrangements regarding the variables that determine its lending capacity so as to maintain the size of new commitments at an annual rate equal to a fixed proportion of its declared capital – say 10 per cent of KD1 billion.
44. For a discussion of this problem, see R. M. Mikesell, op. cit., pp. 108–10.
45. This compares with an annual average during the last three years of about $5·0 billion for the World Bank, $1·5 billion for IDA, $650 million for the Asian Development Bank, $240 million for the Arab Fund and approximately $100 million for the African Development Bank.

Selected Bibliography

Abu Hakima *History of Eastern Arabia* (Beirut: Khayat, 1965).

Adelman, M. A. *The World Petroleum Market* (Baltimore: The Johns Hopkins University Press, 1972).

Adler, J. H. *Absorptive Capacity: the Concept and its Determinants* (Washington D.C.: The Brookings Institution, 1965).

Al-Ebraheem, H. A. *Kuwait. A Political Study* (Kuwait: Kuwait University Press, 1975).

Askari, H. and Cummings, J. T. *Middle East Economics in the 1970s: A Comparative Approach* (New York: Praeger, 1976).

Berrill, K. (ed.) *Economic Development* (London: Macmillan, 1965).

Chisholm, F. H. T. *The First Kuwait Oil Concessions* (London: Frank Cass, 1975).

Dickson, H. R. P. *Kuwait and her Neighbours* (London: Allen and Unwin, 1956).

Earle, E. M. *Turkey, The Great Powers and The Baghdad Railway* (New York: Macmillan, 1973).

El-Mallakh, R. *Economic Development and Regional Cooperation: Kuwait* (Chicago: The Chicago University Press, 1968).

El-Sheikh, R. *Kuwait: Economic Growth, Problems and Policies* (Kuwait: University Publications, 1972).

Hopwood, D. (ed.) *The Arabian Peninsula: Society and Politics* (London: Allen and Unwin, 1972).

Issawi, C. and Yeganeh, M. *The Economics of Middle Eastern Oil* (London: Faber and Faber, 1962).

Little, I. M. D. and Clifford, J. M. *International Aid* (London: Allen and Unwin, 1965).

Mickesell, R. F. *The Economics of Foreign Aid* (London: Weidenfeld and Nicholson, 1968).

Mikdashi, Z. *The Community of Oil Exporting Countries* (London: Allen and Unwin, 1972).

Najjar, I. *The Development of a One Resource Economy. A Case Study of Kuwait* (An Unpublished Dissertation, Indiana University, 1969).

OAPEC *Assayat Sina't Al-Naft Walgaz (Fundamentals of Oil and Gas Industry* (Kuwait: OAPEC Publications, 1977).

Palgrave, W. G. *A Personal Narrative of a Year's Journey through Central and Eastern Arabia, 1862–63* (London: Macmillan, 1865).

Sayigh, Y. A. *The Economics of the Arab World, Development since 1945* (London: Croom Helm, 1978).

Sherbiny, N. A. and Tessler, M. A. (eds.) *Arab Oil* (New York: Praeger Publishers, 1976).

Shiber, S. G. *The Kuwaiti Urbanisation* (Kuwait: Kuwait Government Press, 1964).

Shihata, I. *The Case for the Arab Oil Embargo* (Beirut: The Institute for Palestine Studies, 1975).

Stephens, R. *The Arabs' New Frontier* (London: Temple Smith, 1976).

Streeten, P. P. (ed.) *Unfashionable Economics: Essays in Honour of Lord Ballogh* (London: Weidenfeld and Nicholson, 1970).

Tugendhat, C. and Hamilton, A. *Oil, The Biggest Business* (London: Eyre and Methuen, 1975).

White, J. A. *The Politics of Foreign Aid* (London: Bodley Head, 1974).

Wilson, A. T. *The Persian Gulf: An Historical Sketch from the Earliest Times to the Beginning of the 20th Century* (Oxford: Clarendon Press, 1928).

Winston, H. V. E. and Freeth, Z. *Kuwait: Prospect and Reality* (New York: Crane, Rusak, 1972).

Articles

Al-Hamad, A. Y., 'International finance, an Arab point of view' (Kuwait, Kuwait Fund publication, October 1974).

——, 'LDCs and international bond issues' (Kuwait, Kuwait Fund publication, March 1977).

——, 'Some aspects of the Kuwait Fund's approach to international development finance' (Kuwait, Kuwait Fund publication, December 1977).

——, 'Towards closer economic cooperation in the Middle East, financial aspects' (Kuwait, Kuwait Fund publication, October 1976).

Al-Saadon, J. K., 'Factors contributing to equality of income distribution in Kuwait', *Journal of the Gulf and Arabian Peninsula*, vol. 3, no. 12, October 1977.

Balogh, T., 'Multilateral *versus* Bilateral Aid', *Oxford Economic Papers,* new series, vol. 19, no. 3, 1967.

Bauer, P. T., 'Foreign Aid Forever?' *Encounter*, March 1974.

FIDIC, 'Estimating Costs of Construction,' *Newsgram,* January 1978.

Hamouda, M. A., 'Auditing of Joint Sector Companies', paper presented to the Third Seminar on High Management, Arab Planning Institute, January 1977.

Hill, A., 'The population of Kuwait', *Geography*, January 1969.

Hoss, S., 'The Central Bank and the Monetary Policy in Kuwait', The Kuwait Economic Society, January 1972.

Khouja, M. W., 'Distinguishing Properties of the Kuwait Economy', The Kuwait Economic Society, March 1973.

Khouja, M. W. and Said, W., 'The Kuwait Stock Market, Performance and Prospects', The Kuwait Economic Society, June 1974.

Kubursi, A. A., 'Vocational and technical education and development needs in the Arab world', *Working Paper* No. 77–04, Department of Economics, McMaster University, June 1977.

Middle East Currency Reports, 'Kuwaiti Dinar', vol. 3, no. 1, October–November 1976 (prepared by *International Currency Review*).

Nasr, Z. A., 'The Kuwait Fund scheme for the guarantee of inter-Arab investments' (Kuwait, Kuwait Fund publication, May 1972).

Penrose, E., 'Middle East Oil: The international distribution of profits and income taxes', *Economica*, vol. 27, August 1960.

Pincus, J. A., 'Costs and Benefits of aid: An empirical analysis', in UNCTAD Second Session, New Delhi, vol. IV, *Problems and Policies of Financing*, (New York, 1968).

Pincus, J. A., 'Growth and Aid', UNCTAD second session, op. cit.

Rashid, Y. R., and Shihab-Eldin, A., 'The Future of the Petroleum-Nuclear Balance in the OAPEC Countries', *Journal of Oil and Arab Cooperation*, vol. 2, no. 2, 1976.

Shehab, F., 'Kuwait: A Super Affluent Society', *Foreign Affairs*, vol. 42, no. 3, April 1964.

Shihata, I. F. I., 'The Kuwait Fund for Arab Economic Development, A Legal Analysis' (Kuwait, Kuwait Fund publication, 1973).

Shihata, I. F. I., and Mabro, R., 'The OPEC Aid Record' (Mimeographed paper by the OPEC Special Fund, 1977).

Singer, H. W., 'External Aid: For Plans or Projects?', *Economic Journal*, vol. 75, September 1965.

Welles, C., 'The Rise and Fall of the Arab Underwriters', *Institutional Investor*, September, 1976.

Index